LAST WORDS

SHARI J. RYAN

ISBN-13:978-1976383434
ISBN-10:1976383439
LCCN: 2017952187

Editor: Lisa Brown, Looking Glass Revisions
Cover and Interior Formatting: MadHat Books

CONTENTS

SUBSCRIBE TO MY NEWSLETTER

BE THE FIRST TO RECEIVE UPDATES AND
ADVANCED READER OPPORTUNITIES

https://www.sharijryan.com/subscribe

ALSO BY SHARI J. RYAN

Find all books located here:

https://www.sharijryan.com/all-books

ACKNOWLEDGMENTS

This book has given me peace, understanding, and gratefulness.

It was a journey I'm going to miss greatly, but I'm so glad I went through this story and came out on the other side.

Mom, you spent countless hours weaving through every one of my words, hashing out plot ideas, and editing my raw words to add more detail and emotion into the story. I loved working with you on this, and it means so much to me that you helped me through this difficult book. Thank you for always being by my side. I love you!

Lisa, thank you so much for putting so much passion into the edits. The hours of research and polish you have added to my story is above and beyond anything I could ask for.

My beta readers—I love your excitement to dig in and help me, by offering your honest feedback when the words are fresh and raw. Knowing I can trust you means more than I could ever explain. The time you selflessly offer me is something I'm truly appreciative of: Annelle, Kelly, Cindy, Sue, Barb M., Crystal, Heather, Julie, Samantha, Michele, Erin D., Jocelyn, Renee, Barb S., Tanya, Belinda, Alissa, Shannon, Coleen, Shelly, Val, Tracey, Rebecca, April, Dee, Erin K., Lin, and TK Leigh.

Julie, a special thank you for helping me out when I needed it the most. You have gone above and beyond; proofreading the last round and offering your support throughout this entire journey is something I can never thank you enough for. I'm so grateful for our friendship!

Linda, thank you for keeping me sane, organized, and on track. You regularly offer me a shoulder to lean on, and it means the world to me. I don't know what I would do without you!

Bloggers, Readers, and Author Friends—I love you all so much. Being in this community has given me a different outlook on life, and I can't think of a better industry to be a part of than this one with all of you. Thank you for your support!

My friends—the ones who constantly listen to me yap about my invisible friends. Your support is everything to me. Gia and Annelle, I love you like sisters. <3

Lori—the best sister in the universe—thank you for being my first reader and going chapter to chapter in excitement along with me as I write. Love you!

My family—Mom, Dad, Mark, and Ev—thank you for having faith in me to give this story justice. I love you all.

Bryce and Brayden—my sweet boys—I hope you always remember your family roots and that you have warrior blood running through your veins. You two can accomplish anything you put your mind to, and you make me proud every single day.

Josh—my other half—thank you for continuing to support my books on a daily basis, and for always taking an interest in what my heart is passionate about. Having your encouragement is everything to me.

DISCLAIMER

This fictitious novel is incredibly graphic, made up of many non-fictitious details of the Holocaust. If you are sensitive to violence, this may not be the book for you.

I am a descendant of two Holocaust survivors, from whom I have had the privilege of learning facts of my history and heritage. In addition, hours of research have been conducted to keep historical facts accurately laced in with this story that brings forbidden love to another level.

I have wanted to write this book for many years, but it has been challenging to relive a life experience my grandmother and great-grandmother survived, while knowing the rest of my family did not make it.

With the taboo nature of this story, please know I do not condone or support the typical enemy's behavior portrayed in my story. On the contrary, I have lived in fear of hatred, hiding my religion and beliefs for many years. Therefore, I hope this story is as enlightening to you as it has been for me.

PRAISE FOR SHARI J. RYAN

Last Words by Shari Ryan is a gripping, emotional, spellbinding journey of bravery, redemption, and love. Once I picked up this book, I could not put it down, completely captivated by the story. I felt every emotion the characters went through, one minute my heart caught in my throat, the next overwhelmed with the love these characters shared. I urge everyone to read this book. Allow the story to consume you as it consumed me, and remember the lesson that has sadly been forgotten lately... Love is stronger than hate.

— USA TODAY BESTSELLING AUTHOR T.K. LEIGH

There is absolutely no amount of amazing words I could possibly use, in any language, to describe Shari Ryan's new release Last Words and still do this deeply moving, thought provoking love story justice.

Last Words moved me to the brink of tears, cultivated fear and burned deep in my heart with the out pouring of love it provoked.

Ryan's story was an unexpected one in Nazi German times. Two souls finding love in the most tragic of places. Ryan poured every stitch of her heritage into this emotional novel. By doing so, she has written her best novel to date.

Last Words is one of those books you must absolutely read for yourself to feel the strength and emotion crafted by Ryan. Last Words is special, a different story of love demanding to readers to be read. Don't miss out on this opportunity to read something that'll change your perception of true love.

— EMILY GOODMAN, SOUTHERN VIXENS BOOK OBSESSIONS

There are no words to correctly portray how this book has made me feel. This is honestly one of the most beautifully written, captivating, and heart-felt books I have ever read! I am a huge fan of Shari's - but I'm now wishing I could rate this book higher than 5 stars, because it is some of the best writing she has ever done! I'm not going to lie - I cried like a baby, quite a few times - but I just could not put this book down...I needed to know how it was going to end, but once I got there - I was so sad to say goodbye to the characters. Last Words takes us back and forth from the present to the past, a terrible time in history, during WWII, in the Holocaust. It was very hard to read about this time of history, but the love captured within the words throughout the past and present, helps tie this story together beautifully. 10 stars, an absolute MUST READ!

— HEATHER, EARLY READER

To the survivors who made it through, and the souls who weren't given a chance, your legacy lives on through all who continue to fight for peace, freedom, and love.

PROLOGUE

AMELIA

Since 1945, my story has remained hidden deep within the corners of my mind and blacked out as if with a permanent marker, in hopes that no one else would ever know. I've been holding on to these silent memories for such a long time, but I'm becoming weak. I've always known that the truth might someday be stronger than my will to be silent, but I can't imagine what my secrets would do to those I love.

This may be cliché, but I'm going to start my story with a once upon a time...except my life hasn't been a fairytale—far from it. In fact, for a long time, I believed a happy ending meant death.

During my early years as a child, I had a perfect life. The sun shone golden rays across Bohemia's breathtaking sky and bore its warmth down on the silky, green-grass-covered soil. I lived in color—rich with vivid hues, and I danced through the mustard fields, twirling my dress as my hair blew like weeping willows in the breeze. My heart was protected, my life blessed with knowledge, and I was surrounded by love. There was a lightness in my mind and a feeling of completeness in my soul that made each day feel like a gift from above.

Then, a day came when the sun was taken away. The sky

became dark with heavy clouds, and my world turned gray. Raindrops that once fell from the sky bled into the tears that burned down my cheeks.

I thought darkness was all I had left after losing everything I'd ever known and loved, but through a cloud of dust and despair, I found a glimmer of hope—a smile amongst the sunken cheeks and rotting corpses.

He should never have smiled at me, and I shouldn't have acknowledged him when he did, but once it started, there was no turning back. I never considered the possibility of how it would end until I felt the heartbreak of loneliness again. His smile was gone. The warm touches we shared through my cold shivers would never heat my body again, and the worst part was that all hope was lost.

It was all for nothing. It would have been easier to have never felt that kind of love because once I knew how good it could feel, I didn't think I'd ever feel that way again.

As the world caved in on itself, I allowed the pain and misery to pour from my eyes one last time before making a silent vow to never give another ounce of power to those who wanted to dominate the weak.

I traveled through the phases of bitter denial, revenge, hate, sorrow—and finally, the emptiness that would be a part of me forever.

When the sun returned and the grass grew back, those who had survived slowly allowed their wounds to heal, but there was a numbness inside all of us—protection from feeling the pain of the memories that would last a lifetime.

To forget and move on as if it never happened was the only way to survive. I tried to convince myself that I hadn't lived through the most demoralizing and destructive five years this world has ever seen.

I moved to America, leaving the enemy behind. I lived on, shielding myself from the memories. I lived up to society's moral standards and expectations by getting married and having children. I cooked, cleaned, and supported those I love. Then, over time, my past became a part of the earth like the bones and ashes in that far away land.

There is one exception, though, and it's the part of me I have only pretended to forget—my secret. In fact, some would consider what I did to be as wrong, and equally horrendous, as what the heartless ones did to my whole race.

In my heart, I will never consider that it was wrong, and I will stand by my actions and beliefs because the heart wants what the heart wants. Sometimes, even the toughest warriors who survive the odds and somehow escape the shadows of death, can still fall helpless and weak at the mercy of love.

CHAPTER ONE

EMMA

*G*reat, I'm going to be late again. I glance over at the clock on my car radio, feeling anxiety set in as I wait for my phone to ring. I don't understand how I can be expected to predict the exact moment I will arrive somewhere. Mom thinks that because I work for myself, I make my own hours, but that's not the case. I have a job and deadlines to meet, but Mom clocks in and out of her beloved receptionist position at the town hall, so her lunch hour is the same every day. Even though mine doesn't always match up, I try my hardest to be punctual, but I can't foresee my daily schedule and traffic.

I fly into the parking lot of Panera and see Mom standing in front of the entrance, her hip cocked to one side, an annoyed grimace covering her face, and her fingers frantically searching for buttons on her phone.

Not-so-shockingly, my phone rings five-seconds later, just as I put the Jeep into park. If she weren't busy calling me, she would see that I pulled into the parking lot a minute ago.

I decide to ignore the call as I walk toward her, watching her talking to herself. I'm assuming my voicemail is picking up right about now, and as soon I step foot onto the curb, five feet from where she's standing, she'll begin her, "Emma, where are you?" message. "You're two minutes late, and I'm worried something may have happened. Please call me as soon as you get this."

"I'm right here, Mom," I tell her, smiling in hopes of erasing the angry look on her face.

"Oh," she says. "I was looking for you. You know lunch is at one."

"I was working with a client, Mom, and I'm only two minutes late," I remind her. I give her a quick hug and a kiss on the cheek before taking the few steps over to the door.

"I'm sorry, I'm just having a bad day," she says.

My heart sinks for a moment, going through the list of things that could be wrong for her to have the despondent expression I see tugging at her face. "What happened?"

"Nothing actually happened," she begins.

"Is Grams okay?" I ask. Ever since Grandpa passed away ten years ago, we have been taking turns checking up on her since she refuses to be "taken" from her house and "placed" in an assisted-living environment, or a morgue as she calls it.

"Yes, she is fine but just angry today, I guess."

"Why?"

Mom places her hand over her eyes and shakes her head. "I don't know, Emma. She's getting those palpitations in her chest again, and she's sure she's going to die today." Mom tends to be overdramatic at times, but Grams doesn't typically throw around the topic of death, so I can see why she is concerned.

"I'll go check on her after lunch, and I'll let you know when I find out she's okay. That will put your mind at ease."

Acting as if I didn't say a word, Mom opens the door to Panera and walks inside. I totally understand that she can't handle the idea of Grams not being around, and I feel the same, but she's making herself sick with worry every day.

Mom silently takes her place at the back of the line, squinting her eyes at the menu before pulling her glasses out of her purse.

"You always order the grilled chicken sandwich. Are you getting something new today?" I ask her.

"No, I'm just looking to see if they've added anything new to the menu."

"I don't think they have since last week," I tell her, trying to save her the time from scrutinizing each column. She removes her glasses, then slips them back into her bag and looks around at the few people waiting in line to order. "Emma," she whispers, "do you see him over there?" She's pointing toward the front of the line at a man working the register. Therefore, he must be single and available...unlike me, who is in a relationship. She'd like to pretend otherwise, however.

"No," I tell her. "Don't."

"He's cute, though," she says with a grin. I'm glad she's feeling better now, but it is at my expense.

"Please, stop it, Mom," I mutter without hiding my aggravation.

"I want grandchildren," she responds in a singsong voice.

"I'm only thirty-one," I argue. "I have plenty of time."

"I don't want you to wait as long as I did, Emma. I feel like an old hen around you and I don't like it. Plus, whether you like it or not, your clock is ticking, and you're with the wrong man," she feels the need to add in.

"Do you really think I should get involved with a cashier at a fast-food restaurant? I'm a career woman with some long-term goals and memorizing the value meal numbers isn't one of them."

This is how lunch goes whenever I meet her during the week. I love Mom to death, and I enjoy spending the time with her, but we don't see eye-to-eye on my love life, my career, my lifestyle, or diet. As a matter of fact, sometimes I kind of feel like I'm on a different planet than she's on. "Mom, don't worry about me so much, okay? I'll figure things out."

"I'm always going to worry about you, Emma. You're my daughter. You're not happy, and it's obvious."

"I am happy," I lie, forcing a smile to try and end the conversation, but no one knows me better than she does. I'm like an open book to her.

"You're not living life to its fullest," she argues.

"Mom, Dad left you fifteen years ago, and you've been living alone ever since. How is that happiness? Are you living life to its fullest?"

"You are my happiness, Emma."

Sometimes the guilt is overwhelming, and I think she knows it.

The moment I slip back into my car, my phone buzzes in my bag, and I silently curse. Between work calls, Mom's calls, and Mike's calls, which have increased to an irritatingly excessive level as of late, I rarely have a moment to breathe. I pull out my phone and see Mike's name on the display. I do not want to talk to him right now, but the calls will continue until I pick up, so I exhale heavily and answer.

"Hi," I say cordially, as I pull out of the parking lot.

"Do you have a minute?" he asks, then clears his throat. That's what he does when he's nervous about something.

"Sure," I tell him, though I don't want to hear what he plans to say. Sorry doesn't work for me anymore, and I'm worn out from the endless arguments.

"Em, I'm sorry for what I said last night," he begins, sounding nearly robotic, or like he's on auto-repeat. I've heard the same spiel a million times now.

"Okay," I reply.

"What's going on with us?" he asks. The remorse in his voice deliberate, verging on the line of fake. Things are never about us, they're about him.

"I don't think this is an issue between us, Mike."

8

"Why is it always me?" As usual, he immediately initiates an argument. What else could I possibly want to do at two in the afternoon during my lunch break?

"I wasn't the one who came home in a drunken rage last night," I remind him.

He grunts indignantly and says, "I wasn't drunk."

"I could smell the whiskey from across the room, Mike. Why do you lie about it? I've been very understanding of you going out several nights a week with your friends, even when you come home smelling like weed and perfume. I keep telling myself that you're just a little immature and you'll grow up eventually, but we're in our thirties and I'm getting tired of waiting." My life consists of hopping from one Starbucks to another while seeking work-day scenery changes, meeting Mom for lunch, and checking on Grams, while I dread going home each night to the small, desolate house I share with Mike. "On top of that, the house is always a disaster with your socks tossed in every corner, dirty underwear and towels in the entryway of the hall bathroom, and empty pizza boxes stacked up on top of the full trash can—all strategically placed so I have something to clean when I get home at night." How can I see myself living like that forever?

"So, what, we're breaking up for the fourth time this month?" he asks as if it doesn't faze him. It doesn't mean anything to Mike because I haven't been able to keep my word when I tell him we're done. The worst part is, he's told me so many times before that I don't have the "balls" to leave him, reminding me I have nowhere to go and that being a freelance designer doesn't offer me a dependable salary.

"I don't know if I can be with you," I tell him honestly. I don't love him like I thought I once did, and despite having to admit that Mom might be right, this isn't the life I want.

My current state of calmness is unusual for how I typically come off during one of our arguments, because I'm passionate about what I believe in, so I become overheated easily, but now, I feel nothing. "Fine, then move out. I don't care," he tells me.

That should have hurt me, but I still feel nothing. I don't know what to say, but I know this is the closest I've come to walking away from Mike. I just need to keep going without looking back this time. "I'll come get my stuff tonight," I tell him.

"Whatever," he says. "You'll be back tomorrow, telling me how much you love and need me. We've been through this crap a million times, Emma."

I pull into Grams's driveway knowing that I need to end this conversation with Mike before I go inside. Her feelings on Mike mimic Mom's thoughts. "Are you going to be home tonight?" I ask him with a tone of finality to rush this along.

"I had plans to go out with the guys. Devin is leaving for a month sabbatical tomorrow, so we're having drinks."

"Okay then, I'll probably be gone by the time you get home."

"Right," he snickers. "You'll be asleep in my bed. This drama is unnecessary, Emma, so just stop. I have to get back to work now that I've wasted my entire lunch break listening to your empty threats."

You're the one who called me; I want to tell him. "Okay," I calmly say again. "Have a good day?" I hang up the phone and wish I could erase Mike from my life as easily as I could delete him from my phone contacts. Whatever the case, I need to remove that man from my thoughts for a bit so I can put on a smile for Grams. She can always tell something is wrong by the way I blink.

I let myself into her house, finding her leaning against an end table in her living room. "Grams, what's wrong?" I ask.

She appears startled as she jumps and clutches at the collar of her blouse. "Emma," she huffs. "I wasn't expecting you."

I look past her, toward the microwave. "It's two fifteen on the dot," I say. It's the same time I come by most days. Mom checks in on her in the morning before she goes to work, I usually check on her midday, and Aunt Annie checks on her just before dinner time. Thankfully, we all live in a close vicinity.

"Oh, right, right...sorry," she says.

"It's okay," I tell her as I gently place my hand on her shoulder and guide her into the family room. "Is something wrong?"

"Yes," she says, the word vibrating against the hollow of her throat.

"Are you in pain? What's going on?" I ask, immediately filled with concern, but I already know about the palpitations she was getting earlier.

"I think I'm going to die today," she says, sounding helpless.

"No, you're not," I say as I help her take a seat.

Grams sits carefully, sinking into the plushness of her worn heather gray recliner. "I'm ninety-two, Emma. It's seventy-four years longer than I expected to live."

I take a seat on the arm of the chair and rest my head on her frail shoulder. "Why are you talking like this?" I ask.

With an exhausted sigh and a slight shake of her head, she replies, "I don't know." Her hand drops to her lap, and her eyes go wide as if she's staring through a wall across the room, or staring at a ghost. "It's just the truth. I shouldn't be here." I'm very confused by what she's saying, and I wish Grams would explain herself a bit more. "My heart aches. My hands are shaky and my voice always quakes, but I know I'm not ready for the end."

I spring to my feet. "I'll call 9-1-1, then your doctor. Did you take a baby aspirin this morning?"

"No," she snaps before tugging at my arm so I'll sit back down. "It hurts inside. I'm scared."

"I don't understand what you're talking about?" She doesn't speak this way. She's strong and brave, never afraid.

"It has been more than seventy-four years," she says again.

"Since what?" I ask.

"It isn't important," she says as she presses her head into the indentation she has made on her chair over the years. Her eyelids close, and she places her soft hand on mine. "Emma, you will always be my sweetheart. You know that, right?"

"Grams," I shout, startled. I press my hands into her shoulders and shake her. "Grams!"

No, no, no! I run to grab my phone, trembling as I dial 9-1-1, and the world freezes in time as I wait what seems like an eternity before my call is connected.

CHAPTER TWO

EMMA

*M*inutes have turned into hours as Mom, Aunt Annie, and I sit in the waiting room, panicking with anticipation. How did she know something bad was going to happen today? We don't even know if Grams is alive, and the feeling of the unknown is making us sick to our stomachs, which is evident since there are no words exchanged between us.

"She was acting kind of strange right before it happened," I mutter while plucking a loose thread off my torn jeans.

"Like how?" Mom asks.

"I don't know. She was talking about it being more than seventy-four years for something. She seemed confused."

"Seventy-four years?" Annie repeats.

I place my phone down on the little wooden table in front of us, annoyed by the constant vibrating messages from Facebook, incoming calls, and work emails.

"Who is sending you so many messages?" Mom asks.

"I don't know," I mumble against my fist.

"Well, can you tell them you're busy with a family emergency?"

Rather than doing that, I lean forward to shut the phone off completely, but of course, Mike must call at the exact second I'm pressing the power button.

I pick up the phone since I've already somehow pressed the answer button. "What?"

"Really? We're there now?" he asks with exasperation like he's the one I should be concerned about right now.

"Mike, I don't have time right this second. Grams passed out—we're at the hospital. We don't know what's going on. It's just not a good time. We'll talk later."

"Oh, shit, Emma, I'm so sorry," he says. "Which hospital are you at?"

"Mass General," I say. Not like it matters to him.

"I'll be right down."

"Mike, no, it's fine—" He disconnects the call. It is neither the place nor the time to try and reconcile our problems. I'm sure he has an apology floating around in that empty head of his, and he thinks he'll catch me in a moment of weakness with Grams being ill, but I don't want to hear it today.

"Don't tell me he's coming down here?" Mom groans.

"What was I supposed to do? He hung up on me."

"Well, call him back and tell him no. It's family only."

She's right, and I go to call him back, but just as I find his number, a doctor opens the door to the tiny waiting room we're occupying. We all stand as if waiting to be sentenced in a court-room. "Doctor, what's going on?" I ask.

The doctor is young, maybe fresh out of residency, but I already appreciate his bedside manner, seeing the reassuring smile on his face. "Amelia is going to be just fine," he says.

Without thought, we all lunge at him and wrap our arms around his neck. "Oh my gosh, thank you so much," I tell him. Out of the three of us, I'm probably the only one who can speak since Mom and Annie are crying. "So, what was it?"

We peel ourselves away from the poor man, and he pulls up a chair as the four of us take a seat. The doctor has kind eyes—a look that emanates ease and comfort. His smile is sort of charming, and it's clear he knows how to handle a roomful of teary eyes. "First, I'm Doctor Beck." He places his hand on his chest before leaning forward to rest his elbows on his knees. "I've been the one taking care of your mother—grandmother," he says, looking between Mom and Annie, then me. "Amelia did have a mild stroke, but we were able to dissolve the clot with a special drug meant specifically for these situations. Fortunately, we were able to prevent the stroke from progressing and doing more damage."

"But you just said she was okay?" I question.

"What's the damage?" Mom finally asks.

Dr. Beck sits up and leans back against his chair, maintaining a level of comfort, which keeps us calm. "As of right now, there doesn't appear to be any physical damage other than a very slight weakness in her left arm and leg, but she does seem a bit confused, which is normal after a stroke."

Annie is breathing heavily, losing herself in thought like she often does. I know her well enough to assume she's going through the long list of "what ifs" in her head. "Will the confusion subside?" she asks.

"In most situations, it resolves itself with time. In my experience, I've seen mild cases of memory loss or delusion, but with cognitive therapy, it's something that can improve." Dr. Beck folds his hands on his lap as he continues to explain everything to us in a way we understand. "To be honest, though, we should be focused on the fact that this could have been much worse, and since you acted so quickly, she has minimal damage." Mom and Annie place their hands on my back, silently thanking me for being there when this happened. It was just luck, though. I hate to think what could have happened if I wasn't there.

"When can we see her?" Mom asks Dr. Beck.

"Just as soon as we go over one more thing," he says. "Amelia has a condition called atrial fibrillation. This condition causes an arrhythmic heartbeat. Basically, when the heart is beating erratically, it can cause the heart to spit out blood clots. The clot can then become lodged in an artery, causing a shortage of blood to the brain, which is more than likely what caused this stroke."

I feel like I just heard a whole lot of gibberish. "What does that mean? She could have another stroke?" Annie asks. The tone of her voice is one step away from a total meltdown. I can sense it coming.

"What I'd like to do is place a pacemaker in her chest cavity, which will hopefully keep her heart beating in a regular rhythm. Doing this will help lessen the chances of her having another stroke."

She's ninety-two. This can't be a good idea.

"What if we decide against the procedure?" Mom asks.

Dr. Beck pulls in a sharp breath and holds it for a second before continuing. "Honestly, the likelihood of another stroke is moderate to high," he says.

I look over at Mom and Annie who appear to be struggling with the decision. "Do it," I tell him.

"Emma!" Mom snaps.

"It's the right thing to do."

"What about the risks involved in the surgery?" Annie questions.

"In my opinion, the risk of inserting a pacemaker is small, but the risk of another stroke without a pacemaker is concerning," Dr. Beck says. "You can come on back and see her now. Talk everything over with her and let me know when you've made a decision."

We follow Dr. Beck through the door and into the ICU. The sounds of odd beeps and air pumping through machines behind closed curtains are noises that I never want to hear again after today. My chest tightens as we reach the end of the hall, knowing how hard it's going to be to see Grams lying helpless in a hospital bed.

She has been a force of nature my entire life. Nothing has ever slowed her down or kept her from doing the things she's wanted to do. Up until now, she has driven her own car, shopped, taken walks, and she even goes out for dinner with friends. I can only hope I'm the same way at her age. Now, though, when I enter the room, she's lying quietly in a hospital bed, asleep, with wires hooked up to various parts of her body. She's pale, and her hair is a mess—this is not the woman I know. My heart breaks at the sight of her, and I grab my chest as if that will help me hold its broken pieces together.

"Grams," I say softly, making my way to the side of her bed.

"Mom," Annie follows.

Grams opens her eyes slowly as a tentative smile presses against the corners of her lips into the dimples of her soft powdery cheeks. "My girls," she says, sounding so frail. "I thought today was going to be the day."

"We're not letting anything happen to you," I tell her, taking her limp hand within mine as I stroke my thumb across the wrinkled skin on her knuckles.

"Where is Charlie?" she asks as her forehead furrows with concern?

"Who is Charlie?" Annie asks Grams.

"Oh, you know Charlie, girls." She laughs at us as if we're ridiculous for not knowing this man.

Grandpa's name was Max, so I don't think she'd be confusing the names. "We don't know anyone named Charlie," I tell her.

"Oh, sure you do, silly. Of course, you know Charlie Crane."

I share a look with Mom and Annie, each of us as confused as the other. Dr. Beck has been silently standing behind us, patiently waiting to check in with Grams. "This is the confusion I mentioned," Dr. Beck says. "She was sharing some stories from the past, and I'm not sure she understands what year it is."

"You all have such beautiful hair," Grams says, struggling to lift her hand before twirling one of my waves around her finger. "So...beautiful."

I don't understand why she's talking to us this way. "Thanks, Grams," I tell her, taking her hand back within mine. "You're going to be okay."

"I know, but you three may not be if you don't get out of here soon. I don't want the Nazis to find you in the sick bay."

That word fills my chest with a dark fear. We know little of Grams's history, mainly just that she survived the Holocaust, but her story stopped there. She didn't want us to know details or to live through the same nightmare she did, so we promised never to talk about it.

"Emma," Grams whispers, pulling me down toward her face. "Get my book, will you, sweetie?"

"Book? Grams, I don't know what book you're talking about."

"My special book," she says louder. "Please." She's clearly agitated with my confusion, but I've never seen any unfamiliar book in her house. The only books I've seen are the mystery thrillers she used to read, and I don't think she's referring to one of those. "Please find it and bring it to me."

Dr. Beck places his hand on my shoulder, and as I glance over, he nods his head for me to follow him into the hallway. "I'll be right back, Grams."

Mom and Annie don't seem to notice the exchange or the fact that I've followed the doctor out of the room, but I may have an easier time finding out more information without their emotions getting in the way. After walking around the corner, we stop, and Dr. Beck's eyebrows rise a bit. "I'd like to do this surgery immediately. The faster we can do it, the safer she will be."

I inhale heavily and release the air slowly through my pursed lips. This is so much to take in at once. "I understand. I'll do what I can to convince my mom and aunt that it's what's best. I don't think either of them are thinking clearly."

"Understandable," he says. "I'm sorry you're going through this." The kindness and sincerity written across his face breaks through the last of my strength I tried to maintain for Mom and

Annie's sake. Tears fall uncontrollably from the corners of my eyes, and I cup my hand over my mouth as I squeeze my eyes closed, wishing this wasn't happening.

"I'm sorry," I choke out.

Dr. Beck wraps his arm around my shoulders and walks me down the corridor, stopping in front of the restroom. "I'll make sure to take good care of her, okay?" He dips his head down to grab my attention and focus. "I promise."

"Thank you," I whisper. "You've been really kind and I appreciate it." Most doctors I've been around haven't had such a passionate understanding of how difficult these sorts of events are for families.

"Emma!" As the slightest bit of turmoil briefly lifts from my chest, another heavyweight drops down on the same spot, compressing all my organs into a painful mess. "Emma, there you are." I glance down the hall toward the sound of his voice, wishing I was imagining it as I stifle a groan. Mike is jogging down the hallway with a phony appearance of worry written on his face. Is this a new act he's trying out?

Dr. Beck lifts his hand from my shoulder and presses his lips into a firm smile. "Well, I'll give you some space. I'll be back to check on your grandmother soon."

"Thank you," I offer with sincerity as he takes off in the other direction.

Mike's out of breath as he forcefully pulls me into him for a hug. "How's Grams?" he asks while cupping his hand over the back of my head. The exchange feels awkward and unnatural.

"No," I tell him. "Don't do that."

"Do what?"

"Don't pretend like you suddenly care." He knows I'm weak right now, and that's his game.

He places his hand on my cheek, making a scene, here, in the intensive care unit's hallway. "I love you. What more do I need to say? I just want to show you that I'm here. I want to be here."

And I want to be alone.

~

After a nearly sleepless night mixed with worry and hope, I got up early this morning to search every nook and cranny of Grams's house, searching for the "special" book. Mom and Annie told me not to worry about it—that she must have been confused like the doctor said, but I sat awake for hours last night replaying her words in my head. They must have been right though because I don't see any book out of the ordinary.

I put everything in Grams's room back the way I found it before heading into the hallway. As I place my hand on the door-knob of her bedroom, another tear falls from my eye as I consider the day we'll need to clean this room out. I can't bear the thought of losing Grams.

Just as I'm closing myself out of the bedroom, my focus settles on a small wooden box beneath the bed. I've seen it there for years, but it never spoke to me until now.

I reopen the door, fall to my knees, and crawl forward a few feet until the box is within reach. It's heavy and full, but I pull it out and find that it isn't just an old box. It has intricate carvings alongside the brass hinges and brackets. The wood is tattered and soft as if it had been touched a thousand times before, yet I get the feeling it has sat here, sealed shut, for years.

Feeling a sense of guilt for prying, I remind myself that she asked me to find her book, and as vague as her plea was, I want to honor her request. I run my fingertips across the aged cover before releasing the clasps, then tug the lid open, listening to the groaning creak fight against the weathered metal springs.

Inside the box there are stacks of old photos and a soft, worn leather-bound book with a red ribbon draped over the top. My heart races at just the sight of the book, wondering what it contains, and questioning what Grams may have hidden from us all these years. I'm not one to spy or eavesdrop, and this feels just like that, so I'm nervous to do much more with the contents. As much as I want to know what this is and what's inside, I carefully pull out the book and hold it against my chest, inhaling the scent of aged parchment paper. Beneath the book are several more Polaroids of Grams in what looks like her early twenties, standing in front of the Statue of Liberty with her beaming smile that has apparently never changed.

I have begged for her story, wanting to know what her life was like, but she was never shy about refusing to discuss the past. She always said, "The future is the only thing that matters." In truth, I'm afraid of what I'd learn if she were ever to fill in the gaps of her life, but I also fear the day that her story could be buried alongside her.

Leaving the rest of the box behind, I stand up with the leather book and eagerly make my way out to the Jeep.

Less than a minute passes after settling into my seat when I feel the book staring at me—begging to be opened and brought back to the life it left behind.

My phone rings, and I'm thankful for the distraction as I pull it out of my purse, finding Mom's name on the display. I answer the call with a clear sense of urgency masking my attempt to sound calm. "Is everything okay?" I ask.

"Yes, yes," she says. "We've gone ahead and scheduled the surgery for tomorrow morning. I just wanted to let you know."

Relief overcomes me, knowing I won't have to argue with her about this decision. "I'm glad you agreed. I think it's best."

"Me too," she says, still sounding unsure.

"Oh, by the way, I found Grams's book," I tell her.

"What book?" she asks.

"The one she was asking for."

"I know, but what is this book?" Mom asks.

"I have no idea, but it's old and looks like it contains a lot of stories or memories. I'm taking it over to her now."

"Mike isn't with you, is he?"

"No," I respond through a groan.

"That was very nice of him to stop by yesterday, but we don't need him hanging around the hospital right now."

"Mom," I say, trying to stop any further incoming comments on the subject.

"Emma, you know how I feel about him."

"I do. It's not like you've been subtle about your hatred for Mike. I understand and partially agree with everything you feel."

"I'm glad to hear that," she says. "You should probably stop stringing him along then, and just break it off."

"Mom."

"Emma," she counters.

"I'll only be at the hospital for a little while. I have a deadline for a client this afternoon, and if I don't get the ad design to her, she's going to find someone else." Business doesn't end at 5 p.m. in my world, and therefore, neither do my contracting hours of operation.

"And why can't you tell them you have a family emergency?" she argues.

"Mom, it's my business, and I can't cancel all of my jobs. I'll handle it all, don't worry. I'm going to be right by your side tomorrow morning and whenever you need me to be with you."

"Okay," she sighs. "Just wait there until I get back, so she's not alone. I need to take a quick nap and a shower."

"No problem," I tell her.

Since my phone call lasted the entire drive to the hospital, it broke up the eagerness to open Grams's book, but now that I'm here, excitement is rushing through me as I slide my hands along the warm leather binding. I need to know what's inside.

I guard it within my arms like a lost treasure as I make my way into the hospital and over to the ICU.

As worried as I was yesterday, I must not have noticed how far the walk to the ICU was, and I'm out of breath by time I reach

Grams's room. Though, it's perfect timing as I nearly run right into Dr. Beck.

"Emma," he greets me.

"Oh, hi, Dr. Beck. How is she today?"

"That woman..." he points behind him, "she is a spitfire." He laughs and looks over his shoulder at her. "She's doing well."

"Thank you for taking such good care of her," I tell him.

"It's my job," he says. "Will you excuse me, though? I have to tend to another patient right now."

I'm left without words, a bit mesmerized by his sparkling eyes and engaging demeanor, as well as the noticeable fact that he has the most perfect butt that I probably shouldn't be staring at while he's walking away. However, I've never actually seen a man's butt fill out a pair of scrubs so perfectly before.

"Emma, is that you?" Thankfully, Grams's voice interrupts my inappropriate stare and thoughts, and I enter her room.

"It's me, Grams. I found your book, I think." I rush to her side and gently place it down on her lap. The corners of her lips perk into a smile as she keeps her focus set on the ceiling above our heads.

"The nice doctor told me I might not be able to see very clearly for the next few days, but you know what?"

"What?" I question.

"I can see he's very handsome," she says through weak laughter.

My cheeks burn, knowing Mom is a replica of Grams in every way. Both want nothing more than to point out the obviously attractive men in this world, constantly reminding me that I'm still not married and don't have children. It's becoming a running joke—one with an underlying meaning I've gotten good at sweeping under the carpet. "Anyway," I try to change the subject, "I hope this is the book you were referring to."

"It is," she says, glancing down at it. She lifts the cover, and the spine crackles against the tug as she flips through a couple of pages. Grams appears to be reacquainting herself with the pages as she runs her fingertips down the center of a handwritten page that looks like a diary entry of some sort.

"What is it?" I ask.

"I wrote this after I arrived in New York, back in 1945. It's so hard to remember the details now, but that's precisely why I wrote everything down while the memories were fresh in my mind."

"Memories?" I question. I know Grams arrived in New York around 1944 or 1945, just after the end of the war, but beyond that, I know very little.

She tries to lift the book, but her hands shake while attempting to do so. "Would you mind?"

"Mind?"

"Yes, Emma, would you please read me this page?"

I take the book from her hands and turn around in search of a place to sit. I pull the blue plastic bucket chair over to Grams's side of the bed and take a seat. With the book resting on my lap, I scan the page, admiring her beautiful handwriting along the yellowed lines of the cream-colored paper. "Are you sure, Grams?"

"Why wouldn't I be?" she asks, sounding confused.

"You have never wanted to share much of your past with me," I tell her, assuming that's what is contained within these pages.

"It's time I tell you what happened," she responds without hesitation. "So, please, please read my words. I need to remember Charlie."

CHAPTER THREE

AMELIA

DAY 1 - JANUARY 1942

*M*ama said to close my eyes and take a deep breath when I got scared. It would offer me a moment of distraction from whatever was making me upset. So, I counted as I inhaled, wishing the sounds would go away and leave us to the little freedom we had left. With my eyes closed, I was more aware of my racing pulse and the rhythmic sound of my unsteady breaths.

The clothes covering my body smelled of clean soap—a scent I had always enjoyed after Mama and I brought the dry laundry in from the clothesline outside. I knew at that moment that I wanted to remember the fresh smell because it was home, and that's what they were there for—our home.

Heavy footsteps on the creaking floors sent shivers through my soul. I heard them moving through the darkness of our small house, then a beam from a flashlight bounced off the walls and worked its way through the makeshift cloth doors I was hiding behind.

"Their plates are half full, and the food is still warm," one of them said. "They're in here somewhere." As the voices continued, I heard one of them chewing the food Mama had just prepared for us. It made me sick.

We knew the day was coming, but we didn't know when. I had foolishly suggested we run away and hide, but Mama and Papa said it wasn't a possibility because there was no place to hide.

We were stalling, hoping for a miracle, but there had been no miracles in Prague for quite some time, and the hope we once held onto was fading by the minute.

As I listened, feeling helpless and full of fear, I could hear them in Jakob's room, tossing his books and tearing his drawings down from the walls. Then, a loud crash followed the smaller sounds. A tear skated down my cheek as imagined the noise had come from his bureau or bed.

A groan followed every bang, and wrestling noises ensued. "No, no," Jakob screamed.

"Who else lives here with you?" a man asked.

"No, one," Jakob shouted. "I live alone."

Jakob was a little less than two years older than I, and at nineteen, he was trying to protect our family from what was happening, but even the smartest and bravest couldn't seem to conquer the army of Nazis hunting us down.

"You're a liar." The man continued yelling at Jakob in a thick German accent that was hardly understandable, but then I clearly heard the man follow with, "I can see the nervous look in your eye." Our walls were thin, and I heard every one of Jakob's nervous breaths. He always had trouble breathing in stressful conditions, and that situation was making it so much worse.

The sounds of wrestling continued, and I squeezed my eyes shut while trying to imagine being somewhere else, but it was impossible to block out the truth.

Papa stormed through the hallway, interrupting the interrogation in Jakob's bedroom. I knew it was him by the way his shoes clapped against the wooden floors—it was different from the sound of a boot's thud. "Let go of my son, now!" Papa yelled. "Jakob, run!"

"He was lying," one of the Nazi's said again—the man's voice was calm and apathetic about the torment he was causing our family. "How many more of you are in here?"

"There is no one else here," Papa said. "Take me and leave my son; he is of no use to you."

"You're a liar too," the Nazi said, playfully, as if he were enjoying the anguish. I didn't know how many of those soldiers were in our house, but I was sure I heard at least three different voices.

Boots charged through the hallway, and as the echoes grew louder, I realized they must have known exactly where I was hiding. They were heading straight for me.

The cloth hanging in front of my closet's opening were torn from the rod as the glow of their flashlights pierced through the fabric that was still draped over me.

I was kicked hard—hard enough that I may have normally squealed or let out a cry, but I held my breath through the pain, trying my best to be brave. "What is under here?" a man questioned. I felt as though I was being teased and toyed with, just as Papa was. It continued to be a game for them as the clothes were peeled away, one article at a time, until I was uncovered and exposed as I cowered in the corner while their light blinded me.

My racing heart felt as though it were free-falling through my body like a lead weight, and I felt numb as I was pulled up to my feet. Fear, unlike anything I had ever known overwhelmed all my senses, making it hard to breathe. A hand cuffed my arm tightly, and the soldier yanked me forward, forcing me to trip over my dress as I stumbled to keep up with his pace. "No!" I shrieked. "Leave us alone!"

"Do not fight with us, Jew. Grab a coat and a bag. You're coming with us."

"I have a right to be here! This is our home, and you are tres-passing." Papa often told me that my mouth would get me into trouble someday, but if that were the day, I would rather it be because I was trying to protect my family versus giving in without a fight.

"You no longer have any rights. You are a Jew—you're nothing more than an animal." The Nazi stared down at me, pausing before dragging me out the door. His lip snarled as if he were an angry dog. I couldn't understand what I did to make anyone hate me so much. He didn't know me or my family. He didn't know any of us living in that town, but he hated us because someone told him to feel that way.

"I am a human being, like you." I spoke so softly, my words were probably inaudible, but I had to say it. He needed to hear how I felt, even if it meant nothing to him.

Despite my efforts, however, it was obvious my words had no effect on him. All that seemed to matter was that he knew I was weaker than him, and I didn't have the physical strength to resist his power as he pulled me out of my house. He dragged me by my heels behind him as we followed in the path of Papa and Jakob.

"Please," I heard Mama cry out. "Please don't take my family."

"Mama, go back inside," I shouted at her.

"Let my children go!" she shouted. "Those are my babies. I put them on this earth, and you cannot take them away from me. They're mine!"

"They are not children or babies," one of the Nazis said.

"Let them go, you monsters!" she shouted louder as she tried to jump on the man pulling me. She clawed at his back, pounding her fists against him, but did little, if any, damage. "Run, Amelia. Run!" Mama told me.

The Nazi soldier didn't loosen his grip on me for a second. I could have pulled as hard as I wanted to, but he had me trapped. "I can't get away, Mama."

Another Nazi took hold of Mama and dragged her away. I

watched over my shoulder as she was pushed down to her knees while cradling her hands around the back of her head.

I prayed to God, begging him not to let them hurt her.

"Amelia, turn around and go!" she cried out. I had never heard Mama cry before then, not once in my entire life.

I cried softly to myself, begging them not to touch her. I kept saying, "No," over and over, but none of them heard me. No one cared.

The world froze around me and a cold sweat coated my skin as that Nazi screamed a line of obscenities at Mama before pulling out his gun. I watched as he aimed it at the back of her head, and again, I prayed he was just trying to torture and scare her, but the sound of a loud click changed that thought. "Mama!" I screamed. "I love you, Mama. Please, don't hurt her!"

"Amelia," she sobbed, looking up at me. "Fight and be strong. For me."

"Mama, no," I whimpered as the blast from the gun thumped against the inside and outside of my chest. I tried to escape the hands pushing me along, but when I saw Mama fall, crumpling to the ground like a rag doll, I froze in place—I felt paralyzed. "Mama, please don't leave me!" It didn't matter how much I begged. My voice wasn't heard, and if it was, it was ineffective and too late.

Brokenhearted and shattered, I was shoved into the back of a line of other Jews who were also being shuttled down the cobblestone street.

I stumbled backwards, watching as blood sprayed from the side of Mama's head, painting the old cobblestones burgundy as her life poured out of her and trickled down the street.

I cried silently among the gasps of surrounding bystanders. I thought maybe I had imagined it, but no matter how many times I blinked, the scene was still in front of me.

She was gone and there was nothing left of her.

Tears filled my eyes as agony shuddered through my chest. I

just watched Mama die—she was murdered. I tried to swallow but my throat was drier than sandpaper.

She was just trying to protect us, but without mercy or a chance for real goodbyes, they took her from me. There was no sense of humanity among the soldiers. Just as we had heard thousands of times before: as far as Hitler and his army were concerned...Jews were nothing.

As we were herded like sheep, I leaned to the side, looking for Papa and Jakob. I caught Papa's gaze as he was muttering words to himself. I assumed he was praying and reciting the Mourner's Kaddish for Mama, but it was only a brief second before he was pushed around the corner. His eyes looked empty as if all the life had been sucked out of him.

Mama and Papa had been married for twenty-two years. They were as happy as two people could be together, and in the time-frame of a few minutes, our family had been torn apart, and Mama was dead. While realization consumed me, a hollow feeling in my chest engulfed my entire body, I pulled at the collar of my dress beneath my coat, tearing the material in an expression of my grief. Since I had never lost someone close to me, I'd never had cause to do so before, but as I felt the threads tear, I immediately understood the purpose and meaning behind the Jewish tradition. It was like a reflection of what was happening inside me—I felt my heart shredding to pieces just like the cloth, as if it were made from nothing more than a thin piece of paper.

Adding to my devastation, the fear of where they were taking us bled through me as I continued to pray it was all a nightmare.

A hand squeezed my shoulder, and a woman's voice whispered into my ear. It was as if that woman were placed in that spot at that moment just to tell me exactly what I needed to hear. "You need to stay alive. You must stop crying. I understand your pain, but your mama would want you to be strong now. Do it for her."

The woman kept her hand on my shoulder as we continued to

shuffle behind the line of others. It gave me little comfort, but at least I wasn't alone.

I knew I wasn't the only one who wanted to know where we were going. Despite being told that there would be shelter for us once the Nazis took over our homes, no one knew where the shelter was.

When the line stopped moving, I was no longer able to see anything happening in front of, or behind me. The sun had set, and the streetlights weren't bright enough to offer much visibility.

I needed to be with Papa and Jakob, and I wanted to stop shaking both from the cold and the utter horror I had witnessed. I couldn't stop thinking about Mama and the fact that she was probably still sprawled out in the middle of the street in front of our family's home, lifeless and alone.

There was a time when we had everything, or so it seemed, but in the blink of an eye, everything changed. Nothing would ever be normal again. Carefree, happy days had already been taken from us several months earlier, but I knew then that the hope of finding those times again were gone forever. I needed Mama; she was my best friend, the closest person in my life, and the one who was always there for me—even during her last moments. I did everything I could to hold back the tears. The pain was unbearable as I kept visualizing that scene of Mama's murder repeatedly playing out in my mind. What was she thinking right before that man shot her? Did she know she was going to die? Did she suffer, or had she died instantly? I prayed she didn't live long enough to feel the agonizing pain. I prayed she went to heaven peacefully and quickly. Then, there was a part of me was envious of her because she didn't have to go on with a broken heart like the rest of us would.

I closed my eyes to block out my surroundings, but all I could see behind my eyelids were blurry pools of blood and splattered red blotches painting a landscape of death. There was no way to escape. I wanted to drop to the ground and scream and cry, but I was too scared. It was so hard to hold it all in and accompanying my pain was a mortal fear beyond words.

The woman who stood behind me tugged at my shoulder that she was still holding onto, forcing me to turn around and face her. She was young, maybe just a few years older than I was, but she was pregnant and cradling her belly with her free hand. "Are you okay?" the woman asked.

"No," I whispered. No one was okay. We were all freezing, waiting for whatever the soldiers had in store for us.

The only sounds within the narrow alleyway were heavy breaths from the others, along with a light breeze that blurred the line between reality and hell.

"Do you know where we are going or what they have planned for us?" I asked the woman I was facing. She shook her head as she pulled her wool coat tightly over her protruding belly. "No. They came in, raided our house, and forced us out," she said.

"Are you alone?" I asked her, wondering if I was the only unlucky one to be separated from my family.

She twisted her head to the right and took a man's hand—I assumed he was her husband—and pulled him up alongside her. "It's the two—well, three of us, God willing," she said. "What about you?"

Once again, I looked for any sight of Papa or Jakob, but I didn't see them anywhere. "My Papa and older brother are up ahead in the line," I told her. "But my Mama was—"

The woman placed her hand on my cheek and hushed me. "I know." Her kindness forced a wave of emotion to unravel within me. A lump caught in my throat, but I managed to pull in a bit of air with the hope of maintaining control. I knew I couldn't cry. Along with being terrified that those heartless men would try to make an example of me just as they did with Mama, I also knew I couldn't let them see how much they had taken from me.

The woman lowered her hand to mine and squeezed it tightly. "I'm Leah," she said, peacefully. She was like a brave angel.

"My name is Amelia," I told her in the same soft tone.

"We have to be strong, Amelia. That's all we can do right now."

The meaning of strong had rapidly changed throughout the previous hour. Before that first day, being strong meant holding in my tears when I scraped my knee as a child, or learning to keep my chin up when a boy at school would tease me. I was strong when Grandmother passed away, knowing she had lived a long, fulfilling life. At that moment in time, though, I didn't know how to be strong—not after watching Mama murdered in cold blood.

The worst part was that I had no idea how much stronger I would need to become in the coming weeks.

CHAPTER FOUR

EMMA

One diary entry and the world I thought I knew feels as though it's crumbling around me. The words read in history books don't compare to the ones spoken by a person I love. "Grams, why haven't you ever told this to any of us?" I ask her.

Grams's head sinks into the pillow, and her unfocused gaze floats to the ceiling. "No one told the survivors how to deal with the aftereffects of having their lives torn apart. There weren't many of us around."

"Yes, but there had to be some kind of help, right?" I ask.

Grams chuckles softly as if what I said was a joke. "Emma, it would be like a person who has never suffered from some type of addiction telling an addict that they can move on from their habit, and how to do so. Unless you've lived through it, you can't preach advice to the victims. Plus, most of the memories were too painful to face, and I had to lock them away in that diary." I understand what she's saying, but never talking about it, even with us, doesn't make sense. It hurts.

"Talking always helps me," I tell her.

"I'm talking to you now, sweetie," she says.

"What about Mom and Annie?" I ask.

Grams shakes her head ever so slightly. "I don't want them to know. They're too sensitive, and it's too late to explain why I never answered the questions they have asked so many times before."

Without even thinking, I say, "It can be our secret." As the words came out, I knew it wouldn't be just some simple secret to hold on to. I would be imprinted on my life.

"I want you to hold on to it, so it's never forgotten."

I take Grams's hand and squeeze it tenderly. "I can do that for you."

With a profound inhale, she glances back at me with solidity burning from her gaze. "I don't want the surgery tomorrow."

"No way," I argue. "It's the only way to prevent you from having another stroke. You were lucky this time. It was mild. You may not be so lucky next time. There's no other choice, Grams."

"Emma," she says, complacently, "there is another way."

"What? No, there isn't. You are not going to rot, not after what you've already been through."

"I'm ninety-two. I'm too old for surgery. I'm too old for miracles. It's time for me to make peace with my life and move on." She speaks as though she's been contemplating this for a while, but I don't understand how anyone can so easily become resigned to dying. Death scares me. I thought it scared most people. Though, Grams isn't most people—I know that more than ever now.

"You still have more life to live," I tell her, spitting out empty words with nothing to back up my reasoning.

"Em, I live by myself, talk to myself, eat by myself, and think to myself all day, every day."

"I'll come over more. I'll have meals with you, and you can talk to me whenever you want. Please, I'm not ready to let you go." I'm begging for her to change her mind, but I know the look in her eye. It's the look she makes when she's made a final decision.

"You need to start a life of your own," she says.

"I have a life of my own," I argue.

"You've never been in love, Emma. You don't understand." As I digest her words, I feel hurt by what she's saying, but after a moment of clarity and silently repeating her words to myself, I realize she may be right.

"I want what you and Grandpa had," I tell her. "It's on my list of things to accomplish in my lifetime."

With what seems like all her effort, she presses her elbows into the bed and pulls herself up into a more upright position. "Emma, listen to me," she begins, frankly. "What your grandfather and I had was love, sure, but it wasn't the kind of love some search for throughout an entire lifetime. He was a good man—my best friend for many, many years—and he treated me well, but sometimes we're not always with the right people in life."

Confusion. That must be what this is. "Grams, maybe you should rest." I stand up to fluff her pillow.

"Sit back down, Emma," she demands.

The sternness of her words forces me to do as she says. "I'm trying to tell you something important, and you need to listen."

"Okay," I utter.

Out of the corner of my eye, I see Dr. Beck enter the room, but at the same moment, Grams begins again. "It's easy to settle, Emma. It's hard to push through your comfort zone and take a chance when everyone else thinks it's wrong." I don't understand what she means.

Dr. Beck's hand finds my shoulder. "How's she doing?"

I want to tell him she isn't making any sense, but for some reason, I think I'm the one who can't make sense of what she's saying. "She seems okay," I tell him, quietly.

"So, Amelia, we're going to be giving you a pacemaker tomorrow to prevent any more strokes in the future. How does that sound?"

"No," Grams responds. "I don't want any of that fancy technology of yours in my body."

"Grams, please," I beg.

"No," she says again, sounding more stubborn than I've ever heard her.

"Grams, I'll do anything for you to reconsider." I'm becoming desperate, and I don't know what else I can do to convince her about the importance of this surgery. She should have it. There's no questioning this fact.

Her eyelids close, but flutter, as if she is in deep thought. After a long pause, her eyes reopen and she says, "Fine."

"Really? You'll go through with it?" I ask her.

"Yes, but under one condition," she says.

"Anything, what is it?"

"Get rid of Mike and go on a date with this lovely man," she says, pointing to Dr. Beck.

I don't think my face could become any redder or hotter without bursting into flames. I feel frozen as I stare at Grams with "how could you" eyes, but she simply smiles in return. If this isn't Jewish guilt, I don't know what is.

"Grams," I say, without much to follow with, considering Dr. Beck is standing behind me.

"I'm going to give you two a moment," he says.

"No, I don't think so," Grams pipes in. "You're very much a part of this, don't you think?"

Dr. Beck shifts his weight from one foot to the other, obviously uncomfortable with the situation Grams is putting him in, as well. "You know, for a woman who just had a stroke, you're quite feisty," he jests.

"It runs in our blood," she says, winking at him. "Now, ask my granddaughter out on a date so you can go schedule my surgery."

"How do you know I'm not married, or dating someone?" he asks Grams while pulling up a rolling stool to her bedside.

"There's no ring on your finger, and I've been watching the

way you act when my granddaughter's around—you steal a glance at her every chance you get. I may be old, but I'm not blind," she says as her brow arches with delight at the accusation.

"Grams, stop," I groan.

Dr. Beck drops down onto the stool and leans forward, resting his elbows on his knees. "Uh, Emma," he says.

I'm embarrassed to even look over at this man, dreading what he must be thinking. "Yes," I say, timidly.

"How does dinner tonight sound? I get off my shift at five."

Grams's heart monitor begins to speak for me—the continuous beeps of her pulse escalating just enough to make a scene. This is unbelievable. "She'll be here waiting for you," Grams answers for me.

I smile with incredible embarrassment and agree with a quick nod. "Yes, I'd love to." I believe this is officially the most awkward moment of my life.

"Are you sure that man who was here yesterday is going to be okay with this?" he asks. "I wouldn't want to step in between the two of you or complicate your relationship."

"There is no issue," Grams answers for me. "He cheats on her at least once a week, but she has stuck by him, anyway. It's time for her to turn over a new leaf."

Dr. Beck places his hand on his chest and noticeably sucks in a lungful of air. "Well then, Emma, I'd be happy to take you out for dinner."

"Great," I say softly, shyly, mortified as I feel Grams's stare burn into the side of my face.

"I have a few rounds to make, but I'll be back in soon to check on you, Amelia."

"Maybe you should just start calling me Grams," she says with a chuckle.

As Dr. Beck leaves, I shift around in the seat, directly facing Grams while kindly offering an evil eye. "I can't believe you are using your heart to control my dating life."

"Oh, Emma, what better part of me to use? Plus, you'll thank me someday. I'll probably be dead, but you can visit my grave and pay your respects then."

"You are cruel," I tell her.

"No, I just know what I'm talking about," she says with a devious smirk.

"Oh yeah?" I tease.

"Keep reading, Emma. You'll see."

"Grams, this—" I place my hand down on the diary's cover. "It's a lot to take in." Watching her mother die in front of her eyes, then carrying on alone...I can't fathom a world where that took place. I'm not sure I could have kept going; yet all these years later, here she is, making jokes with me.

"It's a lot to try and forget too," she says.

"Is that why you have never shared this?"

"It's one of the reasons, yes," she says with confidence while taking the book from my hands.

She flips open the cover and turns to the second page before returning it to my hands, then nestles her head back into the pillow.

Grams has always been good at one thing—distracting me. Just a minute ago, I was arguing with her about refusing the surgery, and now I'm staring at her scripted words written on aged paper, nervous about what I might learn next.

"Well then, come on," she says, waving her hands at the book. "I want you to get to the good parts."

The good parts? Of the Holocaust? I stare at her with a blank expression, unsure how to respond, but she doesn't appear to be seeking a response as she keeps her focus zoned in on the open pages.

I can only chalk her irrational behavior up to her medical condition.

CHAPTER FIVE

AMELIA

DAY 2 - JANUARY 1942

*W*hen we were allowed to stop walking, a freight appeared to be waiting for us in the distance. Steam billowed into the night, but there was an unknown destination of where it was headed.

Hours passed as we stood in one line, waiting to board the train. Whether for punishment or thrill, I'm still not sure, but they forced us to stand silently in the cold until sunrise before we were brought inside the train.

Hundreds of Jews, including myself, were ferociously shoved inside the metal freight containers as we smashed into each other or one of the four metal walls. We were left with no space to move or breathe, and I foolishly thought the soldiers would fix the situation once they noticed how many of us were crunched into one metal box, but I quickly realized it was purposeful as laughter grew from outside the train's walls. Suffocation felt imminent, but the small opening above the closed sliding door offered just enough air to keep us alive. After less than a half hour, I considered the situation to be pure torture, but at that time, I had no idea how bad things could get.

The soldiers never told us where we were going. There was no one to ask, and none of the other people were talking. Everyone must have been as scared as I felt.

The tight constriction that was filled with musty body odors and sweat-covered limbs rubbed against me at every angle. I knew the feeling of strangulation was only in my head, but the sensation was so prominent that I felt like a noose had been tied around my neck. After watching what happened to Mama, part of me wanted to hold my breath until death found me since I knew that would be the only way to avoid the next destination, but I was too scared to end my life right then and there.

As the train jerked us all around, the heavier bodies fell on the smaller ones, and I was shoved into one of the vibrating metal walls—my cheek slammed against the cold, flat surface, but I hardly felt the pain in comparison to the abundance of consuming fear. Unable to move, I clenched my eyes and fists as I continuously relived the look on Mama's face at the moment before the gun went off.

I had never felt alone before then. Even when I would walk through the mustard fields on sunny days to seek the quiet sounds of nature, I didn't feel as secluded from the world like I did at that moment.

The vibrations from the wall soothed me into a semi-meditative state, and the surrounding bodies pinned me against the wall hard enough that I knew I wouldn't fall, even if my knees were to give out.

The rumble of the train's metal grinding against the track was the only sound we could hear inside. With as much confusion as I assume we were all feeling, I would have expected people to be talking, questioning our whereabouts, and what might have been happening, but it was as if no one was left with a voice. Even the woman who had been standing behind me earlier when Mama was shot just stood silently with an arch in her back as she cradled her stomach, almost as if she were holding it up. The poor woman must have been very uncomfortable, especially with so many people pressed up against her. I wish I could have helped her over to where I was standing to offer her my spot against the wall, but I couldn't move a hair. We didn't have a choice on where we stood once we boarded. In fact, it was almost as if we were purposely separated when I was shoved against my will toward the far side of the tomb-like enclosure.

I tried to block out the terror I felt, but it was impossible to block anything out as the train's occupants would fall into me every few minutes or so. At one point, the train shifted so hard that the larger woman by my side fell onto me, but she didn't correct her stance afterward. I was stuck with her chest pressed into my back and my long braid caught between us. I reached behind me to free my hair and had to pull firmly to twist it over my shoulder. I didn't know if she was unconscious, or awake and weak, but I couldn't see anything in the dark space, so I didn't say a word to her.

While running my fingers down the tightness of my braid, a painful sensation drove through me as I recalled Mama's fingertips running across my scalp the morning before she wove the strands together. Even though I was seventeen, Mama still enjoyed trying new things with my hair just like she always had, and I let her play with it in the mornings before we would start our daily chores around the house.

Mama was only eighteen years older than I was, and as I grew older throughout the years, the difference between our ages felt smaller and smaller. We shared secrets, told stories, and helped each other in any way we could. Our house was very much the picture of women against men, but not in a negative way. Papa and Jakob did the "men's work," and Mama and I did the "women's work." Papa and Jakob were close like Mama and me, but I was Papa's princess, and Jakob idolized the ground Mama walked on. No one's family was perfect during that time, but I felt like ours came pretty close.

After what felt like hours on the train, a squeal from the brakes screamed through the walls, piercing my ears as everyone toppled onto each other.

Without surprise, it felt like another hour passed before the door finally opened to let us out. We all poured out of the train and into the open air like an overfilled bucket of water. The cold, fresh air was like a slice of heaven, but that feeling was quite brief.

Demands were shouted from every direction, and I didn't know where to look or what to do. Being on the shorter side and having trouble seeing over some of the taller people around me, I thought I might be at a disadvantage, but then again, Mama always told me, "What you don't know won't hurt you." Maybe I was better off not seeing everything at that moment.

I couldn't tell where we were, but I held onto hope that it would be some type of shelter like we were promised. I wanted to scream out for Papa and Jakob, but it was apparent that the only people allowed to speak—or yell, as the case was—were the Nazis. I was frightened to move, let alone speak.

A Nazi made his way through the crowd, pushing us in different directions, but then a pair of hands clamped down on my shoulders and I was shoved into a line. It was immediately obvious that I was segregated into a group with only women and children. The men had been led to a different area, which eliminated all hope of finding Papa and Jakob.

It felt as if we were being herded like cattle. It was so demeaning and humiliating. I couldn't imagine who gave those people the right to treat us like animals.

We were then led beneath an archway and into a dirt pit surrounded by what looked like cement prison cells. There must have been several hundreds of us on the train, but by that point, it looked like the number could have been in the thousands. I had never seen so many people in one place at a time.

Before we stepped on the next train, the Nazis patted down each one of us and took all our belongings. I didn't know what they were searching for, but it felt like they were just stripping us of everything we had and all that we were.

Though I was impatient, upset, and feeling ill, I was relieved that the progression of whatever was happening to the people in front of me, was fast paced since my only objective was to find Papa and Jakob.

As I got closer to the front of the line, I saw several Nazis inspecting each person's body from head to toe. It appeared that whenever they found something of value, they tossed it into a wooden crate before shoving the person ahead, where they were led in one direction or another.

When it was my turn, I stepped up to the Nazi and closed my eyes—it was something I found myself repeatedly doing to block out the reality of my situation. The darkness, however, could only cover up the visual reality. Nothing could stop the sensation of hands roaming freely over every inch of my body and fingers digging deep into my thin pockets, only to come up empty-handed. I had nothing of value, and they didn't seem to appreciate that. The Nazi that searched my body sneered and shoved me harder than he had shoved the woman in front of me.

I was passed to another Nazi, one who was gentler as he tightened his hand around my arm and walked me along the outside of the courtyard until we reached one of the prison-like buildings.

The Nazi brought me inside, where there was a long, dimly lit hallway with a dirt floor, and doors on both sides for as far as I could see.

"Where are you taking me?" I asked with a cautious inflection.

At first, he looked at me as if I were pretentious to be speaking out, but as he stared at me for another short moment, it seemed that a piece of bitterness chipped away from his scowl. "To your assigned block," he answered.

As we continued walking, I took the opportunity to examine

the expression of his profile, noting there was something different about him versus the others. His eyes appeared softer, more innocent, and he looked younger than the other Nazis, almost boyish in fact. I assumed he was around my age. "What is going to happen to us here?" I asked him, knowing the risk I was taking, once again.

He straightened his shoulders and inhaled sharply, making it clear I should have stopped talking after my last inquiry. "Why would you ask such a stupid question?" he responded, though his words sounded rehearsed and unnatural.

"Why are we here?" I asked again. Maybe I was feeding off of an assumed weakness he had, but curiosity had me acting fearless, as well.

The man cleared his throat and gripped my arm a little firmer. "To offer you shelter, of course. Just as you were told."

"One of you killed my mother yesterday," I snapped without thought. Jews were being executed daily for reasons that were unknown. They killed Mama for trying to protect us. They didn't even know who she was other than that she was a Jew. How could I believe those Jew haters were doing something to help us?

"I'm not one of them," he said quietly. Then, a sudden jerk of his arm stopped me in my place as he pushed me into the wall. "We are all different, just like every one of you."

"You're a Nazi, so you are no different from the rest of them," I replied, speaking in a way I should never have been speaking to one of those soldiers. I could have been killed for saying what I said, but unfortunately, defiance grew from my anger—I had lost control of my emotions, and at that moment, I didn't care what the consequences were.

"You don't know what you're talking about," he said, sharply, through a tightened jaw.

After staring me down like a park bully, he regained his tight grip around my arm and continued pulling me down the hall until we reached a door that he threw open.

"This is where you will be staying," he said, pushing me inside.

I was faced with a tiny foul-smelling room surrounded by nothing more than cement walls and columns of bunk beds with a walkway just wide enough for a body to squeeze through. Most of the "beds" had already been claimed by others, but there were a few empty spaces I could share with others.

"This is where I'll be living?" I asked.

"Yes," he answered.

The door slammed behind me, and I walked ahead slowly, scanning the people on the thin mattresses—all of them were women. Some appeared emaciated. Others looked worse; almost skeletal.

The floors were uneven and covered by dirt, there were insects everywhere, and the torn fabric on the mattresses were filthy with stains.

During each of the first few moments I spent in that horrible place, I gained more clarity. None of our people from Prague wanted to leave their homes, but we were given no other choice. I was sure we were becoming prisoners for crimes never committed.

I chose a mattress closest to the ground and dropped into it, feeling the weight of my body collapse from under me after standing for so long. With only a moment's rest, the sound of people moaning and the scent of ammonia trickled in, alerting my senses of the true reality. The peeling paint on the walls and the sealed, darkened windows made me homesick for my beautiful home. Instead, all I could feel in that dismal building was utter sadness and a feeling of hopelessness that was accompanied by the smell of death. In that room filled with strangers, I was all alone.

My mattress was full of sharp, defined coils pressing up against the thin layer of foam and cotton. I was sure it would be some time before I'd be able to will myself asleep with the amount of sheer discomfort I felt.

I prayed for sleep, though.

I was mourning Mama, but the pain was too much to bear alone, and I wanted to turn off my mind for a while.

CHAPTER SIX

EMMA

*a*s I finish reading Grams's detailed entry describing her admission to the concentration camp, I hear her breaths turn into soft snores. Reluctant to leave the book behind, I slip it into my shoulder bag and take the opportunity to find a bathroom and a place to grab food. I don't make it very far down the hallway before I run into Dr. Beck as he's studying a patient's chart. "Emma," he greets me. His voice is deeper than I remember from earlier, but still just as professional.

"Dr. Beck," I respond.

He seems a bit flustered as a paper falls from a folder pinched under his arm. We both lean forward to retrieve the fallen paper, but he reaches it first. While correcting his stance and replacing the paper, a soft sigh hums in his throat. "You can call me Jackson," he says.

"Jackson," I correct myself. "I'm sorry about my grandmother." He moves the clipboard beneath his arm where the folder is and clasps his hands together in front of his waist.

"What do you have to be sorry about?"

"She shouldn't have been so pushy and intrusive," I tell him.

A smile tugs at the right corner of his lips and he shifts his weight from one foot to the other. "This may be hard to believe, but I have a grandmother just like her. In fact, she does just about anything in the world to embarrass me."

With the feeling of awkwardness from our not-so-casual conversation, I reposition my bag over my shoulder. "Well, I guess today is my day to take one for the team," I say, feeling a warm blush color my cheeks what must be a deep shade of pink.

"Take one for the team?" he questions. "Does that mean you'd rather not go out tonight? I promise I won't be offended if you don't want to go out with me."

I didn't intend to sound like I was complaining. "No, of course not," I say as I place my hand over my big mouth. "That's not what I meant."

"Good." A grin stretches across his face, pinching against the bottom of his dark lashes. With that, Jackson gently taps the back of his clipboard against my arm and walks off. "See you tonight, Emma."

My hand is still on my face as I continue walking down the hall. I have a boyfriend. I can't just go out on a date with some guy because he's a good-looking doctor and I'm being lured in by Grams. It's been six years of this. No one in my family has liked Mike from the minute they met him. In my defense, I don't think he was always the person he is now, but maybe I just didn't see it then. I don't know.

After grabbing a couple of snacks from the gift shop, I head outside to the courtyard, finding a picnic bench under a low hanging tree. *Let's hope there's a WiFi connection out here.* I pull my laptop out of my bag, open it up, and place it down on the table. It's only a matter of seconds before dozens of emails pop up, following a lead weight falling to the pit of my stomach.

I can only see the subject lines, but I swear each one says there's some kind of problem I have to fix. My career has always come first, but I can hardly think straight today.

With a deep breath of the fresh autumn air, I open the first email and begin the succession of responses, knowing I'll most likely be doing the actual updates on their projects at midnight tonight.

"I guess I can be thankful that you made it easy for me to find you today." Mike walks around from the other side of the tree and without an invitation, sits down across from me.

"What are you doing here?" I ask him.

"I came to see how Grams is doing."

"Mike, why are you saying that—calling her that? When have you ever cared about Grams? When's the last time you came with me to visit her?" I let out a groan as I run my fingers through my hair. "I guess what I'm truly interested in is your reason for trying to impress me all of a sudden."

He weaves his fingers together and rests them on the table, bowing his head as if out of shame, which I doubt to be the case. "I really do want to be with you," he says, calmly.

"Answer me this, Mike. Did you or didn't you cheat on me? That could mean anything from kissing to whatever else. Look me in the eyes and tell me the truth." I'm not sure what he'll say, but I already know the truth. He has cheated...many times.

I pull my laptop screen down and fold my arms over the top of it, looking past him, rather than at his eyes. Since he didn't immediately tell me he wouldn't do such a thing, I'm hopeful for the truth. It would be a change from his typical lies when I ask him this question. You don't just come home smelling like perfume because you were in an elevator with someone, or because they were helping you with a project for two hours. The stories have been quite imaginative, that's for sure.

After a long minute, Mike lifts his head and does as I asked. He looks me directly in the eyes and begins talking, "I slept with someone," he says with a minimal amount of shame.

A part of me feels relief for knowing I'm not crazy, and for the confirmation that my gut is always true to me. "So, what, she wasn't as good in bed as I am? Is that why you love me so much right now?" It's harsh, but I know Mike well enough to assume his reason.

"Emma," he says with a flustered sigh as if I'm the one being unreasonable. "I don't have the desire to do that again, I swear to you. I was thinking about popping the question and all that jazz. Then I realized how scary forever sounded, and I just got this bug in my head. As soon as it was over, I realized how stupid I was for thinking I needed something more."

The only emotion stirring inside of me at the moment is happiness, and I'm not sure why. "Do you know how long I've waited to hear you say that?" I ask him.

"Say which part?"

"That you were thinking about popping the question." I can't stop the cyclical laughter from oozing out of me. "I'm thirty-one, and we've been together for six years. I've been sitting around waiting for you to mature into the type of man who wants to settle down, all the while, being afraid of moving on from you because I've already missed out on my prime years. I feared starting over and hoping to find someone who would want to be with me and eventually settle down, but in the last five minutes, you've made me realize how much better my odds are of starting over versus what my life would be like if I were to stay with you."

He looks at me with confusion. Clearly, I'm not making sense to him, but how could he think I'd be okay with the fact that he decided to test the boundaries by sleeping with another woman? Maybe I held onto this relationship too long, but I'm not that weak. "So, what are you saying?" he asks, nervously.

Is he seriously that dumb? I suppose I don't need to ask him that part. "I'm saying we're done. I waited long enough for you to love me the way I forced myself to love you, and it's never going to happen."

He huffs a sarcastic chuckle. "I knew you wouldn't understand. How could I be with someone who has no acceptance or the capability of forgiveness? Maybe I was wrong, but the coldness in your heart is eventually going to catch up to you. I'm surprised you didn't remind me of your favorite saying—you know, how people don't change and blah blah blah."

I lift my laptop from the table and slide it back into my bag. "If you need someone to blame, tell me this is my fault. Maybe I'm cold. Maybe I wholeheartedly believe people can't change who they are, yet I still waited for you to become a better person. That makes me the stupid one."

"You can say that again," he says. Mike always needs to have the last word, and I've let him have it through every fight we've endured, never caring what words lingered as I walked away.

I walk away, finally feeling free of the restraints that were holding me back—the ones I couldn't manage to untangle myself from before today. "I didn't just cheat on you once," he shouts. "It was so many times that I lost count." His fit of laughter floats through the air, making him sound like a lunatic.

Tears prick my eyes after his last comment, which makes me angry because I don't want his words or actions to hurt me anymore. Plus, what right do I have to pretend I know what pain feels like after reading Grams's diary entries? I'm lucky to have a choice—to be able to walk away.

As I'm heading back toward the hospital entrance after an unsuccessful attempt to catch up on my emails, I hear the engine of Mike's truck rev, followed by the sound of tires squealing against the pavement.

"How could I have been so stupid? Six years. For what?"

"It happens to the best of us," a familiar voice pipes up behind. Jackson pulls my attention away from the anger and rage I'm fighting against. "I wasn't eavesdropping."

I don't know how much Jackson heard between Mike and me, but I hope he only heard me talking to myself. "It's okay," I tell him.

"See this?" he says, pointing to his ring finger. There's an indent and band of lighter colored flesh compared to the rest of his finger.

I study it for a moment, trying to figure out what I'm looking at, but then it dawns on me that it's his ring finger. "Did you lose your ring?"

He laughs with obvious discomfort. "Definitely didn't lose it."

"Oh?" I question, waiting for a more detailed explanation.

"I was married for eight years, I've been divorced for eleven months, and this stupid spot won't fill in. She's still torturing me."

"Geez, I didn't realize that could happen," I tell him. Seriously, I didn't know skin could shrink like that.

"It can, it did, and she'd probably love to know."

"I guess I can assume you didn't have the best marriage?" Now that I'm evidently going on a date with this man tonight, I suppose I should know a little more about him than just his name.

"That's putting it mildly, but no, I didn't have a great marriage."

I fidget with the straps of my bag, keeping them upright on my shoulder. "So, what happened?" Maybe she cheated on him too. That would just make for a cute coincidence, wouldn't it?

"She was selfish, lazy, mean, and bored. She didn't like the fact that I had to work long hours, but she would continuously complain that we never had enough money. She told me she was too tired to make meals but insisted on being a housewife, and to add insult to injury, she stayed up most nights texting and talking to her friends while I sat beside her, waiting for a moment of her attention after working a twelve-hour shift. If I tried to get near her, she'd push me away. I lost track of how many times she asked me to sleep in the guest room."

"Oh my gosh, that's terrible," I tell him. "I may have the perfect match for her if she's still single." I laugh because I suspect she's going to have a hard time finding a man that's going to please her if Jackson wasn't good enough. On the other hand, he could just be saying all of this. I certainly don't know him very well, considering we just met, but it sort of sounds like my life with Mike, minus the marriage. "She'll eventually realize what she had. I'm not sure what man would cave to those requirements and demands."

We reach the side doors of the hospital and Jackson opens the door, holding it out so I can walk in. "Surprisingly enough, she's already remarried, which is fine by me. I wished the guy good luck when we awkwardly ran into each other in Target a couple months ago."

"Wow. I guess it's a good thing you were smart enough to get out when you did," I tell him.

Jackson scuffles his shoe against the thin carpet while peering down to his feet as he inhales loudly before spilling out, "Yes, except she's the one who left me. I'm not a quitter, so I kept making excuses to myself and tried to make it work."

I'm not sure what to say in response, but I suppose it's good I finally grew the courage to do what I was afraid I'd never be able to do. I'm sure Mike isn't through with me yet, though. I imagine I'll have dozens of texts and a bunch of missed calls on my phone tomorrow after I sleep at Mom's again tonight, but I can't go back to him this time. I don't want to have to tell someone someday that my ex left me because I wasn't strong enough to leave him.

"Well, I guess we have something in common," I tell Jackson.

A hint of a smile pokes at his left cheek. "Hey, again, I know this probably sounds like I've been eavesdropping, which I swear, I haven't been doing, but I overheard some of what you were reading to your grandmother earlier."

"Oh," I say, trying to imagine which part he may have heard. "Yeah, it's pretty heavy. I'm having a hard time digesting some of it. It's why I went outside to clear my head for a few minutes, but evidently, exes always know the right time to make life just a little more sour."

"That's for sure," he agrees. "I can imagine it might be hard reading her words out loud like that."

"She's very detailed with her descriptions, and it's hard not to envision what she went through, you know? I mean, she's my grandmother, and it's just so hard to comprehend her enduring that kind of abuse. On top of that, I never knew any of her concentration camp stories before now. It seems surreal."

"She's lived quite a life," he says. "Thankfully, you're saving it by going out with me tonight." He puffs his chest out, and his face brightens with a silly grin. "It's all in a day's job—saving lives and going out with pretty granddaughters of my patients. What a way to make a living, huh?"

"How many granddaughters have you been bribed into taking out?" I ask—partially joking, maybe a little serious. I'm sure he's kidding. I can't imagine too many grandmothers use their lives as bait for their unmarried grandchildren.

"Oh, you're only the second, don't worry," he says with an accompanied wink. "I have to get going, but if I don't mysteriously run into you again before tonight, have a great afternoon."

"You too." He is like a breath of fresh air, and I can't help the curiosity I feel while watching him walk away. I want to know more about this man who seems too good to be true.

"Code Blue on floor eight. Dr. Beck, paging Dr. Beck." My moment of light-hearted ease is gone as I hear the alert on the loudspeaker. Dr. Beck's name and the eighth floor is an immediate cause for panic since that's the floor Grams is on, and I know what code blue means. However, I don't know how many patients he has on the eighth floor.

I circle around for a moment, looking for the nearest elevator, then break into a run when I spot one. I desperately slap my palms against the elevator buttons until the doors open, and I do the same with the "close door" and "eighth floor" buttons on the inside. *Hurry. Please.* It feels like forever before the elevator reaches the eighth floor, but as soon as the doors open, I hear alarms and beeping noises blaring from different directions. I can't help feeling terrified of the unknown, and the fear has made me forget which room number Grams is in, so I start running in what I hope is the right direction. I must have circled the entire floor before I see nurses coming and going from a room near the end. That's her room. Eight-eleven. *No, no, no. Please, be okay, Grams.*

Though I'm running, I feel like I'm on a treadmill, or like the hallway is growing longer by the second. I can't seem to reach her room fast enough, and my chest tightens with guilt for leaving Grams's side. *I shouldn't have been so worried about answering emails.* When I finally reach her room, I see doctors and nurses working on her. It confirms that the alarm sounds are coming from her room, and her heart looks like it's flatlined according to the flashing monitor. I just pray they just took the wires off to work on her, not because they're giving up.

Jackson looks over at me for a split second. His face is white, and his forehead is glowing with beads of sweat under the bright light. "Emma, you need to go into the waiting room. Now."

"Is she going to be okay?" I cry out.

"Emma, please, go," he says forcefully.

I clutch my chest as tears barrel down my cheeks. Please, God, don't take her from me. I need her. I just want to be selfish a little longer and keep her here. I slowly make my way to the small waiting room that we were in yesterday before we found out what had happened. This time I'm alone, though, and I'm debating whether I should call Mom and Annie now or wait until I find out what's happening before I scare them. I should wait a few minutes. I think this is the right thing to do. I hope it is.

I fold over as I drop down into a chair, pressing my fingertips into the sides of my head while trying to breathe in and out slowly. *Please, let her be okay.*

Minutes pass, and I still don't know what's going on. I feel completely helpless and alone sitting here, so I take the leather diary out of my bag and hug it to my chest. Did I do this? Was reading the diary to her too much for her heart to handle? I don't understand why she wanted me to read this to her so badly.

Charlie. He was the initial reason for me finding the book. So far, I haven't read anything about a Charlie, though.

With each silent passing minute, I grow more impatient, and my hands move on their own accord as I pry open Grams's diary again. I need to feel close to her voice—her words.

CHAPTER SEVEN

AMELIA

DAY 5 - JANUARY 1942

J hadn't moved from the mattress in three days except to squat in the corner of the room to relieve myself. Obviously, the Nazis didn't think we were worthy of a toilet or shower. They could at least allow us to relieve ourselves outside, but we were under strict rules and weren't permitted to leave the barracks aside from their commands. In those first few days, there were no invitations to leave our quarters. It felt like they were desensitizing us from any type of humanity.

I sat on the floor in front of my bed with my aching back arched forward, while I stared at cracks in the cement wall in front of me. I would ponder my bleak existence, wondering when they would let us know what would come next. I had heard a rumor that we would be assigned jobs to earn our keep, but no one had come in to inform us of that yet, so we waited. All we did was wait.

The only time the doors in front of us had opened or closed

was when a Nazi delivered each of us a small loaf of stale bread and a teacup-size portion of cabbage soup.

I was hungry by the end of the first day, feeling the discomfort grow from the bottom of my stomach into an ache I couldn't ignore. The second day, the ache turned into agony. Then, the third day, it felt as if my insides were feeding off my fat and bones. The pains came and went, but the weakness was the fiercest. I could hardly stand, and I wasn't sure I would have the strength to work when the time came.

The woman on the bunk beside me stared at me all day, each day since I had arrived. She was constantly reaching for me, almost as if she were pleading with me to save her. It was what the expression on her face said to me, anyway. She spoke French, and I was never very good with that language, so I had a hard time understanding her. Besides Czech, English was the only other language I focused on learning because I had planned on moving to America someday. Though, someday seemed unlikely by that point. I wondered how old the woman was because I noticed that after days and days without eating much or bathing, age was merely a number. The living conditions made everyone look and feel much older than they were, and for those whose bodies weren't strong enough, death was likely. I was determined to fight, but most of the women living in the block I was in probably felt the same way when they first arrived too.

Our rations were brought in to us early that day, and I devoured the bread and guzzled the soup, silently pleading for more. My stomach craved more food after I finished eating than it did before I took my first bite. However, food had become a necessity that needed to be consumed rather than savored, and it was never enough to eliminate the hunger pains.

"They—are—they nous tuer." It was the only time the woman beside me spoke out loud rather than muttering to herself.

"Non, je ne parle pas Français," I told her, wishing I understood what she was saying, but she made it clear a moment later as she sliced her finger across her throat and dropped her head to the side. For a moment, I was confused, but as she pointed to the door, I put her pantomime together, confirming my fear of what was happening. They were slowly, but deliberately, trying to kill us.

I'm not sure how much time passed between when we finished eating and the moment everyone very suddenly became ill. I also don't know if we were poisoned or if some or all the food had gone bad, but I don't believe much can go wrong with bread and cabbage soup. Almost every woman in our block began to vomit. Soon, the last meal was coming out of everyone one way or another, and the smell that followed could make anyone who wasn't already ill, sick to their stomach. For me it was vomit. I barely made it off the side of the bed before the heaving started. It was pure luck that I made it off in time, or I would have had to sleep in it that night.

When everyone was at the peak of their sickness, a few of Nazis came to the doorway to watch, as if it were their entertainment for the night. A few of them laughed at us as we curled up on our mattresses, miserable, shaking from the cold, but also sweating at the same time. Over the next several hours, most of the other women fell asleep, and all but one of the Nazis left since the show was apparently over.

I rested listlessly on the side of my mattress, staring at that one Nazi, wondering how anyone could find enjoyment in watching people fall so ill.

That particular Nazi didn't appear to have the same type of enthrallment like the others, though, so I had found it odd that he remained in the doorway. When he caught me looking at him, he lowered his hands behind his back, straightened his shoulders, and walked toward me with no expression on his face. It wasn't until he was a few feet away that I recognized him. He was the Nazi who brought me into the barrack three days prior.

He stood in front of me for a long minute, staring down at me as if I were an unrecognizable type of species that he had never seen before.

"Did you need something?" I asked, meekly, using every ounce of energy I had left to force sound into my words. Not only was my stomach folding in on itself again, but my throat was on fire from the acidic vomit I expelled just a few inches away.

The Nazi lifted his hand with a handkerchief balled up inside of his fist, then pressed it to his nose. It made me jealous that he had a way to block out the smell. He then reached into his coat pocket and pulled something out. Whatever it was, it was small enough to be concealed within his hand, and my curiosity was piqued. He knelt in front of me and timidly dropped the object down on the empty space beside me. "Is that poison?" I grunted through a hoarse whisper, studying the piece of bread.

"No," he replied just as softly.

"Tomorrow, they recruit for jobs. You must be well enough to avoid transit." There was a certain kindness in his eyes that confused me. Still, I would have been foolish not to consider that the bread may be poisonous, despite what he said. After all, I had spoken out of turn one too many times with that soldier, so I thought he might want to torture me slowly. "Eat it."

"Why would you help me, and why should I believe you?" I asked.

His eyes narrowed, and he leaned in a bit closer. The scent of his breath was fresh, and it was the most pleasant smell I had encountered since I arrived there. "You shouldn't," he says. His German accent was very thick but understandable enough.

My mind hurt with confusion, trying to read the thoughts floating through his eyes, but it was as if he were blocking me from them. He was still squatting in front of me when the smallest of smiles pressed against the whites of his teeth. "I'm not one of them. I'm a prisoner like you, but a prisoner on the other side."

I didn't know it was possible to feel sadness for those who

have been destroying Jewish lives for so long, but there was something about him that made my heart feel something other than despair. I felt a very small sense of sympathy. He *was* dressed like the enemy and able to come and go as he pleased. Therefore, it was hard to consider him a prisoner in comparison to the way I was living. "What is your name?" I asked.

To me, they were all called Nazis. Just as we didn't deserve the courtesy of an actual name, neither did they.

"My name is Charlie." He seemed apprehensive to share his name as he looked around the room to make sure no one else was paying attention. I didn't think he had much to worry about considering every other woman in the room had either passed out or fallen asleep by that point.

"I've been internally referring to you as 'the girl with the big mouth' over the past few days." His words caused a subtle commotion in my mind, and if I were capable of laughing, I might have done so, but the hunger pains beneath my ribs wouldn't allow that type of movement.

"I have been called that before," I told him. Mama always taught me to speak my mind, while Papa would say that a lady doesn't speak out unless in an agreeable manner. It's not that I've had trouble accepting propriety, but I've had a history of questioning convention simply out of curiosity. After having so many basic rights taken from me, I had an endless number of questions, and I was determined to get answers and learn the truth.

When I first I arrived there, I already knew better than to speak up, but with that man, I couldn't stop myself. He seemed kinder than the others, so I figured it was my only chance to ask the burning questions I desperately wanted answers to.

"I'm not surprised," he said. "What is your name?"

My name. He wanted to know my name? Jews no longer had names. We were called Jews. I was called a Jew girl. We weren't individuals anymore. We were just one entity, and nothing else mattered. Even before I was taken, the only place I heard my name was in my home with Mama, Papa, and Jakob. It was forbidden to use our names anywhere else. It had been that way for years, and sadly, living without a name became normal. "My name is Amelia," I told him.

He reached his free hand out, turning it over, palm up, and I didn't understand what he wanted. He urged his hand forward a bit more as if I didn't understand the gesture. With hesitation, I struggled to lift my hand from my lap and dropped it gently into his. Charlie's hand folded around my fingers as he looked around the room once more for onlookers, then lowered his head and placed a soft, quick kiss on my knuckles. "It's a pleasure to meet you, Amelia," he said.

The sound of heavy steps echoed in the hallway outside the room, forcing Charlie to stand erect. He took another glance at me, then at the bread sitting beside me. "Thank you," I offered in a hush and bowed my head down as I quickly chewed the sweet bread that was much softer than any piece I had been given here.

"You're very welcome," he said. Charlie made his way back to the door, his shoulders back, chin angled toward the ceiling, and left me staring at the back side of the door with wonder as my mind raced with possible reasons for the interaction.

My thoughts were soon interrupted when a conversation filled with laughter and German words ensued in the hallway on the other side of the door. I wanted to imagine he was not one of the Nazis laughing, but what did I know? Their form of entertainment was sick, and it was hard to determine when their laughter was for fun, or in preparation for something far more devious.

I still wondered if the bread Charlie gave me might kill me, but left to choose between the possibility of being poisoned, or sleeplessly lying on the coiled mattress while suffering from starvation for another long night, it was worth taking the chance on the bread.

I finished the bread as fast as I could chew, feeling the crust scrape down the sides of my throat before falling into the empty pit of my stomach. My mouth and throat had become so dry from vomiting and dehydration that it was hard to push the small pieces down, but I continued choking on them until the roll was gone—until every little crumb was devoured.

I rolled onto my side, facing away from the puddle of vomit I left behind, and closed my eyes in hopes of sleep or death. Though, my mind wasn't shutting down easily that night as it replayed the sensation of Charlie's lips touching my bitterly chapped, cold, and dirty skin. It was, however, a pleasant change of imagery after constantly reliving the scene of Mama's insides being scattered along the sidewalk.

The thoughts scared me, knowing what could have happened if anyone had seen the exchange between Charlie and me, but there was a spark of thrill I couldn't deny—a current of electricity that brought just a little part of me back to life, even while knowing I could never trust a man from that side of the war...the side that killed Mama.

CHAPTER EIGHT

EMMA

s I close the book, I feel lost in Grams's old life, a new feeling of discontent holding my mind prisoner. I've learned about the Holocaust from books and in history classes, but what I've read over the past twenty-four hours doesn't do reality the justice it deserves. This time in life became history when all the captives were liberated, but the stories continued on in the lives of the survivors. It's hard to wrap my head around this story while I live with an abundance of freedom.

I glance up at the clock, surprised to discover it's been an hour since I sat down on this seat. I'm still debating whether to call Mom, but I don't know anything, and it would only scare her. The only hope I have now is that no news is supposed to be good news, so I'm sticking with waiting it out a little longer.

I stand up and tuck the diary under my arm before pulling on the door handle of the waiting room. The opening invites in the bright lights to filter in from the hallway and with the gloominess of this room, it's like moving from night to day. I don't hear any beeping noises or alarms, and no one is running around or shouting orders, which helps me remain semi-calm. Everything around me is still and silent as I approach Grams's room, but as I peek inside, I find the room empty. *Where did they take her? Why wouldn't anyone tell me? Could she have passed away, and no one came to get me?*

Terrified from the thoughts filling my head, I run to the nurses' station, placing my hands down on top of the cool wooden countertop, waiting for someone to give me an ounce of their attention. The three-seconds I wait is long enough. "Excuse me?" I call out.

A nurse who is typing something into a computer turns around and walks toward me. "Can I help you?" she asks with a kind smile, one that does nothing to calm me down.

"Do you know where Amelia Baylin is?" The nurse looks past me, over to Grams's former room.

"Are you family?" she asks.

"Yes, I'm her granddaughter, Emma Hill." My fingernails dig firmly into Grams's book as I wait out the longest minute of my life. I may chew a hole through my lip before getting an answer. I know I'm probably impatient, but everything seems to be happening in such slow motion around here, and it's causing me to take quick, deep breaths that are making me dizzy.

She finally sits down at the computer she's closest to and types something in before peering back up at me. "The notes I have here says she's in surgery. That's all I can see from here, though. I'm sure someone will be down to speak with you shortly."

"Surgery? Why wouldn't anyone tell me, or ask?"

The nurse looks confused and apologetic as she holds her hands against her chest. "I'm so sorry, I don't have an answer for you. I can assure you she's in good hands, though," she says, matter-of-factly.

As I stare back at the straight face in front of me, I can't help wondering how many patients she watches come in and out of this department daily because she appears to be unaffected by the emotions of the patients and their loved ones on this floor. I guess to work here, you must become desensitized to a certain degree, but her eyes show a blank slate of emotion. She may be numb to it all, but I'm on the verge of hyperventilating. Leaving a family member without any inclination of what's happening isn't right. Someone must know something around here. My continued stare does nothing to earn me any extra information. Instead, the nurse points down the hall. "The waiting room is just around the corner if you'd like to have a seat in there." As much as I'd like to tell her I've already been sitting in there for an hour, I know it won't do much good.

I should call Mom now. This is going to be bad. I head back to the waiting room, closing myself out from the rest of the world, alone...again. How have I been the only one in this room for so long? It's the ICU. Are there no other patients on this floor with family members who are waiting for answers? I take my phone out of my pocket and dial mom at work, thankful when she answers, rather than her boss who doesn't appreciate personal calls during the day. "Town Clerk's Office. This is Clara, how can I help you?"

"Mom, it's me," I tell her.

"What's wrong?" she asks, anxiously as if someone just jumped up behind her.

"Grams is in surgery right now. I don't know what happened. The alarms were going off when I came to see her, and they told me to go away. I didn't want to go, Mom, but they made me. So, I went back into the waiting room, and when I went back to see what was happening, she was gone. The nurse said...well she won't tell me anything except that Grams is in surgery. That's it; that's all I know, and I haven't been able to find out anything." I'm speaking so quickly that I'm not sure what I'm saying. I think my words seem out of order, but I think Mom understood enough.

"Why didn't you call me sooner?" Her words are just as quick as mine were, but louder. She sounds like she's on the brink of hysteria.

"I didn't want to scare you. I just—"

"It's okay," she cries. "I'm coming over there right now."

I hang up the phone, feeling like a monster. I shouldn't have waited. It's her mother, and she should be here. *What was I thinking?* I'm obviously not thinking straight. Plus, I have a splitting headache, and it's blazing hot in here.

Angry at myself, I toss my phone down onto the pile of magazines scattered along the small table. The thump of my phone landing causes the display to light up and I notice several missed text messages. I was so engrossed in the diary that I didn't feel my phone vibrate.

I can already guess who the texts are from, and I don't want to read them. Mike doesn't give up. I have tried to break up with him so many times, and this is how it turns out each time. He begs and pleads for my forgiveness, resistance fails me, and I give in. Not this time, though. I don't have the time to think about him now. In fact, I don't want to have time to think about him again.

The screen on my phone goes black, and it feels like I've overcome a small hurdle—letting it go. I drop down into one of the seats and lean back as I rest the diary on my lap. Without anything else to focus on, my attention sways to the muted TV.

Who needs sound when all you see is bad news from around the world? Suicide bombings, murders, terrorist attacks—it's all so sad and depressing. I can't bring myself to watch what the news is broadcasting tonight, so I close my eyes and block everything out.

If they're operating on Grams, she must be well enough to undergo surgery, or they wouldn't operate, but I still feel like there's a heavy weight sitting on my chest. I clench my hands around the armrests and try to slow my breaths. *It's going to be okay. It has to be.* I'm not ready to say goodbye to Grams.

The door to the waiting room finally opens. "Mom?" I ask before seeing anyone walk in. I should have considered that it could be anyone walking in and waited to see her face, especially since it's not Mom. "Jackson!" I try to stand but my feet feel like they are stuck in cement, as I fear what he has to say.

Jackson sits down next to me and places his hand on top of mine. "Your grandmother's in recovery," he says.

"She is?"

"Yes, but she had another stroke. Her heart stopped, and we had to resuscitate her. We were able to break up the clot with a clot-busting drug and got to it quickly, which is a good thing. The longer the blockage is present from the clot, the more susceptible the brain and other body parts are to damage. It's fortunate that she was already here in the hospital. It would have only been a matter of time before she had another stroke if we had not placed in the pacemaker. Her atrial fibrillation causes clots to form, and all it takes is one to get lodged in an artery. The procedure was successful, but I also put her on a strong medication to slow down her heart rate. The medication will work in conjunction with the pacemaker which will stop her heart rate from going below sixty beats per minute."

"Is she okay?" I manage to choke out.

"It's hard to tell right now since she was just taken to the recovery room. So far everything looks good, but we'll do more testing once she's fully conscious."

"Wait—" My mind replays something he said a few minutes ago. "Did my grandmother die for a minute?" My face hurts from the tension around my eyes and jaw, and even though I know she's alive, it doesn't ease my other concerns.

"Her heart stopped for a minute, but she wasn't dead in terms of a medical diagnosis. We had to get her heart pumping again, and it was touch and go for a few minutes," Jackson says, squeezing his hand a little tighter around mine. "Did you call your family?"

"I did." I'm trying my best to hold back my tears because he isn't offering me the hope I need, and I assume it's because he doesn't want to say something that may not be true.

"Are you going to be okay?" he asks, gently, dipping his head down to catch my gaze. "You're very pale, and I'm worried about you."

I nod my head because I don't think I can lie and say yes.

The door to the waiting room flies open again, and Jackson slips his hand away from mine, reminding me that doctors don't typically comfort family members as much as he's been comforting me. Mom rushes inside, her hands waving around with panic. "What's going on?" she asks, breathlessly.

"Your mother is in recovery right now," Jackson begins. He retells her the same information he just offered me, and rather than listen to it twice, I focus on Mom's face—the pain and heartache evident by the tears welling in her eyes.

"So, we don't know anything yet?" Mom asks.

"She's alive and hanging in there," Jackson reminds her.

Mom clutches her fist against her chest and takes a seat as her face distorts into a deeper level of distress. "How long before she'll be awake?"

"Shouldn't be long," Jackson says.

"Emma, did Grams sign the health care proxy papers and HIPAA release form?" Mom asks me.

"Proxy papers?" I question.

"Well, she must not have been able to sign the surgery consent forms if this happened so quickly," she continues.

"Actually, she signed off on them last night," Jackson tells Mom while carefully avoiding eye contact with me. I now know that Jackson was aware of Grams's bribe about the surgery, seeing as she already agreed to it. It was a setup to get me to go out with Jackson tonight and he was in on it.

"I'm going to go check on Amelia now," Jackson says while giving Mom a quick shoulder squeeze. "I'll be back shortly."

As the door closes behind Jackson, Mom swings around in her seat to face me. "Were you here when it happened?" she asks.

"No, I was getting some fresh air and answering some work emails."

Mom wraps her arm around my shoulders and rests her head against mine. "I feel like there's never enough time to do and say the things we should, but Grams has lived an extraordinary life, more so than a lot of people her age," I tell Mom. I don't know if my words help, but now that I've seen a glimpse of what Grams has already survived through, this blip on her timeline is nothing in comparison.

"I know," she whispers, then glances down at the diary I forgot I had out. "What's that on your lap?"

"It's nothing. I was just reading something a friend gave to me." I place the diary into my bag and pull the flaps together.

"Looks pretty old," she says.

"Yeah, I'm designing a book cover for it," I lie.

"Oh, that's nice, honey." She's completely unfocused on what I'm saying while she stares through the wall in front of us. We are all so close in our family that the thought of one of us not being here is incomprehensible, especially Grams. She is the backbone of our family.

Mom and I sit in silence until Annie arrives, which stirs Mom back up. Her version of the story isn't quite as tight and to the point like Jackson's version, which causes Annie a lot of stress. She wants answers and isn't getting enough information for her liking.

"If we're going to be seeing her soon, we should probably pull ourselves together so she doesn't see how worried we look. It won't help her," I tell them, knowing I must not look much better.

"She's right," Mom says, pulling a wad of tissues out of her purse and handing one to Annie. Their makeup is streaked down their cheeks, and they both have bloodshot eyes. My heart is breaking for them. After all, this is their mom. As close as I am to Grams, I know there is nothing stronger in the world than the bond between a mother and daughter.

"I broke up with Mike," I tell them, trying to shift their focus a little.

The sniffles stop for the moment, and they both look directly at me. "For good this time?" Annie asks.

"He admitted to cheating on me. It's over. Nice timing, huh?"

Annie takes the seat on the other side of me, and both she and mom hug me, which only makes it harder to stop my leaky faucet of tears. With a sharp inhale, I grit my teeth and look up to the ceiling, reminding myself again that Grams will not want to see us crying. I need to keep it together, especially with the two of them being as upset as they are. Throughout my life, Grams has always told me that *"Crying doesn't solve anything, and for those people who cause you pain, the tears give them a type of fulfillment and satisfaction they don't deserve. Tears are just wasted emotion."*

I try to remember her words each time I'm upset, but I'm not as stoic as she is—I'm not programmed well enough to control my emotions. They work on their own accord, I suppose. Mom and Annie are the same way.

The waiting room door opens again, and this time it's the nurse who had no information for me earlier. She presses her back against the door, holding it open. All the while, she's staring down at a file, paying us no attention, which bothers me as much as her emotionless facade she showcased earlier. Why wear hearts and rainbows all over your pink scrub shirt if it isn't going to represent your attitude? "Amelia is back in her room now if you'd like to go visit with her," she says.

I know I shouldn't be so hard on this nurse. She's just doing her job, and I don't envy her. It takes a special type of person to do what she does, and I definitely don't have it in me. It must harden them after a while—keeping their emotions in tow all the time.

We head down the hall, back into Grams's room, and I'm scared to see what she looks like now. We find her with her eyes half closed and her skin paler than the white sheets covering her. The amount of wires and machines she is hooked up to doesn't look much different from the last time I saw her, though. I rush to her side and drop my bag down against the bed. "Grams, can you hear us?"

A groan gurgles in her throat, so I place a kiss on her cheek and kneel beside her, carefully encasing her hands within mine.

Mom and Annie take her other side and do the same. "She's probably still groggy from the anesthesia," I say, quietly.

"I want—Charlie," Grams mumbles. Her words are garbled, and it's hard to understand what she's saying, but I heard Charlie's name...and it makes sense now.

"Mom, who is Charlie?" Annie asks.

A frail smile struggles against the corners of Grams's wrinkled lips. "He was spec-tac-ula—."

Annie and Mom look at each other, questioning who Grams is talking about, and the guilt hits me since I know, but I'm unable to tell them the truth per her request. She asked me to keep this book to myself, so there must be a reason Grams doesn't want them to know what's inside.

"Do you know of any Charlie?" Mom asks me.

"No, no, I don't know who Charlie is. I've never heard of him before. It's strange."

Grams tries to laugh, but it comes out sounding like phlegm catching in her throat. I squeeze her hand to let her know I understand her, but I think she's confused since she asked me not to share anything about her diary with Mom or Annie, and yet, she's calling for Charlie again.

"How's she doing?" Jackson's voice startles me as he enters her room. "Looks like she's coming out of it, huh?" I don't know how to answer since this is all new to me. Instead, I stand up and move out of the way so Jackson can take a look. "Amelia, how are you feeling?" he asks her.

Grams struggles to lift her hand and moves it from side to side as her lip curls into a slight smirk. "Eh," she mutters.

"Well, we'll get you something to help you relax," he tells her.

"Charlie," she says again.

"Her confusion seems worse," I whisper to Jackson.

"Amelia, can you tell me what year it is?" Jackson questions.

Grams's eyes open a little wider, and she twists her head against the pillow to look at him. "Why such a silly question?" she says.

"It's just a common question we sometimes ask our patients."

Grams sweeps her hand across her forehead, pushing away her silvery white-streaked bangs from her forehead. "It's 1942, of course."

"Grams," I pipe in, afraid she's truly stuck inside of her head during that period of time. "It's 2017."

"Oh, Emma," she says. "Such a funny girl."

Jackson backs away from Grams and nods for us to follow him out the door. As we file into the hallway, he inhales deeply, pausing for a moment, which soothes me more than my own calming breaths. "I'm going to schedule some tests to see if any brain damage occurred while she was in cardiac arrest. Honestly, I don't think that's the case, but I want to rule it out. I'm quite confident her confusion is a result of the first stroke, and then having a second one so soon afterward wasn't much help with progress." Jackson clears his throat and folds his hands down in front of his waist. With his eyes squinted slightly and his lips pinched to the side, he leans against the wall. "As much as I hate to ask you three to do this, we need to avoid upsetting her, which means playing along for the time being. Keeping her heart rate in a normal rhythm is very important right now."

We're supposed to pretend like it's 1942 and she's still in the middle of the Holocaust? I don't even know if she was still a prisoner then. "She knows my name," I tell Jackson. "That should mean something, right?"

"It does," he says. "It means, she's here and there, both at the same time, and that's nothing to be concerned about right now."

I don't think he understands how not okay this is for her.

"Regressing to that time may cause her more issues with her heart than telling her the truth."

Jackson seems fixated on me for the moment, gazing into my eyes with concern as if I were the sick patient. "I think she's going to be okay," he says. "We just need to give her time."

"Thank you so much, Dr. Beck," Mom says. "I can't tell you how grateful we are to know our mother is in such good hands."

"It's my pleasure," he says. "My shift is just about over, though, so Dr. Lane will be covering the ICU until morning. She'll be by to introduce herself if you're still here, but I assure you, Amelia will be sleeping for most of the next twenty-four hours, and I advise you all to get some rest, as well."

"We're just going to spend a little more time with her," Annie says. "Thank you, again." She takes Mom's arm and tugs her back into Grams's room where they pull up chairs to sit beside her. For the moment, I just want to pray that wherever Grams's mind is right now, it isn't as terrifying as I'm imagining it to be.

"If you'd like to reschedule for tonight, I would understand," Jackson tells me.

I think for a second, knowing I have nowhere else to go. It's either I go to Mike's apartment and grab my things, or to my childhood bedroom at Mom's. She goes to bed at eight, so I won't be doing much good by sitting on my bed, working for the night. I suppose I should be working, but a part of me was looking forward to tonight, despite everything that happened today. "I think I could use an escape from my life, even if it's only for a few hours."

"No problem." Jackson scratches at the back of his head as he surveys the hallway—looking everywhere but at me. I don't think he understood what I meant.

"I meant yes, I'd like to still go out with you tonight. At least I'd know if something happened to my grandmother if I was with you, right?" I press a small smile into my lips so he knows I'm partially joking.

"Exactly, I'm probably the best person to be with tonight." His shoulders straighten, and his dimples deepen. "I just need a few minutes to change and sign off my shift. Do you want to meet me in the lobby in about ten minutes?"

"I'll be there," I tell him.

I pivot on my toes, feeling a slight bounce in my step as I watch him walk away. I turn back into Grams's room, finding Mom and Annie with wide eyes and questioning looks on their faces. "Did we just hear what we think we heard?"

I hold my palms out. "Seriously, do you two have bionic hearing?"

"No, you were just talking louder than you think you were," Mom says.

"You're going on a date with him tonight?" Annie confirms while clasping her hands together.

"You can thank me for that," Grams groans.

"What do you mean?" Mom asks her.

"I'll tell you after she leaves. Oh, Emma, don't forget to find Charlie, okay?"

I pause for a moment, reminding myself to play along. "Sure thing, Grams," I tell her as I grab my bag.

"Have fun," Mom says. "Don't stay out too late. I'll be up waiting to hear every detail."

Nothing has changed from the time I moved out of Mom's until now, and it's been at least five years. My life is far too exciting for her to handle, even if I'm not enjoying it myself.

I take the elevator downstairs and drop down into one of the wooden chairs in the lobby. I only have a few minutes before Jackson meets me down here, but maybe it's enough time to read another page or two from Grams's book.

CHAPTER NINE

AMELIA

DAY 6 - JANUARY 1942

*a*fter almost a full week since I arrived at my assigned "shelter," there was still no sign of a future for us. The Nazis had also done their best to strip us of any trace of our past, so all we had left was the present. Our austere barracks were crowded with dirt-ridden bodies surrounded by feces, urine, and other bodily fluids, and the foul stench of death and decay became part of my dismal reality.

Sleep was a rare treat due to pain and fear, but I managed to find a couple hours of peace that night before the door was thrashed open and several Nazis stormed into our already confined space, shouting orders. They told us to get up and stand in front of our bunks. It took everything inside of me to find the strength to hold myself up that day, but the memory of Charlie's warning was the motivation I needed to move.

The clothes I wore were soiled and damp from night sweats, and they smelled as bad as the floors and mattresses. When I had gotten dressed at home the week before, I had no way of knowing it would be the one ensemble of clothing I would have on for the indefinite future. I would have chosen something more comfortable to wear than a form-fitting day dress made of wool.

"Today, you will begin work. If you are capable, you will be assigned a job. If you cannot handle the work, you will be managed accordingly." I waited patiently for my number to be called, barely able to keep my head up as I watched one after another of the able-bodied occupants of my barracks be summoned and marched out to an unknown work assignment. It must have been at least an hour before I heard it—the number that had become my label, in place of my name. I walked over to the Nazi holding the clipboard and waited for the assignment. "Medica."

"Where—"

"Keine!" he yelled. German was another language I wasn't well versed in, though I was thankful to be familiar with at least the basics. The Nazi pointed to the door, and I made my way through the hall and outside, unsure where the medical office was located.

I walked as quickly as I could, fearful of being spoken to by anyone. It was frigid outside, but the sun was bright, whiting out the signs that would point me in the right direction, and it took my eyes a while to adjust to the sunlight after being in the dim barracks for days. I didn't have to go far before I saw an adjacent block labeled as the sick bay. There was a line of other Jews out the door, mostly mothers with their children.

Worried about being too close to those who were sick, I covered my mouth and nose with my sleeve as I snuck inside, to the right of the line. I received looks from many people, most likely wondering if I was skipping ahead of them, but their questions were answered when a Nazi grabbed me by the arm and nearly pulled me off my feet. "What are you doing?" he asked.

"I'm reporting to work here," I told him, trying to speak affirmatively, rather than sounding weak and afraid like I was feeling.

He pulled at the collar of my dress, peeling it away from my skin to reveal my number. Mama had written it there in ink last year when we were all assigned numbers, as well as Jude stars to wear on our sleeves. "Anzahl 24225," he shouted to a female Nazi, whom I believed to be a nurse, according to her uniform.

"Ja," she replied, waving me over. I placed my covered hand back over my face as I approached the woman who was sitting behind a wooden desk with a stack of papers in front of her. Her eyes were dark and menacing as she visually inspected every part of my body. She then stood up from her chair and walked around to meet me, pulling me to the corner of the room. Her fingers tugged through my hair, yanking strands apart in what I assumed to be a search for lice. "Your hair is to be up and tightly secured," she snapped in her thick accent. She then clapped her hands against my cheeks before angling my head in various directions. "Strip."

I swallowed hard as I peered over at the dozens of people staring at me from just a few feet away. The hesitation must have been longer than I thought because the woman's hands furiously began tearing my clothing away. I was left bare and cold, on display for everyone around me. Having been raised to act modest about my body, I felt violated and embarrassed. I tried to cover my private areas as well as I could, but she was quick to force my hands up in the air so she could inspect every inch of my body. I closed my eyes, avoiding the looks and the mortification the others may have been feeling for me. I knew they probably did the same thing to everyone there, but that didn't make it any easier.

With my eyes closed, hiding from the surrounding happenings, I was startled by a poke through the flesh on the inside of my arm. The sharp pain forced me to open my eyes, and to my disbelief, I saw a hypodermic needle, a tube, and a bag. Without my permission, they were stealing my blood. At that moment, I realized I had lost my rights...all of them. It was as if my body didn't belong to me anymore. They weren't just treating like an animal, it was as if I were of lesser quality than livestock on a farm. It was very hard not to ask questions, but I was starting to see that the less I knew, the better off I was.

Several minutes passed as the woman jotted down notes, then stored my blood away in a blue metal cabinet. "Go shower," she demanded.

"Shower?" I questioned. Considering my filthy conditions, I wasn't aware there were showers anywhere.

"Out back and through 'Block A,'" she said.

I picked up my clothing from the floor and held it in front of me as I scurried out of the building and around the side to Block A, where I found a room with cement walls and rusty shower heads protruding from the ceiling every few feet. The room was filled with other people—more people than there were showers, none of whom seemed to care that they were bare in front of each other.

I had always been a very private person, and I hadn't been naked in front of anyone since I was a small child. I didn't like the feeling of being looked at, but after being covered in urine, vomit, feces, and whatever diseases accompany those conditions, the shower was appealing.

I stood under the water, feeling it wash away what was left of my dignity. The water was cold, as I expected it to be, and there was no soap, but I scrubbed with my fingernails, scratching at the dirt and grime that had built up, wishing it would offer a small sense of refreshment.

"Be careful," the woman beside me said. "If you scratch too hard, you'll have open wounds. That's how people die around here."

My jaw fell open, not that I shouldn't have thought of it on my own, but I hadn't considered that fact. "Oh," I responded simply, digesting the truth.

"I'm sorry to scare you," the woman continued.

I rubbed the water away from my eyes and to look at the woman, recognizing her. "Leah?" I questioned. She was the woman standing behind me in line when Mama was shot. I may not have remembered most faces after those first few days of oblivion, but a pregnant belly stood out, especially a naked one.

"Amelia, right?" she returned, smiling a bit.

"Yes. How are you? Your baby?" I whisper.

"Hungry," she says, cradling her arms below her stomach.

I could only gaze at her with sympathy, knowing how hungry I had been—remembering that I was given extra food last night when she needed it more. "Your husband—"

Her brows furrowed and pulled in toward her nose as if she might cry. "I'm not sure. I haven't seen him since we were separated at arrival," she said through a sniffle. "Did you find your papa and brother?"

I shook my head as more comprehension hit me. The barracks were filled with only women. The line at the sick bay was made up of mostly women, though I did see one or two men scattered throughout the line. The shower, though—all women. "I don't think men are living here, other than the Nazis, of course."

Her lips fell into a downward curve. "I know," she whispered.

She stepped away from the shower and twisted her hair tightly to free the trapped water.

I followed Leah, dressing at the same time. "I'm sure we'll see each other again," she said.

"I hope so," I replied, though I didn't know how many people were around in the same location, or how often I would be running into familiar faces.

I hurried back around the corner toward the building but stopped with fear when I came close to running into a group of Nazis who were standing in a circle, having a discussion. I was quick to notice that one of them was Charlie. I caught his eye for a brief second before we both looked away. Part of me wondered if I had imagined the odd interaction from the night before, but by the look in his eye, I knew I most definitely had not.

The men carried on through a roar of laughter, and I walked

around the side of them, ignoring their presence while they ignored mine.

As I snuck back into the sick bay, I was again given a look by many of the Jews who were standing in line, but I tried to avoid the questions in their eyes and focused solely on the German nurse waiting for me behind the desk.

She spared no time upon my return. "You will register each Jew. Their number, ailment, age, and whether they are expectant." The woman was not speaking to me softly, and I witnessed the sickened expressions on the faces of those who were waiting in line.

"Yes, Madame," I replied.

The woman took the chair from behind the desk and moved it to the other side of the room. When she returned, she pointed to the stack of papers. "There you are."

The papers were all handwritten notes about each patient who had come and gone, including only the four pieces of information she asked me to record. I took a stack of fresh paper and piled it neatly onto a clipboard, then found a pencil in a tin can I noticed on the corner of the desk.

I pulled my coat collar up and buttoned it over my mouth and nose, fearful of contracting anything from the sick people.

Immediately, I began questioning the patients standing in a line that was spreading throughout the alleyway of the barracks. It seemed like an endless amount of work.

Without knowing how many hours had passed, I guessed the time from the position of the sun and the fact that it was slowly beginning to set.

A hand on my shoulder pulled my attention away from the woman I was questioning. I turned to see who was behind me and found him—Charlie. Taken aback by his greeting, I struggled to maintain my composure due to the unease I was feeling. "Yes, sir," I greeted him, sounding weary. There was a certain look in his eyes that I couldn't quite understand, and it made me wonder what his intentions were. With everything that had happened to my family and myself, I was smart enough to know I couldn't and shouldn't trust anyone—particularly a soldier of any kind.

"Follow me," he stated with a commanding tone, one that didn't sound authentic.

I did as I was told, feeling even more confused about his intentions, but I dared not ask him anything at that moment. After all, I should have known better than to argue with a Nazi after watching the way they killed Mama, even if I had already tested my limits with Charlie. I followed closely in his footsteps while analyzing his straight posture and how tightly his hands were clasped behind his back. I walked as straight and tall as I could, but had to hold my arms over my chest as if embracing myself to shield my body from the icy cold wind.

We stopped at a small nook between two barrack blocks where there was no one else in sight. I didn't speak first. I had already thanked him the night earlier for the bread, and I didn't know what else he wanted from me. "I'm glad to see you're doing paperwork," he said.

"Why is that?" I questioned.

"Your longevity depends on your assigned job," he answered. There was a seriousness in his voice, and his hands still had not moved from behind his back. I couldn't understand why he would say that to me, and I wondered if it was a warning or threat?

"Are you trying to get me killed?" I whispered. I was not flattered or humbled by his pleasant attitude toward my new job. If we were caught having a private conversation back there, I could assume how it might turn out. I was the enemy, and he was—I'm not sure. I knew what he did not want to be, but if push came to shove, would his allegiance be to those that could have me killed without blinking an eye, or to a Jewish girl he just met?

Charlie's eyes were not one of a Nazi. He had an innocent look that set him apart from the others. I could see hate and resentment a mile away with some of the passing men, but not Charlie. I was not about to admit that to him, though, because I was still unsure about trusting anyone.

"What do you want?" I asked, looking over my shoulder as my level of discomfort escalated. I didn't understand what was happening, but I knew I shouldn't be back there.

"A friend," he said.

I covered my mouth as if trying to hide the sarcastic laughter threatening to erupt from my dry throat. "Nazis are not friends with Jews. That's just absurd."

"Of course. That's what we're supposed to think. That's the way they want us to be. Where's my say in the matter, though?" he argued. "I had no choice about becoming a soldier on this side of the war. I was forced to, and I don't want to be considered a Nazi because I'm not a killer."

"Clearly, it can be worse, so be thankful you aren't Jewish," I replied with haste.

He leaned forward and lowered his voice to nearly a whisper. "I am not comparing our situations. I'm simply answering your question as to why I'm as desperate for a friend as you are. I obviously shouldn't have approached you. My apologies."

The feeling of guilt hit me hard, even though I couldn't figure out why—I had nothing to feel guilty for. He was the enemy. He had the upper hand. He was the lion, and I was the mouse, yet there I was, feeling bad for one of *them*. I figured I must have been on the verge of insanity while being brainwashed to think I was nothing more than a speck of dirt. "You don't need to apologize," I replied. "You scare me. That's all." That's what they all wanted. They wanted us to admit to feeling frightened, whether by words or action. It was their goal. Scare, torture, kill. Jews were their enemy, but what did I do? What did Mama do?

"That's just it. I'm a monster, yet I have done nothing to earn that title," he said.

"You put that uniform on," I told him. Just as I had patches labeling my religion, he had clothing that represented the dictator in charge of all the hate there.

He took my arm and pulled me to the ground, squatting down in the corner as if he were trying to hide us, but without any further coverage. "No," he argued. "I was trained from the age of ten until I turned eighteen, then never given a choice on whether I wanted to live this way. I don't want to be here, and I certainly don't want to do the things they expect me to do. I would be slaughtered if I didn't follow orders, however. Much like you, I'm afraid."

His words terrified me more than they enlightened me. I couldn't understand the meaning of a ten-year-old being trained to hate. Plus, he wasn't sleeping in filth or being treated like an animal from what I could tell. "Well, I would trade places with you in a heartbeat," I told him. I thought it would be easier to hate than to be hated, but I might have been wrong about that.

My eyes narrowed in on his, wondering how he had managed to remain in an authoritative position while admitting his defiance toward Hitler. "Why choose me to unveil this information to? I'm a no one. Why not one of those other women? They're all desperate for help."

His eyes closed for a moment, and I watched Charlie struggle to swallow. "I was sent on a mission to retrieve your sector in Prague. I was the one who pulled your mother off the other soldier's back."

"You killed her?" I yelled as quietly as I could. "That's why you're being nice to me? That's why you gave me an extra loaf of bread? You killed my mother?" I knew I couldn't raise my voice any louder, but the anger was searing through my entire body, igniting a fire within my soul.

"No, no, no, I did not—that was not me, but I was there. I watched you and your world fall to pieces like I've watched so many times before with others, but you were different. The intense pain I saw in your eyes made me feel heartache after being numb to it for so long. I never looked anyone in the eye after they watched someone in their family fall to their death, but I made the mistake of looking in your eyes for just a moment." Charlie took a couple of breaths, as did I. He ran his hands down the side of his face and fell completely into the soil. "Amelia, time stood still for those few seconds, and even though I could almost feel your pain, I also felt jealous of you—that you could love your mother as much as you obviously did. Yet, I'm here because *my* mother forced me to train for this life."

I was speechless and heartbroken all over again at the thought of Mama, and I couldn't clear up the foggy feeling in my head from his explanations. He watched Mama die in front me, and for that, he wanted to be my friend. He wanted to risk both of our lives for a senseless friendship? "People die every day," I told him, simply ignoring the trueness of his confession.

His lips pressed together, and he swallowed hard once more. "I know."

"I need to get back to my job before I'm caught," I told him, needing more air than what was available in that corner.

Friends. For so long, Jews had not been allowed to be friends with anyone except our own.

I began walking back toward the alley where the line was still growing longer, but Charlie grabbed my arm, unknowingly where I had blood taken from just a few hours earlier. I couldn't help but wince at the tenderness. Feeling an immediate release of his hand, I turned quickly to hear his final words on the matter. "I'm sorry," he said. "You look just like her, beautiful and pure. I hate that you have to live on without her—here of all places."

His words hurt me. They cut through me like a knife, scraping the outside layer of my heart as my wounds felt renewed. Charlie may not have intended to hurt me, but I'm not ready to listen to an apology from any of my captors, not even him.

CHAPTER TEN

EMMA

a hand on my shoulder shocks me into awareness, and I jump up from my seat with a gasp. "Aren't you supposed to be reading that to your grandmother?" Jackson asks me with a raised brow.

"Should you be listening in on conversations?" I question, mirroring his raised brow.

"It's part of my job sometimes," he argues.

"Right." With a grin pulling at my lips, I close Grams's book and slip it into my bag before swinging it over my shoulder. "Normally, I might shower and freshen up before a 'date,'" I tell him, making sure to air quote the word date.

"Hey, I offered to reschedule," he says, taking my bag off my shoulder. "What do you have in this thing?" He swings it over his free shoulder, seeing as his backpack is hanging off his other.

"My life," I tell him.

"You have a heavy life, I guess."

"Not really, but my laptop is heavy," I say with a bit of sarcasm.

"Fair enough," he replies while pulling open the heavy glass door to the outside, unveiling a heavy downpour of rain. I hadn't looked out the window since I tried to get some fresh air earlier, but it was perfectly clear with a blue sky then. The drastic change in weather proves how long my day has truly been. I must already look totally disheveled, but now I'll be soaking wet on top of it. Not a good look for a first date with a handsome doctor.

"Why don't you wait here, and I'll come pick you up?" I suppose I didn't consider the whole driving situation either. We both have cars here, but it would feel awkward to drive separately to dinner.

"It's okay, a little rain won't hurt me," I tell him.

"I insist," he says handing me back my bag. "Stay dry."

He runs out, holding his bag over his head as puddles splash up the sides of his jeans that I'm only now noticing he has on. I've only seen him in scrubs, but I like the way he looks in jeans and his leather jacket. I feel my pulse speed up, and I know if he keeps having this type of effect on me, *I* may need a heart doctor.

I watch him until he disappears into the parking lot across the street, and I quickly power up my phone and flip my camera around to see how bad I look. *Please don't have dark circles of worn-off makeup caked up under my eyes.* Somewhat surprised, my reflection reveals that my hair isn't too bad and most of my makeup is still on. *I could look worse.* I guess if he sees me like this, hopefully he'll be pleasantly surprised if there is a second date—one where I have time to fix myself up first.

A dark car pulls into the main roundabout and parks in front of the doors. I don't know much about cars—it's never been my thing, but I know this car is sleek looking and it's a Mercedes, and I've never been inside one before. I guess there's a whole list of "firsts" for me today.

I open the door to run out, but Jackson jumps out of the car with an umbrella and runs toward me. "What are you doing?" I shout over the thunder and rain.

"I don't want you to get wet, I told you." Is he for real? The men I have come across, don't act like this.

I watch him curiously as he opens the passenger-side door and I slide in, still dry as a bone. He closes my door and makes his way back around to his side, closing the umbrella, tossing it into the back, and sliding in. His dirty blond hair is soaked and spiked in every direction and his jacket has droplets of rain dripping down the sleeves. "You're drenched," I tell him, stating the obvious.

"I'll dry," he says, glancing over at me with a small smile.

"You are quite the gentleman. Are you always like this?" I ask with a raised brow. That came out a bit sarcastic. I didn't intend for it to, but I honestly didn't think there was a man left on earth who acted so cordially. I could easily get used to this.

"What do you mean?"

I settle my bag between my feet, but he picks it up and places it on the back seat. "I wasn't aware there was a man around who still opened doors for women and picked them up in a rainstorm. I thought chivalry was dead." Dad certainly never did that for Mom when they were together, and through my years of dating in high school and college, I never witnessed such a good-old-boy act of kindness.

"I was raised by two women, so I guess that has something to do with it," he says through laughter.

"Two women?" I question.

He looks over his shoulder and pulls away from the curb. "Yeah, my dad left when I was two, and my sister is thirteen years older than I am."

"Wow," I say. "Are you still close with your sister?"

"Very. She has her own family now, and I like to be around my niece and nephew whenever I can." All I can think to myself is that he *is* the perfect man; perfect manners, good looks, a great job, cares about people, and likes kids.

"If you tell me you're Jewish, my mother might get a Rabbi to marry us in the hospital tonight," I say, but immediately regret the words. *That's rude.* Regardless of what Mom and Grams like to say about me marrying a nice Jewish Doctor, it's something I should probably keep to myself.

"Hmm," he snickers. "I'm not Jewish; I'm Catholic...and German, so after listening in on some of your grandmother's story, I'm not sure that's what you want to hear." He glances over at me with a quick wink, but his words settle in my head. It's 2017. Religion and origin shouldn't determine who we choose to spend our lives with now. Mike is Jewish, and considering how that relationship went, I can honestly say religion will not be the deciding factor in who I end up with.

"I was kidding," I tell him. "It's not something I'm concerned about, but my mother can be a little over the top sometimes." I laugh quietly, hoping to defuse some of the awkwardness I created.

"Actually, your grandmother already knows, and it didn't seem as though she cared." With a soft snicker, he squints one eye and leans away from me as if I'd punch him or something, which I briefly consider doing as I remember how this all came together today. "Don't forget, we shouldn't speak ill of the ill." His words remind me that I should be nice regardless of this little setup between him and Grams. *He did save Grams's life today.*

"Okay, I'll pretend like we were *both* blindsided by the guilt trip of us going out together." I press my lips into a straight line, trying my best not to smile, but it's hard to avoid while looking at him. "So, where to, Prince Charming?"

"I am kind of charming, aren't I?"

"You *are* kind of charming." I'll give him that much.

"Well, since I know almost nothing about you, are you the wine and dine type of woman or do you prefer something a little lighter and fun?"

I run my fingertips up and down the smooth leather seat cushioning my legs as I think about his question. *What am I?* I guess I'm a workaholic that doesn't fit into either category. "I like to experience life, but I don't have the opportunity to do so as often as I'd like."

"Not that you've answered my question, but you have me wondering why a person couldn't enjoy life as much as she would like to?"

"I work a lot," I tell him. "I'm also alone a lot and sometimes forget to eat, never mind exploring the big world out there."

"So, how do you know you like to experience life?" He has a valid point.

"I guess it was more of a wish than an answer to your question. I'll go with fun. As much as I enjoy wine and food, fun sounds better tonight."

"My kinda girl," he mutters as he takes a sharp turn into a different direction. I guess he had me pinpointed as a wine and dine kind of girl.

How did today end up like this? Never in a million years would I have expected to be out on a date with a different man tonight, let alone a great guy. Mom has always told me I give off an uninterested vibe to people, like I'd rather not meet anyone new or interact with those I don't know. I've never tried to be that way, but I'm unintentionally quiet because I like to observe. It's the artist in me, I suppose, plus there's the whole six-year relationship part I had been dealing with.

As we drive through the city, the street lights and painted lines on the road seem to have a hypnotic effect on me, and I feel unusually relaxed for the first time all day. I gaze out the window at the rain cascading down the glass in a solid sheet of water, lost in thought about Grams and her past. I hope she told that soldier —Charlie—to take a hike. It didn't seem like she was interested in his story, even though it was about him being forced into his position. He was probably up to something. Maybe she keeps calling out his name because she wants revenge on him for being one of the bad soldiers. *I would.* I could imagine it haunting me until my dying day. "Beer or wine?" Jackson interrupts my scattered thoughts.

"Beer," I tell him, turning back in his direction.

He looks impressed as his lips purse together. "Light or dark?"

"Dark," I answer without thinking. "I'm not a big fan of IPAs, and I like the smoky hops."

"Okay, you might be a little too perfect for me, so I'm not sure this is going to work out," he says with a sigh that oozes sarcasm.

We pull into a parking lot beneath a glowing sign with a spinning bowling ball. As Jackson puts the car in park, the rain stops abruptly, as if someone were shutting off a faucet. I can even see a few stars poking out from behind some thick clouds. "Perfect timing."

I let myself out even though he was heading around the back of his car toward my door. "I just have to grab my purse out of my bag." I pull my seat up and lean into the back where my bag is, grab my small leather satchel, and pull it over my head as it falls diagonally across my body.

We walk side by side around to the front of the building and in through the entrance, greeted by dance music, hundreds of large screen TVs, and more glowing lights.

"What size shoe do you wear?" he asks.

"Seven," I tell him. "And you?"

"I'll get them, don't worry." I was trying to be funny, and he's either playing back or taking this date very seriously.

"What size can I get you?" the balding man with a silky, pink button-down shirt asks from behind the counter.

"A seven for her and an eleven for me," he says. "We'll do two rounds."

"Here," I offer, handing him some cash.

"Cut it out." He pushes my hand away. "I was in on the guilt trip with your grandmother, so I'll pay the consequence."

"Consequence?" I snap with a smile.

"Kidding." He gives me a quick wink as he hands over my

shoes. This man sure knows how to make a heart flutter. It's obvious he specializes in that area.

"Lane fifteen," the guy says, pointing to the right side.

We make our way through dozens of couches and modern chairs, finding our alley capped off with a dining table and menus. "This is pretty cool," I tell him.

"You haven't been here?"

"I'm in the suburbs, about twenty minutes away, and I don't get out to the city as often as I'd like."

"So am I. What town do you live in?" he asks.

"At the moment, I'm not quite sure." I'm currently homeless unless I count Mom's house as home. "I lived with my boyfriend in Waltham up until yesterday."

"Oh, yikes, I wasn't aware of how serious it was. You just broke up with him out of nowhere today?" He seems concerned, rightfully so, as I would be if it happened the way he may be assuming it did. I'm sure he's not up for being a rebound guy.

"Oh, believe me, it wasn't out of nowhere. It sounds worse than it is," I tell him. "I've been pulling away from him for a while and spending more time at my mom's than with him. I've been *over* us for a while, but I wasn't forceful enough to make a clean break. However, today was the day he admitted to cheating on me multiple times, and it was enough of a reason to remove him from my life for good. I just need to get my stuff out of his place, and I'll never have to see him again. So, our "date" happened to pop up at just the right time, I suppose."

"Wow, so you've wasted no time getting back into the dating scene, huh?" His face has little emotion, and I don't know what to make of his statement until he breaks into a hearty laugh. "I'm kidding."

"You think you're pretty funny, don't you?"

"Actually, I have been told that I would have been great as a stand-up comedian. It didn't pay as well as being a doctor, though, so I tried to incorporate comedy into my medical career, and I turned out to be a pretty funny doctor. After all, laughter *is* the best medicine for the heart, you know?"

"You're a clever one, aren't you?" I ask with a grin.

"If I can't laugh a little each day, I'd be surrounded by sad, sick people, so I do what I do to get by and try to make my patients smile at the same time."

"That makes perfect sense." Maybe it's something I should consider trying out. I don't leave much time for fun and laughter in my life, and it's suddenly apparent how much I've been missing it.

"I'll be right back. I'll grab some bowling balls for our lane."

The curved bench at the table is welcoming with its plushness, and I stretch out, waiting for Jackson to return with the bowling balls. He somehow manages to do so with one trip, placing them in the holding area of the lane, then slides in next to me. "So, what was this ex-boyfriend's name?"

"Mike," I answer, feeling a tightness in my throat just from saying his name out loud.

"I'm sorry you're going through it. Breaking up is never easy."

"It could be worse," I tell him. Life could be so much worse.

"You're right about that."

A waitress comes over to our table with an order pad, but her focus is everywhere except on us. I can understand with how crowded this place is. "Drinks or dinner?" she asks.

"Both," Jackson answers.

"Do you need a minute with the menu?" she continues.

"Please," Jackson replies. "We could order drinks in the meantime, though." Jackson gestures to me, waiting for my drink order.

"Do you have Smoke and Dagger?" I ask.

"We do," the waitress says while jotting my order down.

"I'll have a Boston Lager," Jackson follows. "You like Smoke and dagger?" He hoots with amazement as if my drink choice is a point in the dating game.

"I told you, I like dark beer."

"I guess so. You have good taste." Up until today, I'm not sure I'd say that about myself, but maybe I can start fresh tonight. "So, I must ask, since I was listening in while you were reading to your grandmother today. Is Charlie your grandfather? She was asking for him before the second stroke happened too."

"No, actually, I'm not entirely sure who Charlie is. It's all a little strange. She's never mentioned his name once in all these years, so why now?"

Jackson seems surprised by all of this, just as I am. "The mind works in mysterious ways, and strokes can have an impact on memories and pasts that have been locked away."

"I suppose. I guess it's just a little unsettling."

"Maybe you should look him up?" Jackson suggests, like it's just a matter of Googling this guy and finding out who he is and what his story was.

"I can't even remember his last name, or if it has been mentioned anywhere in the diary so far, and second, he was a soldier. I'm not about to go looking for some guy who may or may not have killed people. What if he tried to hurt her? I really don't know enough of the story yet."

Jackson shrugs. "I suppose. You should keep reading, but you have to tell me what happens because I'm kind of intrigued now."

"You kind of got yourself intrigued when you decided to eavesdrop, don't you think?" I playfully nudge my elbow into his arm, teasing with a smirk.

He pulls back with a cute smile. "Hey, hey, be gentle. I'm a doctor."

I roll my eyes, "I wouldn't want to damage your arms. Do you have them insured?"

"Maybe," he says with a sigh. "In any case, please keep me posted on the next entry. I am curious about where it all goes."

I open the menu to distract myself from this man's flawless smile and the effect it clearly has on me. I have been easily distracted by Jackson all day.

Focus, focus. Menu. The appetizers seem like the easiest thing to go with since we'll be bowling at the same time I assume. "Hmm…nachos and mozzarella sticks."

"You speak my language too. How amazing is this?" he jokes. "Want to share?"

"I suppose I could do that." I feel like I may be sounding too serious rather than just pushing the dry humor. I'm trying too hard, which is why dating is a bad idea. I'm bad at it, and I end up with men like Mike.

"You don't like me, do you?" he blurts out.

"What?" I ask with a squeak accenting my question. "What would make you say that?" Besides my not-so-funny sense of humor and ridiculous awkwardness. It's so obvious how nervous I am. I must look like a fool right now.

He opens his menu, but it seems as though it's just to busy his hands as a distraction. "You seem like you're trying very hard to figure me out."

"I like to do that. It's like a guessing game for me—you know —if I'm right or wrong on certain aspects," I tell him.

"So, you do like me?"

I can't hide the smile threatening the corners of my lips. "Do you have a confidence issue I should be aware of?" I'm going to go with no on this one, but I'm toying with him.

"I do, and you're messing with it, big time." I release the smile I've been holding back and feel a blush warm my cheeks. "Oh, you've got game."

"How else will I win?" he asks.

"Well, you haven't hit a strike yet, so I don't know."

"That's gutter talk right there," he says through laughter.

"Oh, you are a corny one."

"I have no comeback for that," he snickers. "But how about this, if I get a strike with my first ball, you have to tell me exactly what's on your mind at that exact second? That way I'll know what it is you're observing about me."

"Deal," I say, trying to appear unfazed.

Jackson stands up from the bench, leaving behind a scent of some type of delicious-smelling cologne. The fragrance grabs my senses, and it takes everything I have to hold myself back from running over and wrapping my arms around him. We're basically still strangers, though, and that would be taking things a little too fast for this set-up date we're on.

He picks up the bowling ball and eyes the pins carefully before swinging his arm back. "Don't miss!" I yell at the exact second he drops the ball, but I don't think it had much effect.

"Really?" He turns around and lifts his hands in the air. "You pulled that move?" Without looking at the pins or the destruction of his swing, the word "strike" blares in fluorescent letters on the screen above his head and bounces around amid digital confetti. He just knew.

"Okay, Emma, spill it. Pause your thought and hand it over."

"Wow, I'm impressed with your bowling skills."

His arms drop to his sides. "Really? That's it?"

He's kind of too cute for words, and I hate the thought that this might not move past tonight since this date wasn't exactly our idea. I'm also afraid that he may not want to date someone who might be on the rebound. Maybe I shouldn't have told him that I just broke up with Mike, but I wouldn't want to start something new without being honest. My timing has never been great.

"Fine," I tell him. "I'm worried that I'm having fun with you."

"What? Why?" he asks with a surprised look and a pinched tone to his words.

"You weren't wrong with what you said earlier. I just got out of a long and unfortunate relationship, and here I am on a date with you, just hours later."

"You do know you deserve to have fun, right? We're celebrating your decision to move on with your life. It's that simple."

"I like that," I tell him. It makes me feel better, less like a desperate woman looking to fill a void.

"When your feelings are dead for so long, and someone or something sparks your interest, it's only natural that you're going to have a good time. I've been there."

"You went on a date the day your wife left you?" My curiosity is at an all-time high with this one. He seems to be speaking from experience, but I doubt it's very common to be dating within twenty-four hours of a breakup, especially if it's the breakup of a marriage.

"No, this is actually my first date since then." After all this time, I'm the lucky girl who unintentionally sparked his interest? How did that happen? Is this all Grams's doing? Not that I'm complaining, but my life does not go that way. At least, it hasn't up until now.

I stand up, needing to end this conversation because I don't know what to think, or I don't know what I'm thinking. I'm not sure which. "Now, if I get a strike, you need to tell me why, of all the strangers in the world, you chose to go out with me after being single for so many months. We both know you could have told my grandmother you were busy or taken."

"Deal," he says, adding the tone of challenge to his voice.

I dig my fingers into the holes of the ball and close my eyes, doing nothing but wish for a miracle because bowling is not a talent I have been gifted with, and I don't want him to know that just yet.

I swing the ball, lining it up with the center guide, and release it. I cover my hand over my eyes and wait with anticipation for the sound of my ball crashing against the pins. It sounds loud, so I open my eyes, shocked to see all the pins knocked over. *You've got to be kidding me. No way.*

I turn around and hold my chin up with a proud smile. "That was totally by luck," he says. His wry little grin is totally calling my bluff.

"What? I don't think so!" I argue. "Are you questioning my bowling skills?"

"When your eyes were closed, you missed the part where your ball did this cute little swirl into the gutter before jumping back onto the alley and hitting the pins, but hey, that was impressive."

"It doesn't matter how it was done. It was done, so now you can confess the reality of 'why me.'"

"Why you?" he begins. "Your grandmother told me she knew what true love was and that so few people get to experience it in life because they're too busy settling for the wrong person. She said you were one of those people...too busy settling. Then she asked me about my story, and she told me you would be the perfect one for me. Since the woman seems to know what she's talking about, I took her advice. Plus, you're drop-dead gorgeous, so that helped."

I'm so surprised and embarrassed by his response that I swat my palm against his arm.

"Wow, I tell you that you're beautiful and you hit me. Geez, no wonder you're single." I teasingly hit him again because I like the way he flinches and how his dimples deepen as his smile plays against his laughter.

Somehow, between dinner, a couple of beers, and two rounds of bowling—Jackson taking the game by storm—it's midnight, and it feels like only a minute has passed since we arrived at the alley. Jackson pulls into the parking lot at the hospital and leans his head back into his seat. "I'm going to be so tired at seven tomorrow morning, but it was worth it. I had more fun tonight than I've had in as long as I can remember," he says.

"Me too, Jackson."

"I'm not going to kiss you or anything because I know you're on the rebound. So, don't get nervous or anything, okay?"

"I can't believe you," I groan. "You just can't stop yourself for trying to make things awkward."

"I can't," he says. His smile has captured my attention too many times tonight and I'm falling weak for it. "Oh, don't forget your bag back there. I assume you have a date with your grandmother's diary."

"Is it bad that I'm reading it without her?" The thought has crossed my mind a few times, but I've tried to push it out of my head and replace it with the undying curiosity I'm feeling.

Jackson leans back into his seat and rolls his shoulders back. "Personally, I think it's best to know someone—their past and present—before they're gone. Plus, I think you need to find out more about this Charlie guy."

"I know, right?" It's like I've been let off the hook for spying. It is the reason I began reading without her. If she's asking for this man, I need to at least understand why.

I watch Jackson's gaze float to the time on the dashboard. "You know, I have to be back here in just a few hours so I might just spend the night at the hospital. Therefore, if you want to read out loud, I'm kind of curious to know what happens—or at least find out more about Charlie."

"You're as bad as I am," I tell him.

"Look, I'm surrounded by emergencies, surgeries, and upset family members daily, and sometimes, even the funniest doctors need an escape too."

"I can see that," I agree with his argument.

"Why have I not asked you what you do? I must be very self-absorbed," he jokes, chuckling at himself. It didn't come up, but I hadn't thought much of it. I'm glad I had a mental break from almost everything tonight, including work.

"I'm an artist," I tell him, keeping it vague.

"An artist?" he asks. "I've never gone out with an artist."

"We're an odd breed," I digress while fiddling with the dangling bracelet on my wrist.

"Doctors are a little weird too."

"Touché," I agree.

"What kind of art?"

"Graphics mostly, with some illustration mixed in. I work with a couple of ad firms in the city, consulting mostly—it keeps me busy."

"That's amazing." His brows rise and his lips part, appearing enamored by what I just call work. It's sweet. "I'd love to see your work sometime."

"I'd say the same to you, but seeing as you saved my grandmother's life today, I guess I already have." I reach out in front of me and trace the Mercedes logo on the dashboard, busying myself as I consider all the strange thoughts racing through my mind. My heart is beating a little faster than usual, and it's from such a simple conversation we're having. It feels almost strange that he has this kind of effect on me. I wonder if it's just a relief to feel good for a few moments after such a horrible day, or maybe it's the start of something good.

"Well—" He reaches into his back seat and he grabs my bag. After resting the bag on my lap, he reclines his seat back a bit to relax. "Read me an entry before you go." He looks at me with a strong gaze, affirming his seriousness in hearing more about Grams's life.

"Are you sure you want to listen? It's not exactly bedtime story material."

"I'm sure." His words sound like a hush as he places his hand down on my knee. The warmth from his skin melts through the denim material of my pants, and I find it both comforting and arousing. The mere touch from any part of him makes my entire body shiver.

CHAPTER ELEVEN

AMELIA

DAY 60 - MARCH 1942

*O*nly darkness surrounded me in the early hours each day. I never knew the true time, but I believed it had to be three or four in the morning. At the sound of heavy boots marching around outside and the loud screech of an alarm, I rolled off of my bunk and waited for my eyes to clear. Without electricity, it was easier for my vision to adjust from one level of opaqueness to the moonlit dirt courtyard where I would start my fifteen-hour day.

I pulled my dress down from a hook I had made from stolen paper clips and slipped it on over my undergarments. It was the only sense of normalcy I could offer myself before starting the workday. Small rituals such as those helped me continue to feel human.

The other women around me scurried to prepare for their jobs too, as they did every morning, which made things a bit chaotic in our small block. "Amelia," one of them called out to me, but in a whisper of a voice I could barely hear. "Did you get that bandage for me?"

Alise, the woman around Mama's age who slept on the bunk above me asked if I could sneak a bandage for her. She refused to go down to the sick bay in fear of being marked as injured. I couldn't blame her—I still don't. More frequently, we were seeing people's identification numbers marked with a note, labeling them as sick or injured. Shortly after, they would be transported else-where. We were told they were being taken to a different location where they would receive better care, but we all had a difficult time believing anything the Nazis told us—for a good reason. It was hard to avoid the assumption that the next stop would have better conditions than what we were experiencing.

"I did," I whispered back. I reached into my coat pocket and pulled out the bandage. "May I see the wound?" Not that I could see much in the dimly lit barrack, but the wound looked quite bad the day before when she asked me to help. With absolutely no prior medical training, I wasn't quite sure what I was looking for, but I had been watching the German nurses work, taking notes so I could help wherever and whenever possible.

The irony of my work there was that I had once planned to attend the university with hopes of becoming a nurse. At that point, however, I doubted I see a day where I'd be allowed to take such prestigious classes, so I focused on learning as much as I could by observing the nurses. When my eyes finally started adjusting to the darkness, I dropped my legs down off the side of the bed. My bones felt heavier than my muscles could handle in the mornings, especially after being on my feet with such little sustenance day in and day out. It was taking a toll on my body. It was hard to even imagine what it was doing to the older women.

Alise carefully climbed down from her bed, and I helped her as much as I could until her feet touched the ground. I wrapped my hand around her wrist, noticing it was so thin I was able to close my grip around it a little more than once. It wasn't surprising that everyone was losing weight and starting to look more like skeletons than people. I pulled her arm toward me and gently rotated it to the side. I could immediately see that the wound looked worse than the previous day, and the area of inflammation had spread, but it was still hard to tell exactly how bad it was without much light. "Alise, I'm not sure this bandage will cover the wound entirely," I told her.

"You have to try," she said with fear in her frail voice. "I'll be working in the dirt again today, and I can't let this get any worse. They'll send me away if I become ill."

Each morning, Alise was taken outside the gates to the SS building so she could help with a pool the Nazis were building. She said they were using their hands to do most of the digging, and I could only imagine how awful that must have been. At the end of each day, she would come back covered in dirt from head to toe. Her fingertips were bloody, and she had bruises all over her hands and arms.

"I'm worried about this wound, Alise. I think it needs ointment at the very least, but antibiotics would probably be better. I wish we had some. It may already be infected," I told her. Regardless, I placed the bandage over the area, then quickly hid the wrapper beneath my mattress.

"Do you think you can get some of that ointment or antibiotics today, too?" she asked, pleading as she leaned up against the bed to give her emaciated body some support.

Taking anything from the sick bay was not permitted, and I could be put into one of the prisoner cells for doing anything of that nature, but Glauken, the head German nurse, would often leave to take breaks. She would close me into the nurses' quarters, and I would continue working on the paperwork. It offered me a few moments of freedom from time to time, and it would give me the opportunity to take what I needed to care for Alise or any of the other women in my block.

"I will try," I told her as I placed my hands over the bony area where her shoulders and arms met, offering her some warmth—the same kind I craved. The sensation of bone covered by only a thin layer of frail skin was unlike anything I had touched before. I remember the worry I felt at that moment, thinking Alise was not going to make it much longer without real medical attention, but it also seemed clear that she might have already come to terms with that.

I headed out of the barracks, watching for the soldiers who were continually marching up and down the dirt paths in between the buildings. I did what I could to avoid interacting with them, as it never led to anything good. Though I could no longer run, I was still able to move quickly through the courtyard toward the sick bay where a line was already beginning to form. It was truly endless there. Every day more Jews were brought in, and every day at least half of those were transported away from the camp to another location.

Once inside the sick bay, I prepared the area for Glauken and the other nurses. I organized the supplies and the previous day's paperwork so it could be submitted to the SS officers. I typically finished the pre-day work just as the nurses arrived. They never greeted me or acknowledged my presence, but I tried my hardest to be cordial to them. As much as it killed me to be pleasant, I wanted to remind them that I was human. I also wanted to think I was making it harder for them to replace me. I'm not sure if that was the case or not, though. Had I known what that day was about to bring, being pleasant to the nurses would have been the least of my concerns.

When only a couple hours had passed by, the line of people waiting for care had wrapped around the nearest barrack block. There had to be at least two hundred sick patients in line. Each day, it seemed as if the number of people in line doubled. After making it halfway through the line, I spotted a man draped in dirt-covered clothes like the rest of us, except his belt was tightened so much that the excess leather was hanging down by his thigh. The man's stomach looked concave as his shirt billowed inward from a passing breeze. His face was blackened with soot, and his beard was covered in dirt. His eyes were sunken and hollow, almost as if there was nothing behind them. I studied him for a moment, trying to analyze the torment he must have gone through to make him look that way, but as I stared at his smudged features, I recognized the olive hue of his eyes and the natural auburn highlights strung through his hair in the glow of the rising sun.

My knees began to tremble, and I dropped the clipboard, creating a cloud of dirt at my feet. "Papa?" I whispered.

He was in a state of shock from seeing me—his mouth was agape, and his bottom lip trembled furiously. "Amelia," he groaned with a scratchy rasp. He tried to lift his arms, but it was as if he had weights holding them by his side.

"Papa, where have you been? What have they done to you?" I asked, trying to maintain my composure, though everything inside of me was falling apart all over again. Papa was the strongest man I knew. He worked with his hands, chopping wood for factories. There wasn't much he couldn't do, and he proved that by taking such good care of our family all those years before the war. At that moment, though, he wasn't that man. He was broken, hungry, and by the looks of his sagging pale skin…dying.

I leaned down to retrieve the clipboard, scared of anyone spotting my mistake. "We're in the other section—the ghetto," he answered. His worn, scratchy voice came out in hardly a whisper. "I looked for you every day, but I was sure you had been transported. Even after we heard there were women and children over here, I had very little hope of ever finding you, my precious girl." His voice was so torn up, I could hardly understand him.

"I've been looking for you too," I told him. "Where is Jakob?"

Papa managed to lift a hand and draped it over his chest while using what looked to be all his strength to swallow whatever thickness was in his throat. "He was transported," he said, his voice cracking with emotion. "They took him two weeks ago, but I don't know where."

With so many reasons the Nazis seemed to have for moving us around, I couldn't begin to guess why they took Jakob. Surely, he had to have been working hard. He always had been a hard worker, just like Papa. "Why did they take him?" I placed my pencil down to my paper, making it appear as if I were taking notes.

Papa looked down at the dirt and shook his head with disdain. "Oh Amelia, you know Jakob. He tried to escape."

"Escape?" I questioned with disbelief.

"Don't worry, Amelia," Papa tried to tell me.

"Where was he escaping to?" I felt a pain working its way through my body, wondering what Jakob could have been thinking. "Why would he leave you?"

Papa lifted his heavy arm again, reaching toward me as if he were going to tuck my hair behind my ear like he always had when trying to calm me, but his gaze scanned the surrounding area, and he lowered his hand. "Amelia," he exhaled.

"Why, Papa?" If I had the ability to cry, tears would have been present, but I had worked hard to shut that form of emotion off. I didn't want to cry. It would have been like admitting defeat to the Nazis and Hitler.

"He wanted to find you," Papa uttered.

I cupped my hand over my mouth as if to stop any sounds coming from me. "Do you think he's okay?"

Papa looked away from me and then down at the dirt. "I don't know, Amelia. I've tried to stay as positive as I can but it's impossible not to think the worst—these men have no regard for life. The truth is, I fear that they murdered your brother the same way they did your mother."

I tried to refocus on my papers, but I was suddenly unable to write Papa's name in a straight line. "What are you sick with?" I asked him, sounding as despondent as I felt.

"I don't know," he said. "I've been coughing and vomiting for three days, my head hurts, and I believe I have a fever." I placed the back of my hand on his forehead, feeling the heat radiate from his skin to mine. He certainly had a fever, and I could hear a wheezing noise coming from his lungs when he inhaled.

"Papa, they're transporting all the sick," I tell him, softly.

"I'm aware of that, but I don't know what else to do, Amelia."

I leaned in close, making sure no one else could hear me. "There is a storage closet in the administration building. It's around the back. You need to sneak in during a shift change, probably in two hours or so. Once you're inside, take a left, and it's the second door on the right. It's not being used right now, and you'll be safe there until I can get to you. I'll bring antibiotics tonight."

"Amelia, no, that could get you killed," he argued in the same quiet, but firm voice I was speaking in.

"*You* could die," I reminded him.

"I can't let you do that," he argued. "I already had to watch your Mama die. There is no way I can let you do this."

"Papa, don't leave me. Please, you're all I have right now, and I will do whatever I can to keep you safe, just as you have done for me my entire life. Please, Papa." If the pleading look in my eyes didn't speak loudly enough, I knew that the pain we shared was enough to make him accept my offer.

"There is no safety," he said, shaking his head. "I'm shoving bodies into crematoriums all day, one after the next. We're all dying here. They're starving us and making it so we are susceptible to diseases."

Hearing the truth was different from witnessing it. Papa's words were just illuminating what I already knew but was too afraid to admit to myself. "I know, but I need to keep you with me as long as I can—I will do whatever it takes, Papa. It's the least I can do as your daughter."

"Excuse me," a woman shouted from a few people behind Papa. "The rest of us have been waiting here for so long. When will it be our turn? My daughter has a fever, and we need help." I looked past Papa, spotting the mother and child. The little girl's eyes were half closed and swollen. Her hair was braided tightly behind her head, revealing prominent veins protruding up the sides of her face. The child leaned all her weight against her mother's legs, embracing her with a tight hold. It hurt me to the depths of my soul to know what the future would likely hold for both that mother and her sweet child. After all this time, I still don't understand why so many innocent lives were put through that horror?

Papa swallowed hard, pulling my attention back to him as he mouthed something silently to himself...a prayer, I believe. "So, you think it's just a cold?" Papa asked out loud.

"I do," I replied.

"Thank you," he said while stepping out of line.

It was hard to think of much else throughout the rest of the day. Papa was more than a little sick, and I was scared that it may have been too late for antibiotics to do anything, but I had to save him—I just had to.

The line continued to grow throughout the day, and it seemed endless as usual. Whatever was wrong with Papa was running rampant through the men's barracks. So many of them looked just like him. At the time, I wasn't aware that there were hundreds of men living in a small, tight confinement without beds. They were forced to use one another's backs and shoulders as a form of comfort to sleep. The comprehension of how much worse it could have been, has always been unfathomable.

As I rounded the part of the line behind the nearby barrack, a hand grabbed my wrist and pulled me off to the side. It wasn't the first time I had been pulled away from the line in that spot. It was happening almost daily. I didn't fight it, though maybe I should have.

Charlie would sometimes pull me down to a small, rock-covered tunnel that seemed to be abandoned since I don't believe it was connected to the parts of the camp the Jews were restricted to. There was also a large indentation hidden in the shadows of the inner wall where a person could hide in the daytime and not be seen.

My legs and feet were aching by the time we arrived at the tunnel, but I knew what awaited me, so I complied.

"Talk to me today," he said in the privacy of the tunnel. "Please."

As I did each day, I only stared at his pleading face that was highlighted by the dim light behind him.

His hand rested on my cheek, and I immediately wrapped my hand around his wrist to pull it away. As I did that, I felt bones in his arm, noticing they felt different from the previous time I had moved his hand away from me. Curiously, I placed my hand under his chin and then on the side of his face. I felt a hollowness that appeared to be forming beneath his cheekbones. "Why have you lost weight?" I finally spoke to him. Since the first day of my job at the sick bay, Charlie had been pulling me from the line to offer me extra food—food Jews were not supposed to be given.

"It doesn't matter," he said under his breath. "Here." He handed me a soft, fresh-smelling sweet roll and a chicken leg. As ravenous as I was, I didn't offer my gratitude before taking a large bite of the meat. A moan murmured from my throat, but I quickly remembered the emaciated look of Papa's body, and couldn't find it in me to take another bite of food. I needed to give it to him, but he would wonder why I had such lavish food when the rest of the prisoners had only been fed one stale, hard, bread roll and a small bowl of cabbage soup once a day since we arrived.

"Why are you not eating?" Charlie asked.

"Why are you thin?" I retorted.

"Amelia, I need for you to eat."

"Are you starving yourself to feed me?" I asked him.

Charlie placed his hands around my arms and squeezed gently. "I want you to eat."

"I haven't said a word to you in two months. Why do you care

113

about what I eat?" The sound of footsteps followed my last word, and my heart froze in place as my arms and legs became cold and numb with fear. Charlie's hand pressed against my collarbone, shoving me against the wet rock wall of the nook. His body pressed against mine, and I felt his heart beating into my heart as his arms boxed me in. Charlie's head slid to the side of mine until it touched the wall. As his warm breaths covered my neck, I squeezed my eyes shut to hide from all other sensations.

The gravel beneath a pair of boots crunched towards us at a steady pace, and I thought if tried to ignore it, I could block out the fear I felt. However, I was scared our heartbeats could be heard by anyone who might pass through that small space.

I just needed to focus on something else and forget the rest. It was my only choice.

The warmth of Charlie's body against mine was something I hadn't felt since arriving. It was like a wool blanket and a roaring fire enveloping me in its heat. He was comforting, but if we were to be found, it was likely we would both be executed.

Minutes passed by, and the sound of footsteps finally faded. The soldier was gone. It felt like a small cause for celebration that he didn't find us, but Charlie didn't move. "I have been alone for so long, feeling like a prisoner of this war. Though I haven't been physically tortured like you, I'm here against my will." Charlie told me the same explanation each day, and I couldn't understand why, but I assumed it was to offer himself hope that I would eventually believe him. It wasn't that I didn't believe him, it was that we were two different types of prisoners, and at the end of the day, my life was at risk, and his wasn't, as long as he acted appropriately. I was his prisoner, even if *he* was someone else's.

"Please, believe me, Amelia."

"I believe you, Charlie." It was the first time I admitted to any form of trust with him. "However, it doesn't change the fact that we are not the same."

"You're right," he said. "You are a much better person than I am."

"You don't know that," I said. In truth, he didn't know much about me at all.

"It's in your eyes," he continued. "You can tell if a person is good or bad by peering into their eyes."

"How?" The heat of his body was still moving through me, removing the permanent shiver and ache I had from fighting against the cold. It felt like the winter mornings when I would wake up wrapped tightly in my bed's thick linens at home. It was always hard to climb out of bed those mornings, knowing the cold floors were waiting for me, as well as the drafts that whistled in through our old windows, but I would have done anything to touch those cold floors or hear the melodic sounds of the wind filtering through cracks at that moment.

"When a person can look another directly in the eyes, it shows compassion, understanding, and honesty," he explained. Charlie had always looked me in the eyes when speaking. Considering he had done almost all the speaking for both of us in the previous months, it felt like an odd characterization. However, Mama and Papa had raised me with respectable standards. They taught me to always do the right thing and help people when I was able to. I couldn't understand how he would know that about me by just looking into my eyes. "What should I see in your eyes? Have you hurt anyone?" I asked.

"No," he responded without hesitance. "I'm a guard." His eyes widened as they focused on mine. It was so dark there, but my vision adjusted enough to see the look on his face.

"Am I going to be killed?" I asked him. It was a question that had been running through my head each moment of every day. Was everything for nothing? Was I just waiting for my number to be up?

"I can't answer that truthfully," he said.

"I was afraid you would say that," I replied.

"I was afraid you would ask."

Feeling as though my breath had been stolen from my lungs, I knew I had to return to the line so I could finish taking down the remaining patient information. I had hoped to finish a little early that day so I could tend to Papa. "I need to get back to the line waiting at the sick bay," I told him, needing to digest the reality I had been desperately avoiding. I placed the chicken leg inside my coat pocket and then placed the roll carefully on top of it. "Thank you for the food."

"Thank you for listening to me," he said. Charlie took a step or two back, allowing a cool draft of air to fill the space we were in. He locked his hand around my elbow and guided me out from under the tunnel and back toward the line. Two other soldiers were heading toward us, looking between Charlie and me, and a sick feeling gnawed at my stomach. Charlie's hand unsurprisingly tightened as he jerked me forward for show.

One of the Nazi's elbowed the other as they erupted into laughter before puckering their lips with a clear innuendo. Charlie ignored them and tugged me harder, forcing me to walk up the hill faster than my legs could handle. When we reached the line, he tossed me into a few of the sick people. "Watch yourself," he shouted at me before walking away.

A woman in the line grabbed my arm and righted me on my feet. "Are you okay?" she asked with concern.

"I'm fine," I answered, feeling guilt coursing through my veins. "Did he hurt you?"

"No," I replied, fearful to say anything else.

The woman placed her hand on my back and rubbed gently for a moment before I took the clipboard I had dropped when Charlie grabbed me.

I had to make my way up the line to find where I left off, which wasn't easy, seeing how similar everyone had begun to appear.

My mind was in a fog for the remainder of the day. I found it hard to focus on the words I was writing and the accuracy of it all.

I had yet to make a mistake, and I was terrified of what would happen if I did.

I must have made it through five hundred prisoners that day, all with similar symptoms. Most appeared to have the flu or pneumonia, while others were dealing with wounds that had become infected. Showering once a week was not enough to keep us from the dangerous bacteria in the environment we were trying to survive in, but I considered that to be their plan for us. They wouldn't have to kill us if we all just died off.

At six that evening, the doors to the sick bay closed. A nurse locked up, quarantining those who required overnight medical attention versus those who were well enough to be sent back to their block, or the dozens who weren't evaluated during the available hours. It was time for me to type up my papers from the day and leave them for Glauken to review at her convenience.

The moment I finished my work, I took a small stack of blank paper, along with a needle and vial of antibiotics. Thankfully, I had gotten quick at locating supplies. I then snuck through the adjoining doors between the sick bay and the administration building while creating the appearance of delivering notes, which allowed me to make it past the guards in the hallways near where I told Papa to hide. The area was clear when I made it to the empty storage room, and I opened the door, quietly closing it behind me.

I was afraid to turn on a light, as it would shine under the doorway, so I took caution while entering the room. When searching for a utility closet a few weeks earlier, I had mistakenly discovered that empty room and knew there was a window covered by boxes in the back. Before I called out for Papa, I wanted to be sure he was in there, so I felt my way around the small room until I reached the far wall. I pushed the boxes aside so the moonlight could brighten the room enough for me to see.

A body was crumpled on the ground, up against the side wall. He was in the fetal position with his arms around his knees and his head tucked into his chest. I recognized his belt. It was Papa. The belt was the only part of him that looked familiar. Papa had always been on the heavier side, and the doctors often told him he was slightly above average on the scale and needed to maintain a healthy diet despite his physical labor. Mama would cook for us each night, always dressing up the food in unique ways so Papa wouldn't feel as if he was missing out on his favorite foods. However, when Jews were no longer allowed to shop at the local markets, we could only purchase food in the subsidized Jewish market, and our options were limited. We made do with what we had, and though it wasn't the way Papa had wanted to lose weight, he certainly would have surpassed his doctor's expectations.

"Papa, I'm here," I softly called out to him. I pulled my dress above my knees then kneeled beside his body and placed my hand gingerly on his back. "Papa, it's Amelia. I brought you some food." He didn't move at the sound of my voice, so I reached for his forehead to check for a fever. His head was no longer hot, but rather cool, instead. "Papa, I think your fever broke," I said, trying to force an uplifting sound in my voice.

I pulled his arms loose from his knees, gently rolling him onto his back. "Papa, wake up!" I cried through a whisper.

As the space beside him was exposed from where his face was, I noticed a wet spot on the cement. The site concerned me, so I placed my hand on the side of his face, finding a matching dampness beside his eye. Was he crying before he fell asleep on the floor? "It's okay, Papa, I'm here now."

I didn't ask myself why he wasn't responding because in my heart, I already knew. It took me several minutes before I gained the courage to place my hand over his heart, seeking a beat that I knew I wouldn't find. It took me another few minutes after that to check the artery on his neck for a pulse that wouldn't be there, and one more minute to check his wrist. All three spots were silent and still. Papa died while waiting for me in a small closet. I told him not to seek medical attention because I could help him. Instead, he died waiting for me. Papa died because of me. As I heaved in pain and grief, I tore another piece of my dress, feeling an ache rob another part of my soul as I cried silent tears that would not stop. Papa was gone, Mama was gone, and Jakob was gone for all I knew. For the first time in my life, I was all alone. Papa would always be the one to start the prayer over our deceased relatives, but there was no one here to speak the Mourners Kaddish but me.

Yitgadal v'yitkadash sh'mei raba.

B'alma di v'ra chirutei...

I recited the Hebrew words, trying to remain strong, but my voice broke. The silence took over, and I listened for Papa's voice out of memory, as well as the words I had heard too many times before.

That day was the day I went from being a good person to one who was partially responsible for her papa's death.

I sat beside Papa's lifeless body, talking to him about what I had experienced over the last two months, telling him how scared I was of dying. I told him I was trying to be brave, but the horrors I saw each day while awake were sometimes becoming worse than my nightmares. Part of me felt a little envious of Papa, just as I felt when Mama passed away. He was no longer in pain, no longer suffering, and he was with Mama. *Maybe I shouldn't have been trying so hard to stay alive,* was all I could think at that time.

I sat in that dark room for a long while. I contemplated staying there until I died, but then I realized that would mean Papa had died in vain. I couldn't do that to him. I had to honor his memory by doing my best to make it through that nightmare. I had to find every possible scrap of food and eat it. I promised myself that if Charlie had food for me, I would take it because Papa would want me to do so.

I pulled out the chicken and sweet bread roll that Charlie brought me and I scraped the bone clean. Even though my stomach felt sick, I knew I couldn't let it go to waste. *"Food is a gift from God that should never be wasted,"* Papa would always say, followed by, "It's why I will always be a happy, fat man." At that moment, though, Papa was all skin and bones—limp and lifeless. His frail body was lying in front of me, but his soul, the part of him that made him the man that he was, had left me there alone. I took his hand and kissed it one last time. "Oh Papa, I love you now and forever. Rest in peace."

CHAPTER TWELVE

EMMA

*M*y hands are shaking, and I feel emotionally drained while closing the diary. I'm completely speechless as I stare blankly into the dark parking lot until an ambulance speeds by and pulls up to the emergency doors. The flashing lights force my eyes to focus and I'm brought back to reality, remembering I'm not alone.

Jackson's hand tenderly lifts mine from my lap and weaves his warm fingers between mine.

"Are you okay?" he asks.

"I don't know." Truthfully, I'm baffled. "I feel blindsided."

"You never knew any of that?"

"None of it."

"It explains why your grandmother was telling me how to properly set up a pacemaker," he says with a hint of laughter.

"What do you mean?" I ask.

"She must have gone on to be a doctor or nurse, I assume."

"No, she didn't. She worked with the International Services at the Red Cross from the time she emigrated here until my grandfather died ten years ago."

"Wow," he says. "She seemed to know a lot of medical

information."

"Something else I've never known."

"She didn't talk about your great-grandfather?" Jackson asks.

I place the tip of my thumb between my teeth and shake my head. *I thought I knew her.* "It's probably not something she wanted to remember," Jackson says. "People who experience trauma block out memories without even trying sometimes."

"It's been sitting right under her bed all this time, though."

"I think you're still going to have a chance to talk to her about this," he says, squeezing my hand as a small smile lights up his face.

"Yeah, I sure hope so." My reply comes out through a long sigh.

"Is it weird that I want to hear more? No one ever talks about that part of history, and I'm completely intrigued," he adds in.

"I don't think it's weird at all. I'm flattered that you are interested, and it's nice to have someone to share this with," I tell him. "It's a lot to process and comprehend."

Jackson glances at the time on the dashboard, and I follow his gaze. *How is it three o'clock?* "You must be a slow reader," he jokes.

"Each word felt like a mouthful." It's like I have to stop and absorb every fact to remind myself I'm reading a true story.

"I'm not sure either of us is going to get much sleep tonight, but I suppose it's okay."

"I'm so sorry," I say, feeling bad for keeping him up. He needs his rest to do his job.

"I think Charlie was a good guy," he says. "I know he's supposed to be the bad guy, but I really don't think he was. We always think of all the Nazis as evil, but it sounds like there were young, German men who were forced to serve in the war against their desire."

"I guess we'll find out." I don't know why my heart is racing and my hands feel clammy. Maybe it's because of Jackson, or it's because I just finished reading the most terrifying and sad account of something that happened to somebody I love. Either way, I'm too physically and emotionally drained to analyze my feelings any more tonight. "Well, I should let you get some sleep," I tell Jackson.

"I should try to get at least a couple of hours, I guess." I drop the diary back into my bag and open my door. As I step out, Jackson has already made his way from his seat, outside and around to the other side of his car where I am. "Where's your car?" he asks.

I point toward the end of the row. "Just down there."

"I'll walk you there. This parking lot can be a little sketchy at night."

As we walk side by side, my nerves are on high alert. He is almost too perfect. Nights like tonight don't happen in real life. "This is it right here," I tell him.

I unlock my Jeep with the key fob, and the headlights flash twice. "So, I guess I'll see you tomorrow?"

"I'll be here all day," he says. This is so incredibly awkward. I just had a first date with the doctor who is taking care of Grams. It's not like he can easily avoid me right now, even if he's not interested in me. How did I think this was a good idea? I forgot about all the dynamics of dating someone new.

Jackson is scratching at the back of his neck, looking up at the sky, and I wish I could figure out what's going through his head. I reach for my door and open it, taking a step toward my seat so I can toss my bag inside. If anyone was watching this right now, they could grab a bowl of popcorn and have a good laugh at this scene right out of a high school drama movie.

"Okay, I have restraint. Sorry. I just had to refocus my energy for a second. I don't want to do the wrong thing, especially since I know you've had a bad day." Confused by what he's trying to say, I stop trying to figure it out when he steps forward and wraps his arms around my back. "A hug is okay though, right?"

"A hug is more than okay." I've needed a hug all day. It's the

123

only thing I've needed today…well, besides a date with a gorgeous doctor. I press up on my toes to reach my arms around his neck. "Thank you again, for everything," I tell him.

"Emma, you smell so good that if I don't let go right now, I may not be able to stop at just a hug," Jackson whispers into my ear.

I don't want to let go, either. It feels good to be in his arms. I didn't know it could feel like this.

"It's not a rebound if my past never felt right in the first place, don't you agree?" I can't believe I just said that—the words are obviously flowing on their own accord. I'm not typically so forward with men, but Jackson has a charm about him that I can't seem to resist.

"Since this *is* the first date," he says, "I think it's bad luck to break the rules so soon."

"Rules?" I laugh.

"Dating rules—you know, no kissing on the first date, no talking about marriage, kids, or exes, etcetera." He explains his statement as if there's some well-known book on the stages of dating. Maybe there is, and I haven't read it. It would explain a lot in my life.

"I wasn't aware there were dating rules," I tell him, still holding on to his neck. "We've already broken a couple of them." Exes—the bane of our existence, I suppose.

"Oh yeah, there are a lot of them, but only if you're looking for something more than just a date, you know?"

"So, should I be offended or flattered that I'm not the one-night-stand kind of girl?" I'm pretty sure I just made it sound like I'm easy, and that wasn't my intention.

"I'm not a one-night-stand kind of guy either, so—definitely flattered." He pulls away from our hug, just enough to gaze down at me. His hand releases from my back and rests softly on my cheek. "I really had fun tonight. I need to see you again…and not just in the hospital."

"I would like that," I tell him, trying not to sound overly eager since I know men like the thrill of a chase. At least, that's what Grams has told me countless times; I should never make it too easy for a man.

"How about Friday? Dinner and a boring movie, maybe?"

"A boring movie?" I question.

"Yeah, a boring movie," he repeats. He moves away, takes my door, and opens it a little wider. "Drive safe and apologize to your mother for me. I know she didn't want you home too late." A quick wink flutters through his lashes as I slide into my seat.

"My mom's house," I mutter under my breath.

"She loves you. There's nothing wrong with that. I'd be worried about you as well if you belonged to me."

I'm not sure I was able to sneak in unnoticed at three-thirty in the morning, but I'm going to play it casually with hope of avoiding the unwanted "date" interrogation. I tiptoe my sock-covered feet down the carpeted hall and into the kitchen, trying to not wake Mom up if she's still sleeping. Except, she's standing at the stove in her robe cooking something up. "What are you doing?" I chuckle through my morning hoarseness.

"I don't usually have anyone to make breakfast for anymore, so when in Rome—"

"Make pancakes?"

"Oh, be quiet," she shoos me off. "Soooooo? What do you have to tell me?"

"Oh, Mom," I whine. "I really don't want to talk about it. I want to keep it to myself and daydream about it alone."

The spatula drops against the counter, and she spins around to face me while gripping the sink behind her. "It went well, didn't it?" she asks, excitedly.

"Yes, now stop." I can't help thinking that at least this is giving Mom something else to focus on besides Grams's health.

"No, no, no, no, I need more. I need something, please!" she pleads. "Is he looking to settle down and have kids?"

"Come on, Mom. Is this how you snagged Dad?"

"That's a low blow," she snaps back, narrowing an eye at me.

"Seriously, though, you think I'm going to ask him if he's looking to settle down and have kids on a first date that neither of us initiated?"

"At thirty-one? Yes, I do think it's important."

"You're delusional," I tell her.

"And single," she reminds me.

"See? Maybe if you took it down a few notches, you'd find someone too."

"You're annoying," she tells me.

"I'm you," I add in.

"That's for darn sure." She jogs over to me and wraps her arm around my neck, then plants a wet kiss on my forehead. "Go start the coffee. We need that."

"I'm going to head down to the hospital after breakfast to check on Grams before I have to plant my butt at Starbucks and get caught up on all my work. I can meet you back at the hospital after you get out of work if you want, and I can bring us dinner or something," I tell her.

"That would be perfect, sweetie. Thank you."

Mom plates the pancakes and places them down in the middle of the kitchen table. "So, did he kiss you?"

My head falls into my hands. "Mom, stop."

"Come on, I need at least a little tidbit of information."

"No."

"After everything I've done for you in your life, you won't throw me a small, tiny, little bone to get me through the day. I'm so stressed out about Grams. Just give me something to smile about."

"Moms don't usually smile about their daughters kissing men."

"Moms who want their daughters to settle down and give her grandchildren do."

"You sound crazy," I tell her.

"No, I just want the best for my daughter. There's a difference."

"I just broke up with Mike yesterday; did you forget that? I wasn't about to jump into bed with someone six hours later."

"Okay, wait just a minute. I do not expect you to jump into bed with anyone. I just asked if you kissed. Oh goodness, is that why you didn't come home until three-thirty?"

"Really? You were waiting up until then and didn't call me?"

"You're welcome," she says as if she's done me a favor by not stalking her thirty-one-year-old daughter.

"Thanks, Mom. It's nice to know you trust me after all this time." I roll my eyes just so she knows I'm being sarcastic.

"Do me a favor, though, and make sure he gets tested before you—you do any hanky panky stuff." *Hanky panky. We're there now. This is fun.*

"Yes, Mom."

"I can't wait to see him later," she says, jiggling her eyebrows.

"Okay, now that's weird. *You're* not dating him. You shouldn't be excited to see *your* mother's doctor."

"He might be my future son-in-law, Emma. Why wouldn't I be excited to see him?"

I take a bite of my pancakes, letting her words stew for less than a minute before I drop my fork down onto the glass plate. "Mom, I know you're sort of joking right now, but you better not say any of that to him. Seriously, that would scare any guy off."

"I don't know. He seems like the marrying type. A doctor always wants a nice wife to come home to," she continues.

"Yes, in your dreams, or soaps...whatever—same thing."

"It's important for him to know he's welcome, though. Some

men are scared off by families, and I certainly wouldn't want that to be the case. I would never forgive myself if I thought I could have done more to make him feel welcome."

"One date. That's all I've been on. One date, Mom."

"One date that has you smiling even though you're completely annoyed by me right now." I'm not smiling, am I? I feel the need to touch my lips to confirm this, and as it turns out, there isn't a straight line across my face like there normally is at this time of day.

"Did he kiss you or not?" Mom continues with her badgering.

"No!" I shout. "Feel better?" I smile and force an awkward laugh so she knows I'm not upset about it.

"Oh, honey, I'm so sorry."

I close my eyes because this woman knows how to push my buttons more than any other person in the entire universe, and right this second, I might just lose it. My brain is already on over-load, and I can't handle her drama. "It was a first date, Mom." How many times have I said that in the past five minutes?

"Maybe you weren't smiling enough? You sometimes have that—what's it called? A lazy bitch face?"

"God, Mom, what is with you today? First, it's resting bitch face, and second, I don't have that."

"You don't right now," she says.

"It's not resting, it's purposeful."

"Oh, honey, relax."

By the time I'm done being berated by my ticking ovaries—a.k.a Mom, I've finished my pancakes, and I'm ready to get this day started. I'm going to be losing clients soon if I don't get some work done, and I've already heard my phone buzz at least six times in the last ten minutes.

"I'm going to shower and head to the hospital," I tell her. "Thank you for breakfast. It was great, minus the table talk."

I take our dishes, drop them into the dishwasher, then take a mug from the cabinet and fill it up from the fresh pot of coffee. I'll take it black today. It's definitely going to be black coffee kind of day.

A cold shower too. That always helps. I wash my hair and body quickly, shivering against the frosty water. *What is going on?* I wrap a towel around myself and open the door. "Mom, what's wrong with the hot water?"

"Oh, the water heater's not working. I meant to call someone."

"Seriously? How have you been showering?"

"I've actually heard that cold showers are good for your heart. I read that it prevents some kind of cancer too."

I cannot live here. Nope. Can't do it. "Okay, well, I'll call a repairman for you today."

"Thanks, honey, I guess it's time," she says.

It takes me until I'm in my Jeep and halfway to the hospital before I stop shivering. My hair dryer didn't even warm me up. It's bad enough it's already in the forties in the middle of fall. A cold shower on top of that is a great way to start an already stressful day...*or not.*

The parking lot is fairly empty this morning, and I can't stop myself from parking beside the shiny black car that stimulates a rush of heat in my cold veins as I recall moments from my date last night.

I walk through the front doors, quickly concluding that the receptionist is beginning to recognize me as she offers a big smile while I pass her by. "Tell your grammy Paula says hi," she shouts over.

Oh boy. That's a good thing.

I make my way upstairs and hear laughter echoing down the ICU hall. The laughter isn't familiar, but I can only imagine it's coming from Grams's room. It takes me less than a second to confirm my thoughts as I walk into her room, finding half of this floor's nurses laughing at whatever Grams just said. "Oh, and this is my granddaughter, Emma," she says, introducing me as if she were a game show host.

"Hey, Grams." I'm slightly uncomfortable as I walk into a roomful of nurses who are all staring at me with questioning looks. "What's all the ruckus in here?" I place my bag down by the side of Grams's bed and kiss her on the cheek.

"There is no ruckus," Grams says. "These ladies were just keeping me company." It seems to me like she was keeping them company.

"Mm-hmm," one of the nurse's hums. "Definitely."

A second nurse hoots and slaps her hands against her thighs. "Yes. This is perfect."

"So, what am I missing?" I ask, smiling with discomfort.

Without a response to my question, a couple of the nurses leave, giggling like school girls on the way out. "How was your date last night?" Grams asks.

"It was nice," I say, hesitantly, as I glance around at the others still standing here. Is that what this was about?

"Just nice?" Grams asks.

"I guess you're feeling better today, huh?"

"I'm sore, but laughter *is* the best medicine," she says.

"True, so whatcha laughing at, Grams?" I'm giving her a mirroring raised brow to the look she has always given me when I've been up to no good.

"We saw Dr. Beck this morning—Jackson, if you prefer," she says with a relaxed exhale. "What a breath of fresh air that boy is."

"Oh, you did, huh? And what did Dr. Beck have to say for himself?" I am so scared to hear this response. I don't know him well enough to assume what he may or may not have said to Grams.

"Let me see if I can quote him correctly." Grams pushes herself up a bit on her bed and winces at the stiffness before continuing.

"Do you need something?" I ask her, reaching out to help.

"No, no, I'm fine."

I fluff her pillow anyway, doing what I can to make her more comfortable.

"So, he said, 'Your granddaughter is the most beautiful woman I think I've ever laid eyes on, and it's very rare that you come across a person who is as equally beautiful inside as they are outside. You are a very lucky woman to have so much beauty and love in your life, Amelia.'"

"That's exactly what he said," the nurse, who's right behind me, agrees. "It was so, so sweet. He's a winner. Whatever woman ends up with him is going to be one lucky lady." I see exactly what they've been laughing about now—at my expense, of course. I assume Jackson gets a lot of attention from the middle-aged nurses here. "We've been trying to set him up with women for months now, but that boy does not bite the bait. Yet, your grandma comes on in and offers you up, and it's like the clouds have parted their way to heaven's golden gates for Dr. Beck. He was definitely floating on air this morning."

I can try to hide the warm blush I feel creeping from my cheeks to my ears, but I'm afraid my reaction has already been noticed by each woman in this room. "You're welcome," Grams says.

I groan a little and pull a chair up to the side of her bed. "Grams."

"Okay, ladies, I think I need to talk to my granddaughter alone, or I'll never find anything out," she tells the four nurses who are eagerly waiting for more gossip.

"As you wish, Amelia. We'll be back to check on you soon, hun."

"I'm so glad you're here, sweetie," Grams says to me.

"Why are you telling the staff about Jackson and me?"

"Oh please, don't even pretend like you didn't have the best night of your life."

"I'm not saying I didn't have a great time, but don't you think you're jumping the gun a little, and that it's mildly inappropriate to be playing matchmaker with your doctor?"

"It's not *for* me," she says.

131

"Still, his personal life should probably be left out of the ICU."

"Life's too short for that, honey," she argues.

"Speaking of which," I say, entering unchartered territories. "I still have your diary. You remember asking me to bring it to you, right?"

Grams pats my hand that's resting beside her leg. "Yes, Emma, I remember asking you to bring the book. My mind is still intact, despite what you all might think."

"Well, you've had us all a little worried because you keep asking for Charlie," I tell her.

A smile grows across her frail lips. "Oh, Charlie," she says breathlessly—his name sounds like a quiet lullaby humming from the depths of her throat.

"Grams, you've never mentioned his name before."

"Not to you, your mother, or your aunt—you're right." The sternness in her voice defines a reason for hiding her stories, but I'm still not sure what the reason might be.

"I don't understand. Why would you keep your past from us, and who is he?" Not that I don't kind of know who Charlie is, but she doesn't know I've continued reading the diary on my own.

"You have been my granddaughter for thirty one years. I know you've read at least a quarter of my diary by now. Don't play me for a fool, Emma." Geez, I should have known better than to think she doesn't know everything I'm up to. Just like Mom. The two of them are basically the same person.

"Well, why haven't you told us?"

"Honey, I married your grandfather, Max. We were married for sixty one years and raised two girls. There isn't always space for the past when you're busy planning a future."

"Then, why now?"

"My future is in the past now, Emma. My days are coming to an end, and you know what I've been mostly worried about these last few years?"

I take her hand, wondering what she might say. "What's that,

Grams?"

"When I get up there, you know…to heaven, I've been worrying about what would happen if Charlie *and* your grandfather are both at the gates waiting for me. Your grandfather didn't know much about Charlie, and Charlie certainly didn't know about your grandfather. In any case, it was just a silly concern, since I thought I would see at least one of them earlier when I flatlined, but neither of them were there waiting for me." Trying to push away the thought of her dying, It's hard to wrap my head around the rest of her explanation.

"Charlie died?" I ask.

"You'll see when you finish reading my diary," she says as she gently closes her eyes, settling into her pillow with a look of relaxation. "I don't want to spoil it for you."

"He was a soldier, Grams." I'm not sure why I feel the need to point this out to her, but I have to know what she has to say about it.

"Yes…and…?" she replies.

"Well, you're Jewish. You were a prisoner."

"He was also a prisoner, just in a different way."

"I don't understand," I tell her. I read Charlie's explanation on the matter, but it seems like Grams agrees with his declaration now.

"It's because you have never felt the desire to give up your life for someone who would give up theirs for you."

"I just—that's kind of wrong, though, right?"

"Wrong?" she snaps. "Who's making the rules in your life… you, or the world around you?"

"I suppose I understand, then." Or, at least I'm trying to.

"You know, I have spent seventy-four years asking myself the questions that so easily fly off the tip of your tongue, but after a long life, full of experiences both good and bad, I've decided that no one can tell me how to feel. I made a mistake, Emma, one that cost me my great love story. I settled for what fit into my life

133

instead of entering the dangerous, uncharted territory of forbidden love. The difference is larger than anything imaginable —one option is scary, and one is easy. The scary choice isn't for everyone, but I now believe in my heart that if you're daring enough to take the chance, it could be worth every breathless second of making it work."

My mouth opens and closes at least three times as I try to find words to respond with, but I'm come up short. I'm speechless. "Why didn't you—" I wouldn't be here. Mom wouldn't be here.

"There are some things I can't speak about, Emma. The pain of the past is an emotion I've shut off permanently, and the only way to maintain that promise to myself is by keeping my feelings in the diary—where they belong."

"Were you not happy with Grandpa?"

"I was happy with Grandpa," she insists. "He was a good man who worked hard to take care of his family, but Grandpa and I were more like best friends than anything else, and that's why we made it work for all of those years. Marriages are built on friend-ships, trust, and loyalty. We had that." She left out love. "But when you've had more, there's no going back afterwards."

"So, you were in love with Charlie?"

"Those aren't the right words to describe what Charlie and I had."

"Ladies," Jackson's voice booms from the doorway, and I'm sitting here with my mouth agape, my mind trying to absorb what Grams is telling me. "Everything okay?"

"Everything is just fine," Grams responds. "Oh, Jackson, be a dear and get my purse over there. I meant to pay you earlier for what you did last night."

I don't think I've ever stood up so quickly in my life. The chair I was in hit the wall behind me, setting off an alarm which is currently calling for a nurse. "What?" I look between the two of them. "Are you kidding me? This is a joke, right?"

Jackson has his hand splayed on his chest, laughing quietly

with his eyes closed, and Grams is smiling like a troublemaking child. "Gotcha," she says.

Still laughing, Jackson walks up behind me and places his hand on my hip as he reaches behind me to shut the call button off. The touch of his hand feels warm through the thin layer of my yoga pants. That warmth is igniting a fire in my body that I haven't felt before.

"Okay, now that the pranks are out of the way, it's time to check the ticker," Jackson tells Grams. I'm the one clutching my heart now as I put the chair back in its spot. Still embarrassed, I sit down without saying a word and readjust my bag against the bed to busy myself as Jackson checks Grams's vitals. "Everything is looking good. If your numbers continue improving, we may be able to move you out of ICU soon."

"Will you still be my doctor then?" Grams asks.

"Of course," he tells her. "I'm the cardiologist on your case, so you're stuck with me."

"That's what I like to hear." I press my elbows into my thighs and drop my head into my hands. It's abundantly clear that Mom and Grams are both equally determined to arrange a marriage for me. At least they've picked well this time. "All right then, it was nice to see you again. Emma was just about to read to me for a bit, but I look forward to our next check-in."

Jackson laughs at Grams, just like everyone else on this floor seems to be doing. I don't know what she would do if she didn't have an audience and someone to make the center of her jokes all the time. "Emma, can I borrow you for just one quick second? I'll return you to your reading duties after."

I stand up from the chair, still not sure if I should be angry or laughing "Don't worry; I'm not going anywhere," Grams says.

"I wasn't worried," I tell her, sticking my tongue out as I leave the room.

Jackson walks ahead of me, guiding me down to the waiting area, which worries me that he may have bad news about Grams's

135

vitals, though he didn't seem concerned while he was looking at the reports.

No one else is in the waiting room, and he closes the door behind us. "Is everything okay?" I ask, feeling my words catch in my throat.

"Yes, she's doing great considering what she went through yesterday. I honestly think she's going to make a full recovery."

"Oh," I exhale, clutching at the neckline of my shirt. "Thank goodness." I let out a few more heavy breaths before I remember that he said he needed to talk to me. "So, what did you want to talk to me about?" Could it be the fact that his personal life was put on display this morning without my knowing? I hope that's not the case.

"I was stupid last night," he says.

Disappointment fills my chest, and my heart feels as though it is splitting down the middle. Last night was too heavy. "I'm sorry, I shouldn't have involved you in that story or—"

"What?" he asks, appearing confused.

"I'm sorry if I made things uncomfortable for you."

"You made things incredibly uncomfortable for me," he says, placing his hands on his hips.

His words wind me because I was trying to be extra careful last night. I didn't want to seem desperate like Grams probably made me out to be, and I was honest with him about Mike. I don't know what I could have done differently. Dating is obviously not my thing, and I'm starting to see Spinster Cat Lady as my future title.

"I'm sorry, Jackson. I can make myself scarce around here. I never meant to cause any problems...honest."

"You *should* be sorry," he says, matter-of-factly. "I was trying to do the right thing last night, and as a result, I couldn't sleep for those last few hours of the night I had left. It's because of you that I have already had six cups of coffee this morning."

"I'll get going," I tell him. "I just need to read to my grand-mother for a bit, and after that, I'll be out of your hair."

"No," he says.

"What do you mean?"

The glossy look in his eyes has me pinned, and I don't understand the look written across his face. I take a couple of steps back, but he follows in my footsteps, causing my heart to pound. I don't understand where he's going with this conversation. My back hits the door, and yet, he doesn't stop moving toward me.

His hands cup around my cheeks, tilting my face so I'm looking up at him. With his body pressed against mine, Jackson lowers his face slowly, and I think my racing heart has stopped short, or maybe my lungs have stopped working. Either way, I might need resuscitation from the distress he's causing me.

His mouth hovers over mine, and I inhale a slight scent of cologne, as well as the coffee he must have been drinking—I can taste it, but none of my other senses are working. "You have been making my head spin, and I knew if I didn't say goodnight last night—" Without giving me a second to understand what he's saying, his lips connect with mine, his fingers weave through my hair, and I can't feel a thing except for his mouth on mine. *What is happening to me?* I need air, but I don't want him to stop. My knees feel weak, and I let the weight of my body fall into him. His arms loop around my back, keeping me upright as my head falls against the wooden door. I must be experiencing the true definition of a kiss because every other kiss in my life up until this moment has been nothing in comparison. This is so much more. This is two people sharing something beautiful and passionate, an intensity I didn't know existed.

I don't know how many minutes I've gone without breathing, feeling, hearing, or seeing, but when our mouths part, a burning tingle remains on the flesh of my lips. I'm at a loss for words, and I'm not sure if I remember how to talk. "Wow, I feel better now," he says. He takes my hand and pulls me away from the door before placing one last kiss on my cheek. "I might need another cup of coffee now."

"Yeah," I say, sounding a little mindless. "Coffee."

"I'll let you get back to your reading, but I'm going to hang out in here for a few minutes." His statement strikes me as odd, and since I'm trying to figure out what he is talking about, I probably seem a little naïve as he says, "Sorry, scrubs leave little to the imagination, and I can't leave this room without risking my job." I assess him, still not understanding until I see what he's talking about.

"Oh!" I gush as if I just figured out the answer to life. "I'm sorry!" I grab the door knob. "Oh my, um—yeah, I ah feel the same way, it's just not as apparent." Oh my gosh, I can't believe I just said that. My face must be redder than a fire hydrant.

"Lucky you," he says through laughter. His cheeks are also quite red, and it's more adorable than funny, but I can't stop giggling.

"I'll see you a little later. Good luck with—yeah." I let the door close, and pinch my lips together, savoring the effect of the kiss as I mindlessly make my way back to Grams's room. Wow. Wow. I need to pretend like I was just talking to Jackson rather than experiencing the best kiss of my entire thirty one years, but there's no way to wipe this expression off my face.

I reenter the room and Grams is patiently waiting for me with her hands folded on her lap. An all-too-telling smile is impassively lined across her lips, but she doesn't say anything.

I sit down and pull out her diary, also without saying a word. "You can continue wherever you left off. Don't worry," she says.

"You sure?" I ask.

"Yes, oh and sweetie, you have a little smudge of lipstick on your cheek. Here," she says while reaching over with a tissue, then presses it to my face. Her pursed lips and deep dimples tells me she knows exactly what just happened. *Just perfect.*

I take a quick minute to regain my composure before opening the book to the page I left off with last night.

CHAPTER THIRTEEN

AMELIA

DAY 120 - APRIL 1942

*T*he turnover rate in my barrack had been more than fifty percent. Anyone over the age of sixty eventually passed away from starvation or pneumonia, and the others had been transitioned to a new location.

The loneliness had begun to take a toll on my mind as I stopped talking to the other women with whom I shared tight quarters with. Becoming close to someone meant heartache when they would die or be taken away. Therefore, many nights were spent lying awake, staring into the stained ceiling above my head as I pondered if death would be the same, better, or worse than the life I was living. I continued to feel jealousy of those who passed away, leaving me there to continue on with the hard labor my body was enduring on such little sustenance.

With desperation at a high, an idea clouded my head. While it seemed to hit me out of nowhere, I knew the thoughts had been percolating, drip by drip, into the empty cavernous space my mind still had available. Being a puppet for the Nazis freed me of my own thoughts, leaving me capable of conjuring a way to free myself from that life.

April fourteenth would be the day I survived or died, or so I convinced myself. I couldn't go on being a prisoner, living among disease and swill. It was only a matter of time before someone would notice I had not thinned out as the others had. It would be obvious that I was being helped by a person of power.

I set up my papers for the day, leaving the reports on Glauken's desk. She had stopped watching me so closely after some time, evidently convinced I was doing as directed without a fight. I was easy to manage and hoped her trust would work in my favor.

With a line for the sick bay encompassing most of the camp, there was an opportunity for me—one set up by an attempted escapee who did not make his way out. Charlie said he was executed for trying. I told Charlie that execution sounded like the exit door. I was done being someone's puppet. I was going to run.

The sun was rising slowly above the thin layer of clouds, casting a dim shadow over the russet-colored dirt. My eyes felt larger and my pulse faster, possibly because I hadn't considered a plan for what would happen past my attempt of escape. I figured anything would be easy to navigate after surviving hell for six months. My first priority was to regain freedom. I knew my odds of surviving were slim to none, but if I managed to escape, I would figure the rest out later.

As I got closer to the opening on the opposite side of the hospital block, I went over the plan in my head. It was a matter of going inside and climbing out of the second window, then shimmying along a ledge that would lead me to the open field between the prison and freedom. I didn't hesitate when the open door came into view.

I looked around, meticulously inspecting every person in the area, noting there were no guards in sight. I moved with caution, inconspicuously bringing myself within feet of where my journey would begin. The sensation of fear was no longer present, as I had already lived in fear for far too long. In addition, death no longer scared me. Instead, the idea of winning that battle was feeding adrenaline through me like a powerful drug, offering me the strength to continue.

Less than a step away from the entrance, hands clamped around my shoulders. I was pulled away from my plan and dragged across the dead grass to the shower room where I was faced with another goodbye.

I learned not to fight when being pulled against my will because it would only cause more pain. Therefore, I waited for the hands to release me before I turned to find Charlie at the other end of what I thought to be threatening hands. My heart thudded against my fragile ribs, slowly, but hard enough to cause a ripple within my breaths.

"What is this?" Charlie shouted. I didn't know if he was shouting at me or my friend, Leah, who stood before us naked, with a distended belly. She was clutching her stomach, and there were red marks from the pressure of her fingernails across her thin skin. Blood pooled at her feet as she began to hyperventilate.

"Amelia, you must help me," she cried out. I turned back to Charlie, wondering what was going through his mind. He had to keep up the charade in front of Leah and everyone else in the vicinity, so understanding what he expected me to do, left me at a loss. "He's going to kill my baby and me."

I knew Charlie would do no such thing, but I couldn't explain that to Leah. Charlie needed to put on a show of hatred for my people, or he would be noticed, expelled from his position, and likely murdered for not following regulations. Charlie hadn't told me that, but I had no doubt it would be the outcome if either of us had let our guard down. He was my friend—my best friend, a comrade with a different view, a human who didn't hate humankind, a son, a brother, and a man who wanted a future in finance, not murder.

"You take care of this situation and tell me when you are

through. You are aware of protocol, yes?" Charlie gritted through his clenched jaw.

"Yes, sir," I replied.

"What's happening?" Leah whimpered.

Charlie turned on his heels, leaving the shower room as he closed us in by the metal door. "The shower has been locked for maintenance," I heard him shouting. "Go elsewhere."

I took Leah's hand, offering her all the compassion I could, knowing she was the only person who was there for me when Mama was murdered. "Everything is going to be okay," I told her, hoping my words weren't a lie.

"I'm so scared," she said, shaking beneath the cold drizzling water drops. We weren't given the luxury of towels, but there was a dress left behind by another prisoner who likely died somewhere in that space. I took it from the wet floor and placed it down on the ground. "Come here and lie down," I said. I helped Leah onto the ground, wondering how I would assist her further without any knowledge of delivering a baby. "Do you know how far along you are?"

"It has been more than nine months," she said. "I'm overdue by a week."

I carefully separated her legs, staring down into the bloody mess. "I'm not sure if you're ready to push," I told her honestly.

"I can't stop myself," she cried out in pain.

"How long have you been in pain?" I asked.

"More than a day," she groaned.

Leah didn't look the same as she did the last few times we had run into each other. Her face was almost skeletal, as were her legs and arms, but her belly was swollen, just not as large as I thought it should be at the end of a pregnancy. The poor girl needed food to nourish her unborn baby, but instead, she was being systematically starved to death. A scream escaped Leah's throat as her pale face turned red. She clenched every muscle in her body, followed by a wave of exhales as the contraction subsided. I peered down between her legs again, that time seeing a fleshy-colored dome moving in and out along with her uneven breaths. "I think if you push once more the baby will come out," I told her, unsure if what I was saying held any truth. I feared hurting her or the baby, but if I called for help, I knew what would happen to them.

Leah held on tightly to everything within her reach. Her toes curled with each contraction, and sweat dripped down her face even though there was a chill around us.

The baby's head was nearly halfway out, giving me an opportunity to assist her. "Push a little harder, Leah," I said, trying to keep her calm.

She pushed again through a silent groan, and I guided the baby's head out. My hands were covered in blood, but my only focus was on that innocent baby being born into the hellhole we were in. I didn't need to tell Leah to push again because she did it on her own, delivering a tiny little girl that fit snugly between my two hands.

I wrapped the baby in a kerchief I found in the corner of the room. It was dirty and torn but better than nothing, and I handed Leah her baby, watching the immediate bond between them. The outside world temporarily disappeared as she took in a moment that no one could steal from her. My only hope at that moment was that she would have a lifetime to share with her child.

As I watched Leah and her baby, I realized I would probably never experience another moment like that. It was as close as I would ever come to experiencing the miracle of birth. However, the only miracle needed then was a way to help Leah and the baby. I had no medical supplies on me, no blankets to keep the baby warm, and no tools to cut the umbilical cord from the placenta. On top of it all, blood was still pooling from Leah, and I didn't know if that was normal. All I did know, was she needed more time in that current moment—anything life could grant her. However, without air, the baby would die, and until I cut the cord, she would have no air.

I pressed against my knees, bringing myself to my feet as I walked to the metal door, knowing I was about to reveal the crime of a hidden pregnancy. The door opened, and Charlie was waiting on the other side with a blanket and a small medical bag. "You must go quickly."

I couldn't help the look I gave Charlie at that moment. Something within me was so moved by his compassion that it filled me with a type of emotion I had long forgotten. Seeing people wanting to help others was a dying trait among the survivors of the war. Each person was out for themselves, and all of us were pitted against each other like dogs fighting over a steak bone.

The door shut quietly behind me as I handed Leah the blanket. I rummaged through the medical bag, finding scissors to cut the cord. I cleaned Leah up with the excess material of the dress hanging below her and found her clothes across the room.

"Let's get you dressed," I told her.

I helped with the her clothes, then held her baby girl while she secured her buttons, listening to her soft moans with each movement. The baby was unscathed, unaware of what she had been born into, and I prayed for her to find peace.

It was a struggle to help Leah up to her feet, but as I did, we bundled the baby up inside the smocked dress, and I carefully led her through the back exit. "You must go to your block, hide there, feed your baby, and do whatever you can to keep her safe and quiet."

Tears ran down Leah's pale skin as she leaned forward and kissed me on the cheek. "I will never forget you," she said. "You are a gift."

"No more tears," I reminded her. "We can't show our weakness, remember?"

She sniffled and offered a faint smile before shuffling off behind the barracks.

I reopened the metal door, finding Charlie still standing guard.

"She and the baby are okay," I whispered. "I sent her to her block."

Charlie looked at me with a dark stare. "They're going to kill them when they find her," he said.

Without replying to his statement, I swallowed hard, pushing away the thought—the truth. "I'm leaving," I told him.

"Amelia, you can't."

"I'm making a run for it," I told him again.

"How many times have we talked about this?"

"I think I can do it," I argued.

"No, Amelia. No."

I stared at him so hard I thought maybe I'd be able to see a hidden motive within his eyes, but instead, all I saw was the unmistakable worry in the creases of his forehead.

Charlie closed us back inside the shower room and placed his hands on my shoulders. "Amelia, no one has managed to escape. Not one person in over a year."

"Why can't I be the first?"

"Because if you're not successful, you'll be executed like the others."

I shrugged since I didn't care much anymore. The difference between death and the state I was living in couldn't have been too different. In fact, I imagined heaven to be a very peaceful place in comparison. "Charlie, I don't care if I die trying."

"I do," he said, sternly, through his clenched jaw.

"We're friends," I told him. "You have fed me as I've needed food, you've made me smile when I shouldn't be capable of such an expression, and you have made me feel less alone, but you're going to walk away, and I'm not."

"You don't know that," he argued.

A gentle smile pressed against my lips. "In my heart, I know I'm the only person who can save myself."

"They won't get away with this forever," he said. The look in his eyes pleaded with me to change my mind, but I had to try.

"They have already done too much damage. Look around at how many forevers are over now."

"Don't leave me, Amelia," he blurted out.

At first, I wanted to tell him he was selfish, and I almost did, but I calmed myself first while trying to understand why he cared so much. "What about me?" I asked.

"I'll never leave you," he muttered through a sudden hoarseness in his throat.

"We're only friends, Charlie. Sometimes friends must leave each other, especially friends who should never have been friends in the first place."

"You're not my friend, Amelia." The broken sound in his voice was gone, and replaced by a firm tone of determination.

My breath felt sticky in my lungs as I was struck with the shocking truth his statement revealed. I had wrongly assumed that the time we had spent together and the help he given me defined a friendship. Maybe he was just going for sainthood while the rest of his kind were running toward the gates of hell. In any case, no matter what his reasons, he would always have a place in my heart for what he had done for me—giving me hope that there was still kindness peppered into a world full of hate. "I understand," I told him.

"No, you don't." His hands squeezed tightly around my shoulders as his eyes blazed with darkness.

"Charlie," I whispered as I tried to tug myself free of his grip. I should have been scared by the unfamiliar look in his lake-blue eyes, but I had never feared Charlie before. I believed his acts of aggression weren't a portrayal of who he was inside.

My world stopped spinning when his unequivocal gaze ravaged my breath. I couldn't read him or understand why his chest was rising and falling so fiercely. "Are you okay?" I asked.

He nodded his head with little movement, then inhaled sharply as he crashed his lips into mine. My heart thawed, creating a thick fog in my chest. His lips were warm, soft, and just large enough to engulf mine. Within the bliss of kissing him, I was acutely aware of how awful I smelled and how bad my breath must have been, but I tried to put the thought into the back of my mind as his arms slid around my back to hold me a little closer. He didn't seem to care about the things I was worried about, and it meant everything to me at that moment. I needed air, but if I could, I would have gladly suffocated against his lips and endured that way of dying over anything else. I would have willingly given up my last second of life for that moment—one, I was sure I'd never experience. Charlie's kiss took me by surprise, but I didn't want it to stop. For the first time in so long, I felt alive again. I didn't want Charlie to know, but that was my first kiss, and I wasn't sure how to kiss him in return. I had hoped he didn't notice my inexperience, but maybe that's what intrigued him about me.

Time felt as though it was running away as my thoughts continued to race. How was I blind to the fact that Charlie had those feelings for me?

Tingles ran up and down the length of my body, and I was sure my feet were no longer touching the ground as Charlie's hands slid up to my cheeks. The pressure from his lips softened, and he pulled away with more trepidation in his eyes than he had just a few minutes prior.

Not knowing how to respond, I said, "I'm sorry. I must smell so terrible. How could you want to kiss me?"

"Amelia, don't be ridiculous. None of that matters to me. Besides, your circumstance here is beyond your control. How could that possible influence how I feel about you?" he asked. "To everyone else, we're so wrong, but what does that matter when nothing else in this world is right? Amelia, I—I'm in love you. I love you."

I couldn't speak. I was too surprised by Charlie's confession, and I was trying to process whether the feelings I had for him were just friendship or something more. Maybe I was in denial to protect my emotions because I knew I couldn't handle someone else being taken away from me.

In that instant, though, my thoughts changed as if they were on a switch. I questioned whether it was reality or a dream, but as the cold air touched my lips, I knew it wasn't a dream. "I won't leave you," I told him without hesitating—or thinking—for that matter. He loved me. I was not alone anymore. Somebody loved me.

His lips curled into a smile and his eyes squinted against the rise of his cheeks. "Charlie, if I tell you I love you, you'll leave me just like everyone else I have ever loved, so I'm sorry I can't offer you the same affirmation in return," I told him, fearful of speaking the truth of how I felt about him. It was love, which was why I couldn't repeat his words.

He didn't argue. "I don't care if you love me. I don't care if you do and never tell me, but I needed you to know that I love you, and I will do whatever I can to protect you."

CHAPTER FOURTEEN

EMMA

I can't help pressing my hand against my chest, feeling guilty for peeking in on a kiss that should have remained private. "Grams," I say through a breathless whisper.

"Now, mind you," she says without missing a beat, "I had nothing to compare that kiss to but what I can tell you is this. Nothing has ever come close in comparison."

Grams stares through me, appearing lost in her memories. Her bottom lip quivers briefly before she pulls in a sharp inhale and shakes her head around. "Are you okay?" I ask her.

"Don't be silly," she waves me off with her hand. "Of course, I'm okay."

"You know, it's all right if you're not. You can tell me anything."

"Emma Hill, don't you talk like that," she scolds me.

A nurse meanders into the room and lifts the printed reports of Grams's heart monitor. "What is going on in here, Ms. Amelia?"

Grams doesn't answer her, causing me to glance back at her frozen stare. "Grams, what's going on?" I ask, standing up from the chair and placing her diary down in my place.

"Amelia," the nurse says, more sternly this time. "I'm going to need you to focus for a minute."

A variety of odd beeps on Grams's heart monitor suggests that her heart rate is erratic but slowly regulating to a normal rhythm. Immediately, Jackson reappears, and the nurse greets him with a slightly panic-stricken glance as Grams smiles gently and murmurs, "Charlie, where are you?"

"Grams, Charlie isn't here," I tell her, but Jackson's hand falls softly on my shoulder, stopping me from saying any more.

"Emma, let her be until she can calm down, okay?" Jackson tells me.

I can't just sit here and let her suffer, if that what's happening. Is she suffering as she smiles and asks for Charlie? None of this makes any sense to me.

"Charlie, why didn't you find me? It was our plan." A lump forms in my throat, and I'm not sure I'm strong enough to sit here and listen to her delusions and maintain my composure. I don't know what else to do, so I take Grams's hand and hold it against my cheek, hoping she feels the connection, so it draws her back from wherever her mind has taken her. "Charlie!" Her voice is stern and demanding, as if he were standing here, ignoring her plea.

"Grams," I call to her softly.

"Emma," she replies in a mirroring tone, as if she's trying to find me. "He's not here. Why isn't he here?" A tear falls from her left eye.

I stroke my hand across her cheek, trying to calm her nerves. "I'm not sure, Grams."

"You have to find him, Emma. You have to!"

I don't even know if this man is dead or alive. If he's alive, I have no idea where he lives or how to find him. He could be in Germany or the United States. He could be anywhere, for that matter. She's never once mentioned his name to me before this week.

"Amelia, Emma will see what she can do," Jackson says from behind me. I whip my head around and give Jackson a questioning look. *What is he telling her?* I can't agree to this. I don't know anything about this man other than they were friends and shared a kiss decades ago. I can't just hunt him down. If he is alive, he is an old man and probably has a wife and a family somewhere. I can't do what Jackson is saying, just to appease Grams's confused thoughts.

Jackson nods his head toward the door, and I follow him. "I don't think I can read to her anymore," I tell him as soon as we're out in the hall. "It's obviously causing her serious distress, and I don't want to be the cause of that, especially after the trauma she has been through this week."

"I agree with you one-hundred percent," he says, looking down at me with sincerity. "But, as I've been saying, we have to try our best not to upset her. She needs to heal and get well, and agitation is going to make that more difficult for her."

"Don't you think this stress is going to hurt her even more?" I argue.

"Maybe you should consider trying to find this man," he says again. Is he serious? When he first mentioned it, my immediate reaction was a firm, "No." Even though I'm slowly uncovering the fact that Grams has been hiding something from me her entire life, I feel like I need to know what the outcome of their relationship was. I don't know if I fully understand how someone can be married to one person for more than sixty years while longing for someone else at the same time. That would make me miserable, but Grams has always seemed so happy. If she was so in love with this Charlie, why didn't she try to find him and undo whatever decision she had made? Unless the part of the story that she doesn't remember yet, is that he's dead...

"I can't," I tell Jackson. "My grandfather was a wonderful man, and he would be absolutely crushed. None of this feels right to me."

"This isn't about you, Emma," he says.

I'm not sure why Jackson feels so passionate about this situation. We only met a couple of days ago, and he isn't part of our family. While I understand that Grams is his patient, this is going a little above and beyond his responsibility with her care.

"I can't even make my own decisions, so how can I make them for her? Clearly, I'm not the best person to decide someone's fate."

Jackson presses his hand into the wall beside me. "You're being a little hard on yourself, aren't you?"

"I'm thirty-one years old and I just found the courage to end a six-year relationship that was bad right from the beginning. Then, on a bribe from my grandmother, I accept a date with a charming, eye-catching doctor who just kissed me like I've never been kissed in my entire life, so obviously, I'm a bit challenged when it comes to making rational decisions."

Jackson's infectious smile reappears, illuminating his eyes under the fluorescent lights. "Better late than never."

Better late than never. Is that what's going through Grams's head right now, too?

"If you want my advice, which I know you don't," Jackson begins. "Finish reading the diary. Find out how the story ends, then make your decision based on what would be best for her... and you. The reality is, Charlie has got to be in his nineties and may not be capable of doing much of anything at all, let alone coming here to see your grandmother. Then again, he might be—"

"I know."

"You know you're going to keep reading it anyway, so figure it out afterward. In the meantime, we'll pacify your grandmother and keep her calm, okay?"

I look up into Jackson's piercing eyes and the reflection of the light highlighting his gaze. He has more common sense in his pinky finger than I have in my whole body. "Okay," I agree with a slight nod.

"On another note," he says, looking around briefly. "Are you having any ex-boyfriend troubles before I ask you to have drinks with me tonight?"

"I thought we had a date set for Friday?" I ask, keeping a coy sense of control over this situation.

"We do, but what if I were to get hit by a bus tomorrow?"

"I probably wouldn't know about it because I don't even have your phone number yet," I play along.

"We'll have to fix that problem, and I'll make sure to label your number in my phone as 'Contact If Hit By A Bus.' Now, you don't want to pass up a chance to hang out with the guy who just kissed you like you've never been kissed, do you?" he asks with a smug grin, seeming quite amused with himself.

I can't stop the laughter from pouring out of me. "A funny doctor. I didn't believe you at first, but you really are multi-talented."

"I'm the whole package, you know? I come around once in a lifetime." His words sway along with an exaggerated fake yawn as he groans and stretches his arms above his head. I slap him in the gut with the back of my hand, and he buckles forward with a chuckle.

"I need to go get some work done after I make sure Grams is okay, but where should we meet for drinks?" I just keep falling for his ploys—such a charmer.

"Landsdown at eight?" he offers.

"Sounds good to me."

"Meet me outside of Landsdown, though," he says.

"Why?"

"Just because."

I playfully roll my eyes and brush past him, rejoining Grams, who has fallen asleep in the time I've been gone. Hopefully, she'll be more relaxed when she wakes up. At least I know she's in good hands here.

I take the diary from the seat and slide it into my bag before tiptoeing out of the room. In the large elevator, I fall heavily against the wall and close my eyes for a moment, overwhelmed by everything in my life. I concentrate on taking in a full, deep breath, feeling as though I have forgotten to do so in more than a few days. I feel like my life is spinning out of control, and I'm having a hard time finding something to hold on to. It's a bit like Alice in Wonderland, falling down a hole into uncharted territory, with no way of knowing exactly what happened or where I'll end up.

The words sinking into my mind aren't easily digestible because I can't relate to the circumstances and sensations she experienced. It's hard coming to terms with the fact that I may not ever truly comprehend what she has been through, and now it's causing this invisible gap between us that has never been present before. Grams has been living with this all these years, knowing she'll never have the chance to experience what she should have during those impressionable years, and worse, her young love was filled with torture and torment. I thought for sure that we were similar, but I know now I'll never be able to be half the person she is. I could never be as strong as she was. She is a survivor in the truest sense of the word.

My thoughts carry me out to my Jeep and I toss my bag inside before sliding into the seat. As I go to close my door, I see a note pinned between my wiper blade and windshield. I stare at it for a second, realizing it's an envelope. *That's weird.* I lean back out, pull it free, and bring it back inside.

The envelope isn't sealed, making it easy to retrieve the note. Unfolding the unevenly folded paper, I find Mike's messy handwriting.

Please, no more apologies.

Emma,

    Please don't throw this note away without reading it first.

I have messed up more times than I can count. After having some time to think, I can honestly say that I was a lousy boyfriend. I don't know how to be a good one, and I guess that doesn't say much for me. I realize it shows immaturity on my part, but in my defense, I've never had a role model to follow when it comes to treating another person the way they deserve to be treated.

I'm aware of how much I have hurt you and cheating is inexcusable. I don't expect you to forgive me for what I've done, especially after how well you treated me throughout the last six years. I gave you nothing in return, and I know this note might be tossed out your window in a matter of minutes, but I couldn't walk away without at least trying to do the right thing by you.

No more promises from me. I know I can't keep them. I can't tell you I'll stop drinking because I'm pretty sure I have a problem, just like my stellar father. I treated you like shit because there was never a woman around in my life to show me how one should be treated. I've been blind to it. I know I don't deserve you, and I didn't deserve the last six years of your time, but I hope you'll forgive me someday, even if it's just for wasting your time.

You may never believe me, but I do love you, and it hurts as I slowly come to the realization that we are really over this time. I have boxed up your things and dropped them on the back patio of your mom's house. If you need anything, you know how to find me. Thank you for trying to fix me. I guess some things are just too broken to repair.

Love you always,
Mike

Wow. I didn't see that coming. Maybe it's a little sad that my first thought is that someone wrote this for him, but on second thought, this must be his final attempt to gain my forgiveness.

I lower my head down to the steering wheel, as tears form in the corners of my eyes. I was never trying to change him, but I did hope he would see how much I cared about him and wanted us to work out. Investing so much time into something and then closing the door to walk away is difficult—nearly impossible—for me, but at this point, I don't know what it means to be happy in a relationship. I used to feel it when I made him smile, but that's just it. It was always me making him smile. He was never willing to put any effort into making me happy. The note falls from my hand, landing on my lap as it leaves me with nothing but an emptiness that fills my chest. I won't miss him because there is nothing to miss. He gave nothing, and that's why it's finally over. Six years was a long time to waste, but it's better than a whole lifetime.

I drive toward Mom's but turn off the road when I spot the Starbucks I frequent the most. I sweep Mike's note off my lap and take my bag with me. My focus is set on my usual table in the corner, but Chelsea stops me before I'm all the way through the door.

"Hey, girl," she says from behind the counter. I've been coming here for so long, I've become friends with the staff. Since I don't have a normal office, these people are the closest I have to coworkers, so I like to come here when I need social interaction. They're easy to get along with, they make me coffee, and they don't hover.

"Hey." I wave and pull my bag off my shoulder, letting it drop to the chair I had my sights on. By the time I reach the counter, Chelsea has my grande coffee waiting for me.

"You look like you've been hit by a bus today," she says, handing me the cup. I laugh at the irony, remembering Jackson's threat of being hit by a bus tomorrow.

"It has been a seriously rough week," I tell her.

"I was wondering why I hadn't seen you here."

"Honestly, I may need a shot of whiskey in this coffee before I fill you in on the story," I joke with her.

She glances over her shoulder and pulls her apron off. "John, can you cover for me? I'm taking my fifteen."

I drop five dollars down on the counter for my coffee and tip, then head over to my table where I'm supposed to be working.

Chelsea plops down in front of me. "You know I don't like to be nosy, but Mike was in here earlier," she blurts out with an apprehensive squint to her eye.

I press my hand against the side of my face. "That is not what I wanted to hear," I tell her.

"He was looking for you."

"I guess he's smart enough to know I won't answer his calls if he were to try," I tell her. Chelsea is well versed in all things Mike, and as I think back, I realize it's been years since I had something positive to say about him.

"What happened?" She twists off the cap of her water bottle and takes a quick swig.

"I broke up with him. Again."

"For good this time?" She sounds as skeptical as Mike did, but laughs a little because it's been an ongoing joke in my life. Evidently, everyone is aware of how weak I am. How can I be the descendant of someone so strong willed, yet, I have such a difficult time figuring out how to make a change in my life?

"I had a date last night," I tell her, chewing on my bottom lip, waiting for the excitement that will likely follow her gasp.

"Wait, wait...when did you break up with Mike?" She's leaning forward on the table as if this is the most exciting news she's heard all week.

"Yesterday," I utter, and wince.

"Dude," she laughs.

"It's been over for so long that I felt like it was just a matter of me making it official. I don't think he ever would have broken up with me, even though he was cheating. He had the perfect set-up; a girlfriend for when it was convenient, and the freedom to sleep around whenever he wanted to."

"I totally get what you're saying. It's just that you've broken up with him so many times before. Are you sure you want to bring someone else into this so quickly and possibly hurt him? I mean, are you sure you're not on the rebound?"

"If whatever that one date was last night doesn't work out, it won't be because of Mike."

"One date, and your eyes are suddenly sparkling at the mention of it," she says with an arched brow. "What's his name?"

"Jackson," I tell her.

"See, there it is again, another sparkle."

"Stop it," I laugh.

"What does *Jackson* do for a living?" She scoots forward and brings her leg up underneath her on the chair, elevating her height a few inches.

"He's a doctor at Mass General—a cardiologist."

Chelsea places her hand on her chest and jerks her head back. "Well, excuse me. Yeah, I guess it would be safe to say buh-bye to Mike now."

"I'm sort of going out with him again tonight," I tell her.

"And you're getting married tomorrow?" she continues, a grin now plastered across her face.

"Possibly, and maybe I'll have his baby on Friday."

"Be careful, okay, Emma? You're so used to feeling hurt that I don't want you to fall into another mistake. You deserve more than what you've had." She places her hand on top of mine. "Take your time."

"I appreciate your concern, but I promise you, this time, it's about me. I'm suddenly hyperaware of how fast life goes by, and I've been so busy watching it pass me by that I'm ready to go all in and experience what I've been missing."

"Ah, you want good lovin'. Now you're speaking my language," she says, poking my nose with her finger. "You go get your happy on, girl. You deserve it."

My cheeks burn at the thought. I've been trying to calm my

pulse from our kiss, never mind what comes after that. "You're so sweet...and romantic," I jest.

"You know, I've heard that sex releases a chemical that makes you more creative. Maybe it can even help you with your work stuff."

I lift my cup to my lips, hoping it's cooled down enough as I take the first sip. With a mouthful of the steamy brew, I narrow my eyes at Chelsea. "You know, you should be a therapist. I don't know what you're doing pouring coffee all day. You just—you give the best advice anyone has ever given me."

"It's funny you say that. Three other people said the same thing to me this week." *That's Chelsea.* I love this girl. Everyone needs someone like Chelsea in their life. She looks over at a line growing in front of the counter and purses her lips. "I think my break is over."

"I have to get my work done anyway. Thanks for listening to me," I offer.

"Anytime, but next time, don't forget your co-pay," she says, leaving me with a wink and an air kiss.

"You got it, Dr. Chelsea."

Am I rushing things, or am I just living for once? Is there a difference? If so, why don't I know what it is at thirty-one? I don't know who made these stupid rules that people live by, but everything inside of me wants to see Jackson tonight, and I'm not going to sit around and grieve my six-year relationship for a month just so I can say I'm officially over him. It's not just Mike I need to be over. I'm over living solely for someone else's wants and needs. This time, it's for me.

For the first time all week, I get through several projects over the course of three hours, and my phone doesn't ring once. It's like a small miracle. I respond to the six emails waiting for me with questions about upcoming projects and look down at my phone to see I still have a couple of hours before I need to get to Mom's, shower, and ready for tonight.

My bag stares at me from across the table, and the addiction I'm feeling to Grams's story is like a good book I can't put down, except this is real. It pulls at my heartstrings, and though I feel like I owe my heart a rest, there's no way I can stop now.

CHAPTER FIFTEEN

AMELIA

MAY 1942 - DAY 150

I had been able to block out the stench in my block since the beginning, but one particular night in May, it was more potent than normal, making it difficult to sleep. Still, I knew how hard it would be to function the next day if I didn't get a bit of rest before the whistles blew and the shouting began.

I folded my hands over my head and turned toward the wall, trying to visualize the mustard fields of golden hues, remembering the scent of flowers that intermingled with the breeze. I would have done just about anything to smell that field once more, to feel the tall grass tickle the back of my knees, and enjoy the sun's heat, rather than feeling it scorch my skin.

The door to our block opened and then closed immediately. I avoided looking out of fear for what I might see. Some nights the late-hour entrants were just prisoners who were forced to work extra hours. Other nights, it was a Nazi coming to claim what wasn't his. It's why I chose to lay so close to the wall, wishfully thinking if I remained in the darkest shadow, I wouldn't be a target.

However, it appeared luck wasn't on my side that night. Hands found my bare shoulders, but they didn't hurt me as I would have expected them to. They grazed soothingly up and down my arms, and I wondered if I might be hallucinating—only imagining a gentle touch rather than the roughness we're all treated with.

I was pulled from my side onto my back as a whisper tickled my ear. "It's me, Charlie. Don't speak."

If I had spoken, someone would have heard our conversation—someone may have realized I was okay with a soldier being inside our barrack. At the same moment, though, I wasn't sure what he was doing there. He had never come to visit in the middle of the night before.

"We need to talk," he said. His fingertips stroked the side of my face, almost guiding me into the sleep I desperately needed, but there was no way I could sleep while Charlie was beside me. "I'm going to drag you from the room, okay?"

I offered a slight nod, unsure whether he could see my gesture in the obscurity. Charlie helped me with my dress that I began wearing down by my waist in order to comply with the unexpected demands faster. He pulled me from the bed, and I allowed him to drag me, stumbling as we departed from the block. He jerked me along until we were outside and behind the barracks. We continued until we came upon a secluded area behind the building that held the prison cells for attempted escapees, or those who failed to abide by rules and regulations.

"What's the matter?" I asked him in a whisper.

Before answering me, he handed over a piece of sweet bread. I devoured it, trying my hardest not to lose any of the crumbs, but before I could finish swallowing the delicious food, he placed an ear of corn in my hand too. I tried to nibble on it, but my teeth ached from eating mostly soft foods for so long. I was always conscious of my hygiene, wanting to keep clean and prevent pains in my mouth from decaying teeth, but it wasn't an option there.

Charlie noticed my struggle, and he wove his fingers through the loose strands of my hair that had fallen free from my knotted braid. "We didn't get much tonight," he explained.

"You don't need to justify it," I said. "You've given me more than I ever could have asked for."

"Amelia, I'm being deployed," he blurted out.

"What? What do you mean? Aren't you already deployed?"

"The war is getting bad, and they told me I was being sent to Prague to help on the front lines."

"No!" I shouted, louder than I should have. His hand cupped over my mouth as he hushed me.

"I don't have a choice," he said. I knew he had a little more say over things than I had, but it didn't mean I had to agree with it. "How long will you be gone?"

He shakes his head and peers down to the dirt below us. "I don't know."

"I don't want you to go." It went without saying. Throughout the previous month, our relationship had continued to blossom even within the walls of hell. We were each other's hopes and dreams amidst the horror and destruction around us, but our young feelings hardly had a chance to develop into what they could have been because we had to hide our relationship. We were supposed to have hatred for each other, and I wondered if his deployment was a punishment for abandoning his dictated beliefs —maybe someone found out about us. If someone knew, I considered that I may be punished too—even if it were just for the simple fact that a Jew was smiling under those circumstances. It was not acceptable.

Our wordless conversations between our lips—exploring the inner workings of each other's minds in silence was what we'd grown accustomed to, but I was about to lose my savior, and he was being sent to a place where he would be the one who needed to be saved.

Charlie's arms wrapped around me, and he held on tightly. His hand gently pressed against the back of my head until my cheek rested on his chest, allowing me to listen to the fast rhythm of his beating heart.

Fear was prominent. His heartache was apparent. Loss was in our future, and there was nothing we could do about it. When he deployed, I knew we may never see each other again.

"I love you so much, Amelia, and I'm terrified you won't be here when I get back."

"I'm terrified you won't come back," I told him.

Neither of us could promise each other a different outcome because neither of us knew what our futures held. Waking up each day was a miracle as it was.

"When do you leave?" I asked.

"In the morning."

"So soon?" I whispered, feeling my heart fill with despair.

"Yes," Charlie replied, sounding as heartbroken as I felt. "They just told me before I came to you."

There would be no time to spend together before he left. There would be no time to make memories that I could carry with me for the rest of my life—however long that could be. My heart hurt for the first time since I rested next to Papa. I touched Charlie's face as I had done so many times before, but that time I was trying to memorize every detail—the feeling of his cheekbones, the shape of his eyes, the small cleft in his chin that I had teased him about, and most of all, the warmth of his lips. I needed to make sure I remembered everything before I said goodbye—possibly forever.

The pain was unbearable. I had learned to feel love for that man, and once again, I would have to endure the good in my life being torn away from me. I wanted my heart to stop hurting. I wanted to pull it out of my chest and throw it away so I could stop feeling, and be at peace like Mama and Papa.

I wanted to die.

"Amelia," Charlie said, placing his fingertips under my chin. I submitted and glanced up into his worry-filled eyes. "Will you promise me something?"

I knew what he was going to ask me to promise, and we wouldn't be able to see eye-to-eye. I wanted to run, and he wanted to follow the rules. I shook my head with a silent disagreement, but his hands held my face tightly, stopping me from saying *"no"* without words. "I know you won't tell me you love me, but you show me every day, and if you do, in fact, feel that way about me, you'll stay—you'll keep yourself out of that prison, or worse."

"What if you never come back?" I asked.

"I will find you, Amelia. I promise I will find you."

"What if you die trying?" My words sounded empty...without sentiment. Speaking of expiring was common for us. Death was not something we feared anymore; we merely avoided it.

"What if *you* die trying?" he snapped back at me. "Please, let's try and stay alive for each other."

It hurt my heart to disagree with him because we had so little time left, but at the same time, waiting for him felt like it would be harder than accepting death as the final page of our love story.

Our senseless bickering went silent as his lips met mine in the darkness of the night. Melting into his arms, I instantly complied with his touch as I had each time he enveloped me in that way. We would kiss until our lips became numb or until one of us desperately needed more air. Our minutes together came in short increments, leaving us with brief chapters and cliffhangers—ones that left me yearning for more.

We moved back into the enclosed darkness provided by a tree that hung over the side of the barbed wire fence, and my heel caught on a loose rock, causing me to fall. Charlie's arms caught me in time to soften the landing, and he followed me down, planting his knees into the dirt. His hands slid up to the back of my head, offering me a place to rest as I stared up into his beautiful eyes.

He relaxed beside me and draped his arm around my stomach. "Do you think there are people outside of these gates looking at the same stars, wishing to escape from their lives too?" I asked him.

"Not everyone knows how bad it can be," he answered.

"We do," I tell him.

"How do you say 'we,' Amelia?" Charlie asked. "You're supposed to be at a university right now. You should be enjoying your life. Instead, you're watching your people suffer and die. On top of that, you're suffering too."

"Charlie, neither of us wants to be here. That's all that matters." However, I wasn't sure if what I was saying was true. I had lost Mama, Papa, and most likely, Jakob. Beyond the suffering, though, I was busy working fifteen hours a day, which didn't leave me much time to think. That was a blessing to me. However, at that moment, I felt everything crash down. Once Charlie was gone, I would have nothing...and no one...left.

"Are you okay?" he asked, catching me staring past him into the night.

"No, I'm not," I said.

Charlie leaned in closer, stroking his finger in circles on my cheek. "You're beautiful."

"I'm scared to know what I look like," I rebutted.

He chuckled softly as if my concern about my appearance was ridiculous. "I see two eyes that gaze intently at life, perfect lips that have had my attention since the day I saw you the first time, and a woman with determination in her every step. Your beauty is natural, and it matches everything inside of you. You've lost your family, yet your strength is unimaginable. Every part of you captivates me. You are everything that is perfect and beautiful in this world."

The soft crunch of dirt beneath us tickled the insides of my ears as he leaned over to kiss my neck, sending shivers down the length of my spine. He paused briefly to look up at me with a question lingering in his eyes, and I answered by tying my arms around his neck, then pulled him toward me.

His hands roamed unreservedly, leaving his warmth behind on every inch of my skin. His touch was gentle and cautious, unlike the scenes that repeatedly played out within my barrack. I watched as women were abused and taken against their will, all while crying out in pain. They weren't given a choice to say no. We were informed that the Nazis had needs, and we were to comply or suffer the consequences. I worked so many hours and tried my best to make myself scarce in every possible way that I somehow managed to escape the wrath of their unforgiving attacks.

"Is this okay?" Charlie asked in a whisper as his lips brushed against my ear.

"Yes," I said with only my breath. He struggled against me for a moment, freeing himself before pushing my dress up above my waist. My heart was pounding, scared of feeling the pain some of those other women had experienced. "I've never been with a man before." I felt the need to let him know. It was as if I left home being a young girl, and over the course of time I had been there, I became a woman who had seen too much.

His smile displayed a sense of contentment in response to my confession, and his mouth fell to mine, distracting me from every thought as a new connection forced my eyes wide open. Charlie was careful with me, taking his time while proving his movements were out of love rather than anything else. It was painful at first, but not so much that I wanted it to stop. I watched his face for a moment—the way his eyes closed, and how his lips parted while giving in to heavy breaths. A shooting star in the sky briefly stole my attention until a sense of pleasure caught me off guard and moved through my body like a current. Instinctively, I gripped my hands around Charlie's arms, needing an anchor to keep me grounded because with each movement, a small piece of me melted into the soil beneath us. My heavy eyelids gave in, shutting the world out while I imagined the most beautiful sunset liquefying into a crystal-clear body of water. It's how I felt—the rush of lapping waves upon a sandy shore that was fed to the tide and pulled farther and farther away until I was completely lost amid the sea.

A warm sensation filled every part of me, and I realized I had been pressing my fingernails into Charlie's arms so hard, I may have cut him. He didn't seem to notice, however. He was too busy staring at me with a worried gaze. "Are you okay?"

"That was amazing," I told him. "You're amazing."

He released a heavy, held-in breath and lowered his head to my chest. "We will forever have this night, Amelia," he said, and my thoughts instantly returned to the apprehension of Charlie leaving the next day.

"Don't talk like that," I told him.

"We'll never have to wonder now," he continued.

"Charlie!" I scolded him once more.

"I need to be honest with myself, Amelia."

"I need you to remain positive," I argued in return.

He looked like he was about to fall ill, so I wrapped my arms around him, holding him with all my strength until it became difficult for me to breathe through our embrace. If crying was still a natural emotion for me, it may have been one of the few times it happened, but I had forgotten how to release my tears. Crying was no longer an involuntary response to human emotions. I was conditioned to do what my body was supposed to do in order to stay alive. I had been dehumanized by the monsters who killed for their own amusement.

Charlie righted himself and his uniform, then returned my dress to where it belonged. He helped me up to my feet and laced his fingers between mine. "I want to hold your hand. I want to walk side by side with you and tell the world you belong to me—that we were brought together when my soul came back to life."

"We don't live in that kind of world," I reminded him. "We're a secret that no one would understand or accept, but we're also living proof that some people can't control everything."

"I suppose this is one battle that we won in this ugly war, Amelia—us."

"Come back to me," I told him. "Please."

"If I don't—" he began. I didn't like where his words were going, but I let him say what he needed to say because I couldn't be in denial about our life. "Survive for as long as you can, fight until you can't fight any longer, and if this damn war ever ends, I want you to run as far away from here as you can. Never look back. Start over, fulfill your dreams, and live the way you deserve to live."

"These sound like your last words," I whispered to him as I began to shake.

"If they are, they need to count," he said.

I knew I owed him my last words in case it was the final time we would ever be together. "I want you to go to that university and become a businessman. Wear a suit, hold your shoulders back and your chin high. Find a woman who makes your heart race, have a family, love your children more than you love yourself, and take them to a place where they can forever run free through meadows of flowers. Give them the freedom to be themselves, a freedom we couldn't have."

"I don't see how I could ever be happy without you," he said.

"Don't make those your last words," I huffed through anger.

"Fine. I love you, Amelia."

I stared at him for a long minute, knowing I couldn't say the same to him. I couldn't tell him I loved him even though I did. I still believed it would become a guarantee that he would never return.

I pressed myself up onto my toes, cupped my hands against his cheeks and kissed him with everything I had in me. "May the world keep you safe wherever you go," I whispered with a choke in my throat as a single tear escaped from the barren desert of my emotions. "Goodbye, my Charlie."

Those were my last words to him.

What a waste of words.

I ran as fast as my legs could carry me, sneaking quietly back into my barrack where I curled into a ball on my thin mattress. I felt as though a knife had plunged into the depths of my heart and soul—a pain so deep, it seared through every vein and fiber in my body. I knew I would never be the same again, but at least I could rest knowing there was one good man amongst so many terrible ones.

Humanity was not entirely lost.

he diary is flicked out of my loose grip and falls to the table as the pages fan to equal sides of the binding. My chest is aching, and I feel breathless while sitting quietly at a table in the middle of Starbucks.

"I figured I'd find you here at some point today," Mike says, hovering over the table with his arms folded across his chest.

It's only been two days, yet it feels like a year since I've seen him last. During the last two days since I broke up with him, so much has changed. My life has spun into a maze that I'm not sure how to find a way out of. I don't know which way is up or down, and everything is scattered in my head. "What are you doing here?" I can only hope he isn't here to cause a scene.

Charlie was gone. Grams had lost everyone. How could life be so cruel?

Mike had been talking, but my mind was elsewhere, lost in a goodbye I wasn't even part of. *Her last words to Charlie were "good-bye." He told her he loved her, and she couldn't say it back even though she did love him. How terribly sad.*

"Earth to Emma," Mike says, waving his hand in front of my face. "What is that thing, anyway?" He points to the diary as if it were today's newspaper, full of nothing more than celebrity gossip.

"Nothing," I tell him, removing the diary from the table.

"It sure doesn't look like nothing to me."

"What are you doing here?" I ask again.

"Did you get my note?"

"I did," I answer cordially, ignoring his presence as I reorganize the belongings in my bag to make space for the diary.

"And?" he continues.

"Who wrote it for you?" I can't believe I just asked him that. Not that he doesn't deserve it, but the thought did cross my mind earlier, and seeing how he's acting now, I'm almost sure someone told him what to say. Either that or he Googled "how to win your ex back."

"Really?" he counters.

"In six years, you never said something so full of thought, and then out of the blue, after I tell you I'm done, you leave me a note that sounds as if it came from a different person. Now, I'm supposed to fall to my knees and forget everything?" I was wondering when my anger and rage would catch up to me. It's building inside, overflowing like hot lava on top of the millions of emotions Grams's diary is stirring up.

"Haven't you ever heard the saying, 'You don't know what you had until it's gone?'" he has the nerve to ask me. I don't know if he's implying I should be thinking this, or he's thinking this, but in any case, I don't care.

"Yeah, Mike, and for some reason, I didn't realize what I was missing until you were gone." Witty comebacks aren't my thing, but for once, the words come out when they should, rather than an hour later when I'm talking to myself, thinking of what I *should* have said.

He leans forward, pressing his palms onto the top of the table. "Six years, Emma. We can work this shit out." That's all I've ever been to him. Shit.

"Why do you want to be with me so badly, Mike? What is it about me that is so important to keep around?" I lean back into my chair, hugging my bag into my chest.

"I love you," he says.

"You don't know what love is," I tell him.

"Oh, and you do?"

I squeeze my hands tighter around the bag. "Yeah, but not from my own experience."

"Okay, okay, fine, what do you want from me? Want me to make a scene here? Get down on my hands and knees and beg for your forgiveness, beg for you to take me back?" The thought of him doing that sickens me. He's such a loose cannon that I could see him doing something so stupid and pathetic. I shouldn't be wondering why it took me so long to break up with him. I shouldn't be having this conversation with him. I should have done the right thing years ago.

I take a sip of my now-lukewarm coffee to break up the conversation, giving me a moment to collect my next thoughts. "What I want from you...is to leave. I want you to forget about me. I want you to figure out what is going to make you happy in your life because it's so, so clear that I'm not the person for you, and you're definitely not the person for me."

Mike presses his lips together and exhales sharply through his nose. "You're wrong," he grunts. "I want to be with you, Emma."

I glance down at my cup, fixating on the recycled cardboard sleeve. Am I making a mistake? Is he my great challenge? Am I supposed to endure this, live through it, and dig until I find the good inside of him that gives us both a lifetime full of happiness? A relationship surely shouldn't be this hard, but love knows no bounds.

"Emma," he says again as his hand gently falls to my wrist. "Please, give me a chance to show you I can be a better man."

I force myself to look up at him, staring into his dark eyes while trying to find the part of him I was once so deeply attracted to. I'm sure it must be there somewhere. His brows buckle, and his forehead crinkles with lines, pleading without words, causing me to feel guilty without cause.

As I take the extra few seconds to *really* look at him—the man I have told myself I loved—I can't seem to find one single part of him that makes me feel any type of emotion, not even a twitch.

"I can't," I tell him.

"Fuck, Emma," he shouts boisterously, forcing his voice to echo off the walls within this small cafe. "Is there someone else, or something?"

"You're asking me if there's someone else when you admitted to cheating on me?"

"Yeah, I'm asking you if there's someone else," he repeats.

I'm not sure if Jackson's short presence in my life can count as someone else, but in the time I've known him, he's offered me more than Mike did in the six years we spent together. Jackson is someone good, and he's opened my eyes to a world I didn't know existed. "Yes, Mike, there's someone else." I take my phone from next to my leg and hit the display to check the time. "As a matter of fact, I need to get going so I can go shower and change for my date with him tonight."

Mike looks around as if I told a joke others might have heard too. "A date?" he asks, laughing cynically.

"Yeah, I realize you're unfamiliar with the concept of spending time alone with the person you supposedly love, but some people still practice the ancient method of courting."

"Courting?" he questions while throwing his head back.

"Forget it." I stand up with my bag and laptop, ready to get as far away from him as possible.

"So, this is seriously it?" he asks. Obviously, I haven't been clear enough. There has always been one definitive line with me that can't be crossed, and I was clear about it. I won't put up with cheating. Dad cheated on Mom so many times before she called him out on it, and once she did, he disappeared from our lives as

174

if we were never important to him. There is no way I'd put up with that for as long as she did, or at all for that matter.

"This is it," I confirm. Mike's shoulders slouch in defeat. "Next time you have a good girl to come home to—don't cheat on her. Treat her like she's important—like she matters to you." I wrap my arms around his neck and offer him a quick hug. "Goodbye, Mike." How could my last words to Mike be the same as Grams's last words to Charlie, yet have such a different meaning? *It couldn't have been*. There's more of Charlie in this book. I know it.

I head toward the door, mortified from the scene Mike caused. "Bye, Em," Chelsea shouts from behind the counter. I turn around, taking a couple of steps backward to the door as I wave goodbye. The look on her face tells me she heard everything that happened and my phone will most likely be buzzing in an hour when she gets out of work.

I haven't been on an actual date where I've been given the opportunity to dress up my normal wardrobe, curl my hair, and put on a little makeup since college. I've missed that feeling of anticipation and excitement.

The drive back into Boston is quick and easy, and I find a nearly empty lot in front of the restaurant where Jackson said to meet him. I pull down the visor to check my reflection one last time, and when I see my face, I notice something I haven't witnessed in a while: My cheeks are pink, and my eyes look brighter. I've lost that worn-out look I so often had when Mike and I were together. I feel different, too. I feel a sense of unfamiliar happiness.

I step out of the Jeep, balancing myself in a pair of heels I haven't worn since a wedding I went to last year, and head across the parking lot toward the street parallel to the restaurant.

Jackson is standing where he said he'd be waiting, and he's

smiling at me as if he hasn't seen me in a month—as if he's truly happy to see me.

"Well, hello, gorgeous," he says, shamelessly checking me out. My heart flops around in the bottom of my stomach, and my cheeks ache from the smile I'm trying to downplay. I'm forced to pinch my bottom lip between my front teeth as a rush of warmth reels through while I take in the sight of this amazing man in front of me. He's dressed casually in a pair of jeans-ones that look like he was the one reason jeans were invented. In addition, his casual, blue-and-white plaid collared shirt is fitted, showing off a toned body he's hidden beneath scrubs. I'm suddenly aware of the fact that he is even farther out of my league than I originally thought, and I don't know how the heck I ended up here.

"Hi," I offer in return as I come within an arm's length of him. He doesn't waste a second before stretching out his hand and taking hold of my elbow to pull me in toward him.

"The last few hours have been the longest hours of my entire life," he says. "I couldn't stop thinking about you." I feel utterly speechless. No one has ever spoken to me this way before.

For most of my adult life, I have had the notion that some girls are the type that men woo over, and others, like me, are the ones men settle for when they're looking for simplicity. Jackson's making me feel like I'm on a whole other level than I thought I was.

"Me?" I question. I can't help wondering what it is about me he couldn't stop thinking about.

His thumb and forefinger gently pinch my chin as he leisurely —slowly—bends his neck down to kiss me so softly that my lips quiver as if they were touched by the tip of a feather. Oh, wow. I can't think straight.

"Why did you want to meet me outside?" I ask him.

"I needed this moment before we were surrounded by people."

My heart aches from beating so hard. I should not be falling for him so quickly. I could get hurt. I could fall in love. I can easily see myself intertwining my life with his—just the idea of being with him is compelling, and I've known him for less than a week. I don't do this sort of thing. I take my time. *I waste my time.* I spent six years with a person only to realize I hate him.

I should stop following rules.

"How did your work go today?" Jackson asks while opening the heavy wooden door to the restaurant.

"Good. I got enough done to be somewhat caught up. I schedule projects in increments to try and maintain a somewhat normal schedule. It's hard to stick to, but I've been working hard at cutting back for the whole work/life balance thing everyone is always talking about." I chuckle at what I'm saying because I'm talking about a busy schedule to a doctor who most definitely works more hours in any given week than I do.

"It's definitely a tricky accomplishment to find a balance like that, but I've seen my fair share of people going crazy from a lack of fresh air."

"I can only imagine."

"A table for two please, in the back if you have anything," Jackson tells the hostess.

She takes two menus and heads toward the back of the restaurant where we're brought to a round booth. We both slide in and sigh at the same time. "You too, huh?" I ask.

"You know, sometimes the day just gets away from me, and I realize I haven't taken a full breath until the moment I sit down," he says. I don't know how he stays on his feet all day like that. I'm exhausted and I usually sit all day.

"So, do you mainly focus on cardiovascular health or do you practice any other type of specialty too...you know, besides comedy?"

He points at me and winks, appreciating my comedy joke, but then begins answering with a sense of seriousness. "Cardiology is about as much as I can handle for now. It's a lot, and there is a constant influx of patients, so I'm never bored enough to look for more trouble." He smirks as he hands me one of the menus while taking the one underneath for himself. "I have to say, I'm envious of you getting to change your scenery up whenever you want to. Is it nice working from different locations? It must be good inspiration, huh?"

"I suppose," I tell him. Though, after days like today, I sometimes think I would be better off in an office than roaming around looking for a quiet place to sit.

It only takes him a minute to look over the menu before he places it back down and leans forward onto his elbows. "Can I admit to something that you might make fun of me for later?"

"Uh oh," I joke. I shouldn't be, but I'm a little worried about what he might say.

"I've caught myself daydreaming about you today, twice. Doctors can't be doing that kind of thing," he says as he places his palms on the sides of his face.

Impulsively, I cup my hand over my mouth because I'm not sure what to do with the amount of heat rushing through my face. "Well, I apologize for being such a distraction, but I can't promise I'll be going away anytime soon. My grandmother is in your hospital, after all."

"Good," he says, reaching across the table for my hand. "I mean, that you're not going away...not that your grandmother is in the hospital."

"I was going to say...wow, what kind of doctor are you?" I scoff with laughter.

"Emma, you are *so* distracting," he continues.

I know I'm blushing. I take my menu and open it up, glancing up and down the list of options. I'm having a hard time focusing, but the chicken finger platter catches my eye.

"So, your grandmother was talking about Charlie some more this afternoon when I went in to check on her."

The change of subject shifts my nerves from one distraction to another. "What was she saying about him?" The eagerness inside me is desperate for answers I know I haven't gotten to in the book yet, but the suspense is killing me.

"She asked if you had gone to look for him and was telling me what he might look like now. Then she said the sweetest thing." Jackson chuckles with his breath at the recollection. "She said...and I'm quoting her, 'But even if he were bald and covered in wrinkles, I'd still only see the blond-haired, blue-eyed soldier who had too much compassion for the world to have any space in his heart for the hatred he was forced to show.'"

"I think I know why she's suddenly talking about him," I tell Jackson.

"Did you find something out while you were reading today?"

"No, but she said when she—when her heart stopped for those few minutes, she was sure Charlie would be waiting for her, and he wasn't there."

"You know, what happens after death is all hearsay, right?" Jackson asks. I don't think he's trying to diminish Grams's thought, but scientifically, he's correct.

"Of course, but we can have our own opinions on the matter."

"You're right about that. I also agree with the hearsay. Unfortunately, I've heard more than a few patients talking to loved ones while passing away."

My chest tightens, considering the truth of it all. "If it's true, maybe Charlie isn't dead."

"Who said he was?" Jackson asks, curiously.

"Well, I was rudely interrupted while reading the part where Charlie was deployed to the front lines and had to say goodbye to my grandmother."

The waiter comes over with an order pad and greets us. "What can I get for you two?"

We place our drink and food orders, then the waiter leaves us to the cliffhanger of my story.

"You were saying you were rudely interrupted?" Jackson asks, eagerly.

I glance down at our intertwined hands, noting once again, how fast everything is moving in my life. "Evidently, Mike had spent the better half of his day hunting me down," I tell him, worried about the reaction he might have.

He looks upset rather than angry. "Really? What did he want?" There's a sense of apprehension laced between his words, but I'm sure he's smart enough to know I wouldn't be here with him if Mike was able to work me over.

"He wants things to work out with us," I tell him.

"And what do you want?"

I appreciate his question and can't stop the small smile from stretching across my mouth. "Well, I would like...to see how things work out between you and me."

As much as I thought Jackson would eat up my words, he doesn't smile in return. There's a serious concern wavering through his mesmerizing eyes. "Take me out of the picture for a minute. If you hadn't met me, would you have broken up with him, and if you had, would you have been persuaded to go back to him today?"

His questions cause me to consider the truth. "I can't lie and tell you I know I would have been strong enough to do what needed to be done, but I can say that after knowing you for the short time I have, you gave me enough reason to see that there are people who are worth spending my time with, and people who are not." I don't know how I would feel if I were in Jackson's shoes, or what I'd think if his ex-wife just showed up out of nowhere, begging for him to take her back, but I can't lie about this. He knew this just happened, and I'm sure I'm not the only one who has gone through the trials and tribulations of a breakup.

"So, what you're saying is, you're not going back to him because of me?"

I'm not sure there's any other way to put it. "Would it cause you to get up and walk away if I said yes?"

"No," he says with the slightest hint of accomplishment

written into his grin. "It makes me want to pat myself on the back. I can now say I've saved over two hundred sick patients—and one healthy woman—from destructive heart conditions."

"Aw, another doctor joke?" I jest.

"Kind of cheesy, huh?"

"Kind of adorable," I tell him. I feel like I need to fan myself, but I settle for nervously brushing my hair behind my shoulder.

"So, after dinner, would you agree to come back to my place so we can—" he clears his throat, *and my gosh that's forward*. I'm not complaining—not even a little—but wow. I wasn't expecting him to just come right out and suggest it. "—read a little more of the diary. I can't stop thinking about it."

With even more of a need to fan myself now, I struggle to catch my breath as uneasy laughter sings like an injured bird from my throat. "Yeah, wow, I—definitely."

"Sorry, was that rude of me to ask?"

"No," I reply in a high-pitched squeak, which only comes out when I'm uncomfortable about a topic or when I'm lying. "It's way better reading it with someone than doing so alone."

"You sure now?" he asks.

"I'd love to see where you live. Actually, where do you live?" Why has this question not come up yet? We started talking about it, and then we never finished that conversation.

"Brighton," he says. "And you?"

"My mom lives in Needham, but it's only temporary until I find my own place."

"Oh nice, only a few minutes down the road."

The small talk ensues, and I have a rough time eating while trying to get the food past the bundle of nerves expanding throughout my body. I forgot how awkward this dating thing could be. I know his intentions are true, but I suspect there's more than my grandmother's diary on his mind. There's certainly more on mine.

Once our plates are cleared, the bill arrives, and Jackson

snatches it up faster than I can reach for it. The time seemed to disappear, and I'm feeling a little panicky. I'm going to his apartment. I've only been with two men, and the first one was twelve years ago in college—not much to brag about there—then there was Mike, and I'd rather forget about him completely. I could be getting ahead of myself, though. Jackson might just be lonely and want a little female companionship, or maybe he is just interested in Grams's diary, and I'm reading way too much into it.

The moment we leave the restaurant, Jackson's hand finds mine. It's easy with him. There's no thinking or planning. Everything just flows smoothly. He walks me to my car and leans over to kiss my cheek before I slide in. "Can I have your phone for a second?"

I reach for my phone, knocking over my sunglasses and lip gloss that are sitting on my middle console. He has me so flustered, and it's making me clumsy. I hand him the phone, watching as he struggles not to laugh at me. "I'm just putting my number in here and plugging my address into your GPS in case you lose me in traffic."

"You're spoiling me," I tell him.

"What in the world are you talking about, crazy girl?"

I realize how pathetic I just made myself sound, but I might have never known there was a thoughtful, decent man on this earth if I hadn't met Jackson. Up until now, I have only met up with the ones who are clueless about life and being gentlemen. "Not everyone is as considerate as you are," I tell him.

"It's time you start interacting with some nicer people," he says with a quick wink.

"It seems you're taking care of that little problem."

Jackson leans down and ducks into the Jeep. "If you think I'm being nice now, you haven't seen anything yet," he whispers before kissing away the chance of a response rolling off the tip of my tongue.

With his words being the last before my door closes, I watch him make his way over to his car across the lot.

The late-night hour makes traffic easy to navigate, so following him through Boston and into Brighton is quick and easy.

Apparently, Jackson has his own parking garage underground. *How fancy!* I didn't know these existed here. I thought street parking was the only option on the outskirts of Boston. Shows what I know from living in the suburbs.

There's a string of silence between us as I follow him to the elevator and up to the top floor of this apartment building. I've told myself many times before that I can learn about a man from the way he lives, and right now, I have no clue what I'm in for. The elevator brings us to a hotel-looking hallway, lined with bright white doors, fancy trim, and gold-plated numbers centered perfectly on each apartment door. "This is so nice," I tell him.

"After I left my ex, Dana, I went on a bit of a spending spree," he says. "It was my way of coping."

"Hey, I can appreciate that."

He unlocks his door, and it opens into endless square feet of dark brown hardwood floors and windows for walls across the back side. You can see the whole city from up here. In the kitchen, there are modern, stainless steel appliances surrounded by dark granite countertops and sharp contrasting gray cabinets. Everything else is white. The decor is very masculine but neat and trendy. The best part is, the entire place smells just like him. "I love your apartment. It's so clean and new."

A crooked smile perks to one side as he unbuttons the cuffs on his sleeves to roll them up. "It's funny you say that. It's exactly how I feel too, except I'd rather feel like I'm home, and it hasn't exactly felt like that for me yet." That breaks my heart because I think I know exactly how he's feeling. I'm in the same boat, but I'm home, home, like my childhood bedroom home where my comforter is neon pink and blue with cheetah print patches. There's got to be an in-between spot we're both missing out on.

Jackson pulls me over to his couch and takes the bag from my grip. "White or red wine?"

"White, please." The couch is plush and comfortable. It's easy to tell this was one item where he went for comfort rather than style, although it looks nice too. "You really do have an amazing view from up here."

"Yeah, it's nice, but honestly, when I'm not working nights, I drag myself to bed and watch TV until I fall asleep." I see another side of Jackson that I wasn't aware of—there's sadness in his voice, and I think I can tell he's not the kind of person who likes to be alone. It's the same thing that got me stuck in a relationship that went on for way too long.

"I think we have a lot in common," I tell him. I don't live in a place like this, but I think he's already seen a hint of the common traits we share too.

He walks over with a bottle of wine and two glasses he's already filled halfway. "Get that book out, Emma. It's time." After placing the glasses and bottle down, he rubs his hands together with excitement and sits down on the couch beside me.

"You're really into this story?" I ask, needing more validation. Mike was never interested in any part of my life. This is all new to me.

"That woman knows what she is talking about, and I want to learn from that kind of wisdom. You don't just find people walking around who have lived the kind of life she has lived. Her story is the type to change someone's way of thinking, and from the parts I've heard, I'm already impressed with her strength and desire to push through a situation without hope—alone at that. I don't think I could do something so heroic, and it amazes me to hear about those who can make it through hell and come back from it all."

I get it. Her story is altering my entire view of the world. I don't think I'll ever be able to look at life the same way again.

CHAPTER SEVENTEEN

AMELIA

MAY 1943 - DAY 520

I couldn't think of one moment worth writing about from the time Charlie left Theresienstadt until almost a year later. As I learned more about the situation I was held hostage in, I found that the definition of a ghetto had changed during the prior years to my imprisonment. A ghetto was formerly defined as a place where segregated religions would gather and live in a communal area. In 1942, however, the definition had apparently changed, becoming a place where prisoners were kept against their will between barbed wire fences.

Honestly, I wasn't sure how I was still alive after more than a year of starvation, brutal work conditions, no sanitation, and so many people around me dying from various diseases and ailments. It was beginning to feel as though God had chosen to keep me alive for a reason, one I didn't think I'd ever understand. Misery was my only companion after the one reason I had for happiness went away, just like all the other precious parts of my life.

I clung to Leah during the days following Charlie's departure.

Helping her with baby Lucie was a slight distraction from the permanent pain in my heart. Without hope of future happiness, each ache and pain became abundantly noticeable, and I lost the will to keep pushing myself as hard as I had been.

Keeping Lucie quiet was very challenging, considering a baby doesn't understand the danger her mama could be in if she was heard. However, by the luck of something larger than I could understand, somehow, a whole month went by before Leah was reported for not showing up at her assigned job in the administration building. It was the middle of the day, and I was outside in the sweltering heat when I saw a group of Nazis heading for the barrack Leah was living in. My heart ached because I knew it was not end well. Then I heard one of the Nazi's shout, "There is a baby inside."

My clipboard fell from my hands, and I ran as fast as my bony legs would carry me. My heart pounded in my chest as I followed the Nazis from behind. I had seen enough to know that something terrible was about to happen to Leah and Lucie, and there was nothing I could do to stop it.

I stood to the side of a barrack block, watching and waiting, scared and hardly breathing through the fear overwhelming my mind. I heard a shriek, followed by an infant's wailing cry that I hadn't heard from Lucie since she was born. Despite her circumstances, Leah cared for her so beautifully that there was hardly a need for her to cry.

Leah was dragged out of the barrack, her thin arms locked tightly within the grip of two Nazis' hands as her bare heels dragged through the gravel-ridden dirt. They were shouting at her in German as she screamed at the top of her lungs. But it would make no difference. Her pleas for mercy would change nothing, but at least screaming gave her an outlet to express the palpable fear and pain she was experiencing. Hopefully, that would slightly help her face the impending wrath of the guards. She had broken the rules, and she had deceived them. I was unsure if her punishment would be a whipping, imprisonment, or an immediate transition to the next stop which I was sure at that point was off a cliff somewhere.

I didn't move from the corner of the wall I clung to, gripping at the brick finish so tightly my fingertips began to bleed. After Leah was halfway down the alley between the barracks, another Nazi came out with Lucie locked firmly within his hands, holding her as if she were nothing more than a sack of dirt. The soldier screamed at her—damning her for being born a dirty Jew.

I wanted to murder the Nazi.

I wanted to destroy him for the words he was screaming at an innocent baby, and for the way he was handling Lucie. She was not old enough to hold her head up on her own yet, and it was hanging to the left and bouncing around as the Nazi carried her toward the sick bay where I was not tending to my job as I should have been.

I raced for my clipboard, passing by the Nazi with Lucie in his hands. I retrieved the clipboard and continued questioning the others in line.

As the Nazi and Lucie disappeared inside of the block, I continued down the path where the other Nazis were taking Leah. The direction was opposite of where the prison was, and I wasn't sure if that was a relief or not.

I soon found out how little a relief it was that she was not taken to the solitary cells. Instead, she was brought to the execution field. She was forced down to her knees as one of the Nazi's took his position across the way, aiming his rifle directly at Leah's head. I wanted to move, run away, avoid the scene that would permanently be marked in my soul forever, but I was paralyzed as I watched.

Leah didn't cry. She was done screaming, and her face was void of all emotion. She knew the end had come. Our eyes met one last time, just seconds before the shot rang out. She blinked once and looked up to the sky right before a bullet struck the center of her forehead, knocking her down with so much force I was sure her body would leave a permanent indentation in the soil.

All I could think at that moment was they murdered the poor woman because she had given birth to a baby. Monsters. The birth of a child is the purest, most beautiful thing that can happen in life, and for those men to take her life away for that, was unconscionable.

I wanted to drop to my knees and beg for the nightmare to end, but if I did, I too would have been killed. I made a promise to Charlie to do as I was told and end my plan to escape, so I breathed in the air that was laced with death, inhaling as deeply as I could to stifle all my emotions as I turned and walked away. I felt guilt and remorse for not being able to do something to help Leah, but I knew in my heart there was nothing anyone could have done to save her.

That day changed everything for me. We were part of the war. We were the target, and they were using us like game pieces for their own amusement. I couldn't understand how so many people could be brainwashed to think all Jews were the reason that the Germans lost the first war when so many of us weren't even alive then. It was pure, unfounded hatred for our people.

Months dragged by and I kept quiet, doing as I was instructed, eating the small rations I was given, watching as my limbs turned into skin and bone. Daily, I would wonder how I had the strength to stand when so many of us no longer had that ability. There were living bodies draped over one another in my barrack, taking up every free inch of space as we ran out of room in the camp.

Life was like a revolving wheel I couldn't step off of, and my mind became as numb as the rest of my body while I waited for death to find me, all along wishing there was an easier way out than just waiting for my time to come.

In 1943, on May twenty-fourth, at what must have been high noon, there was a commotion at the front entrance of the camp. I wasn't sure what could have be happening, but I didn't have the energy or desire to pay attention to it. I had a line to get through, and that was my only goal for the day—for every day. Looking at the people as I passed them by, it felt as though I was looking at mirrors of myself. I didn't know exactly what my appearance was at that time, but I imagined it was as emaciated as everyone else. All of us were given the same rations, but some of us were placed in worse working conditions than others —those were the people to die first. Some dropped dead while waiting for me in the line. When that happened, I had to call a guard to remove the body, which was immediately transported to the crematorium. *There were so many dead bodies; they had to create a place to burn them so the space within the camp wouldn't be wasted.*

The Nazis' commotion grew louder as some began to salute a man walking through a man-made path. "Welcome home, soldier," many of them said. It was not a usual occurrence, as many of the Nazis were exchanged daily for deployment or guard duty, depending on their ranking and abilities. Familiar faces were long gone, and the camp felt more like a train station than anything else. Why I had remained in one place for so long was an unanswered question I considered daily.

As the group of Nazis passed by, I turned to watch for a moment, and to my utter surprise, Charlie was the man being praised. Decorations of medals and patches lined his coat, and there was a certain look about him that showed years of aging rather than the year he had been gone. I was in a state of shock as he passed by, peering at me with a subtly through a peripheral glance.

My heart began to beat erratically for the first time in a year, but I wasn't sure what Charlie was feeling in that moment. I didn't know if he would even recognize me in the state I was in. I was afraid he had been brainwashed to believe I was in fact the enemy rather than his best friend and the woman he claimed to love the last time we were together. So many thoughts and fears ran through my head in a matter of seconds, but at the same time, there was a glimmer of hope I wasn't sure I should have.

I had spent the last year trying to block out anything that would cause me more pain, and I would be damned before I'd allow anything close enough to hurt me.

I went through the motions for the next eight hours, pretending it was just another day, but my thoughts were in a fog. I didn't know what to think or feel.

As darkness began to set in and the doors of the sick bay closed, I made my way over to the block where the children were contained, peeking in through the window to check on Lucie, who began to walk a week earlier. She knew nothing of her dear mother, but she also knew nothing of fear or pain. That helped me sleep at night, knowing that the German women were caring for those children under horrendous conditions. Lucie was the youngest child in the block, but the other children were always around her, taking care of her as if they were siblings.

With the daily dose of relief I got from seeing Lucie's precious face, I dragged my worn-out body back to my barrack before settling down on the floor where I was relocated to months earlier when my bed had been taken by another Jewish woman. She was brought there in the more recent months, therefore stronger than many of us and more bullish than those who had been there for over a year. It wasn't worth a battle, and if we were caught fighting, it would likely end in a hanging or execution. The overcrowding was a problem, and the Nazis were doing what they could to control it. Unfortunately, that often included executions for small transgressions.

As I willed myself to sleep that night, my thoughts of Charlie forgetting about me sent an agonizing pain through my heart, and for the first time since Leah was murdered, I wanted to scream my hatred away. I thought maybe a shriek would make me feel better, but instead, I took several deep breaths, squeezed my eyes closed, and tried to bury the thoughts.

I refused to be a victim of the Nazis or my emotions.

Nazis were no longer coming in to pillage the women in our barrack since we were all far too weak to be of any use to them, or so we assumed. Therefore, an interruption in the middle of the night was a rarity. Yet, no one would move an inch if the door were to open.

We had all been scared into pretending we were lifeless on the floors. Unsure what to think, I was startled when my body was lifted up with just a scoop of an arm, right off the ground, and strewn over a firm shoulder. I struggled not to scream, as I knew it would do no good. The Nazis took what they wanted, when they wanted it, and screaming only made things worse.

I kept my eyes closed as I was brought outside. I prayed that the arm around me belonged to Charlie, but he hardly twitched as he passed by me earlier that day, so the hope I had that he was alive became overshadowed by my new fear that he had turned into a monster like the rest. I wouldn't want to know him if that were the case. I would rather think he was dead.

I was lowered to the ground, still unsure of where I was, but I refused to open my eyes. If I was to be executed, I didn't want to watch it happen. It was the last bit of power I had over my life, and under no circumstance would I let them take that away from me.

"You're alive." His voice was gruff and hoarse as if he were sick, but I recognized it. I nervously opened my eyes, forcing myself to face the truth. It was hard to see much at first after clenching my eyelids shut for so long, but as clarity set in and the moon's glow assisted in lighting the enclosed area, I saw a nearly unrecognizable man accompanying the voice. There were tracks of scars lining his face as if someone had taken knives and dragged them in a row across his skin. I reached up to touch the scars—the texture of the indents and bulging skin. "What did they do to you? Are you all right, Charlie?" My fear-saturated words floated above us within the thick, humid air. He didn't answer. Instead, he traced a finger along the rigid bones of my cheek as a tear fell from his eye. "Charlie, speak to me." I couldn't help but slightly fear the man I should have never fallen so attached to because it seemed like it was taking forever for him to answer me.

"We need to escape," he finally said.

Relief flooded my body with so many sensations; I felt as if I were imploding from the inside out. I had stayed there for him because of the promise I made, and it was apparent he was living up to his word, as well. "Thank you," I whispered.

"The Red Cross has announced a visit to this camp, and the SS is making drastic changes in its appearance to fool them into believing this is the ghetto they proclaimed it to be. From what I gather, it seems that anyone who appears to be ill or dying will be transitioned immediately, and you are on a list to be taken to Auschwitz at the end of the week, Amelia," he said.

"Auschwitz?" I questioned. "What is that? Is it a new ghetto?"

Charlie shook his head, and a sickened look draped over his face like a dark shadow. "It's a death camp, Amelia. That's where all the Jews are being taken when they are transitioned from here. They are forced to work in far worse conditions than they do here, and it's only a waiting game until they're forced into a chamber that's filled with a poisonous gas, which kills them immediately."

"Jakob," I called out in a whisper. I had held out the smallest bit of hope that he was alive somewhere, but the truth became clear in that moment...

"He was gassed on the second of March last year."

I couldn't scream, and I couldn't breathe, but I wouldn't let myself break either. There was nothing I could do except stare into Charlie's eyes, with anger for the world I was forced to remain in while everyone else left me behind.

Another rip of my collar—another shred of my heart, gone. The collar of my dress was officially destroyed, just the same as my life. "They're all gone."

Charlie watched as I mourned for a brief moment, praying

Jakob was in a better place. I had to avoid the thought of what he went through—the suffering he endured.

"I'm so sorry, Amelia." Sorry. I don't think I ever understood that word, and I don't think I ever will again.

"When are we leaving?" I asked him.

"As soon as we can," he said.

"I can't leave Lucie," I told him. I promised Leah if they came for her, I would watch over Lucie until I was no longer able to. I couldn't abandon her, even if I hadn't promised Leah.

"Lucie?" he questioned. "Who is Lucie?"

"Leah's daughter. Do you remember—"

"She's alive?" Charlie asked with shock, as a glimmer of hope echoed through his voice.

"Lucie is alive. Leah was executed."

Charlie lowered his head to my chest, still kneeling over me.

"It isn't fair," he said, his hand gripping my arm with force. He shook as he took in a few breaths, digesting the information, though nothing should have felt surprising. The true shock was that I was alive, and so was Lucie.

"What was it like out there—outside of these walls?" I asked him, unsure I truly wanted to know, but I had no idea what he had been through, and by the look on his face, I knew it was bad.

Charlie pulled in a deep breath and straightened his back. Without a quick response, he unbuttoned his coat and shrugged it off, allowing it to fall to the ground behind him. It took me a moment to see the tied-off sleeve on the upper portion of his left arm. "Your arm, Charlie," I growled with anger.

"They took that, but they couldn't have the rest of me, Amelia. I fought so damn hard."

I couldn't bear the thought of what he suffered through. Why was I living in a world filled with death and destruction? Why? "Oh, dear God," is all I could mutter. Starving didn't feel like much in comparison to losing a limb.

"I nearly died due to the amount of blood I lost, but after a month in the hospital, they released me and sent me back here for guard duty."

I wrapped my arms around Charlie's neck, pulling him down on top of me, clutching him with everything I had. More tears pooled in his eyes, leaving a warm, wet spot against my chest. "I fought to stay alive so I could come back for you. My eyes were opened to the destruction this world is living through, and I couldn't leave you here alone."

His words melded into the light breeze, and his lips dropped to mine, pressing against them with a force that ached, but I couldn't manage to break away. I never thought I would see him again, let alone touch his lips or feel his body against me.

"I love you, Amelia. I still love you. I love you more than ever, and I need to get you out of here."

"Thank you," I told him, still knowing there was no way to admit my love for him verbally. I truly believed he was only alive because I spared him of those deadly words.

"We'll take Lucie with us," he continued. "We'll care for her as if she were our own. She deserves at least that much. An innocent soul is easy to love and I will give that poor little girl what I can." My heart thumped in my chest, knowing he understood the importance of keeping that beautiful baby safe. "Tomorrow night, after the rations have been distributed, we'll do it. I'm due to seek weekly medical check-ins for my arm, and the hospital is hours away. Therefore, I would need to leave guard duty at night."

"How will we get by the guards?" I asked. It seemed impossible, and as he told me before, no one had ever escaped. Anyone who had tried over the previous year and a half had been executed. However, I would be dead by the end of the week anyway, so I had nothing to lose by trying. My only fear was that if we were caught, Lucie's life would be in jeopardy, as well. It was a chance we had to take, though. It would only be a matter of time before Lucie would contract an illness at the camp, and she could die from that just as so many of the other children had.

"Trust me," he said. "I came back for you, and I'm not leaving without you."

I clasped my hands around his cheeks and pulled him back down to kiss him—my beautiful enemy who would commit a war crime for the sake of our love.

"I'll never be able to repay you, Charlie."

"You survived a year in Terezín because of a promise you made to me. You have already given me more than I could ask for."

CHAPTER EIGHTEEN

EMMA

$\mathcal{M}$y hands are shaking as I close the book, and Jackson's head lifts from my shoulder. "That's intense," he says.

"All this time, I thought she had been liberated. I didn't think she escaped," I tell him, confused by the muddled facts I've picked up on throughout my life.

"I guess we won't know until you finish reading," he says, sounding as tired as I feel.

"I don't think I can read any more tonight. I feel like it's all I can focus on, and it's taking me to a place I'm not sure I'm ready to go yet." A long sigh exhales from my lungs as I hug my arm around my knee. "I don't know if that makes any sense..."

"It's hard information to digest. It would be for anyone," he tells me. "You probably need to do something after reading to shut it off for a bit. It's not healthy to hold yourself hostage in a situation you can't control." He squeezes his arm around my shoulders...to comfort me...I think.

"Is that the doctor in you speaking or—"

"Experience," he says. "Maybe both."

I shift my body, bringing my other knee up onto the couch to face him. "How so?" We've learned a lot about Grams in the last few days, but I don't know a whole lot about Jackson, and I'm curious to find out more about him, aside from the fact that he's a doctor and a divorcee.

"I lose patients, possibly more than other areas of the hospital. I see so much pain-stricken grief in patients and their families that sometimes it's hard to come home at the end of the day and redirect my attention to something happier, you know?" He places his empty wine glass down on the table in front of us before continuing. "For a long time, I felt guilty about compartmentalizing it and putting my feelings about patients aside when I'm off duty, but I've learned over the past few years that if I don't force myself to shut it down, I'll become consumed and miserable."

He's looking at me with such intensity that I can almost feel his words, and they make me ache for the loneliness he battles in his head. "I've wondered how doctors do it, but I've always looked at them more like super humans than anything else. I figured they could manage it, so that's why they were meant to be doctors. I know I'd never be able to handle serious illnesses, deaths, or any of the other associated emotional pain on a daily basis. I honestly can't imagine going through that all the time. I don't think I'd be strong enough to turn it off on self-command."

Jackson rests back into the cushion behind us and glances up toward the ceiling where his lights are creating an aura of colorful diamonds. "We don't have that option. I wouldn't make it as a doctor if I didn't figure out how to separate my personal life from work. That's one of the first things you have to commit to if you want to have any kind of life outside of the hospital."

"That makes sense." With his gaze still stuck on the ceiling, I look around the room for a moment, noticing the lack of pictures on the walls and coffee table. I know men aren't typically the type to show off photos the way women do, but he doesn't have artwork up either. "You said you have an older sister, right?"

"Two older sisters, actually," he says. I know he had told me one, so I'm slightly confused by the change. "They were twins, but one died in a car accident ten years ago. Drunk driver."

"Oh my gosh, I'm so sorry," I tell him. I'm taken aback by this, and it opens up a new set of questions about Jackson. It's like I'm slowly peeling away his layers, trying to find out what's inside of him.

"Life happens, right?"

"That type of life shouldn't have to happen because of someone else's recklessness," I tell him. "What was she like?"

"Carly was a force to be reckoned with," he says through quiet laughter. "Strongest person I've ever known. She stayed alive for about a week after the accident, but her vitals kept failing, and the doctors were having trouble finding the source. They said they did every test there was, but nothing showed up as a cause. Evidently, her sternum had broken so badly that a piece had shattered off and punctured her aorta. The tear was very small and could have been repaired if found in time, but it wasn't."

I tend to picture stories when I hear them, and this one nauseates me to think about what he went through at such a young age. "Is that why you're a cardiologist?" I ask, almost knowing.

"I was already in med school at the time, but I was originally planning on specializing in internal medicine. I changed my plan after Carly died."

He maintains a straight face through his entire explanation, and I'm not sure I could be as strong. "How are your mom and other sister?"

"Eh," he says. "They had a tough time getting through the first couple of years after Carly passed. Now they have their moments, but mostly they spend their time harassing me to get remarried and have a family for *them*." We both laugh simultaneously because I'm sure he's heard my grandmother's demands of me, not to mention her ridiculous bribe. To find out that his family is similar seems ironic and makes me feel less uncomfortable about my situation.

"Our families would get along well," I tell him.

"It would be a little scary, actually," he says, leaning forward and pouring a bit more wine into each of our glasses. His comment makes me wonder what he sees in his future, not that I'm exactly sure what I see in mine, but I know it isn't living with Mom forever.

"We're supposed to be changing the mood here," he says, handing me my glass.

"Well, what do you do to cheer yourself up after a bad day?"

He leans back into the couch and takes a mouthful of Pinot. "Hmm, that's a tough one," he says.

"Well, you said you watch TV a lot," I say, encouraging his answers.

"I play a lot of Candy Crush too, but don't judge."

I'm not alone. It's amazing. "No judging. I do the same, and please don't take this as an insult, but I'm glad to have finally met someone just as lame." The laughter flows freely between us. At my age, I shouldn't be playing Candy Crush until I fall asleep at night, right?

"We're sad," I tell him, swallowing a mouthful of the tart wine.

"Not right this second." He places his glass back down and leans toward me as if he wants to kiss, but I place my hand on his chest, stopping him in place. "Wait, how old are you?"

"How old are you?" he responds with surprise, asking as if I had a reason for questioning him.

"Thirty-one," I reply.

"I had you pegged at twenty-four, but was suddenly concerned you might be seventeen or something," he says, sounding relieved.

"Seventeen? What grandmother would be interfering with the love life of a seventeen-year-old?"

"Maybe yours," he says, fairly.

"Good point."

"I'm thirty-three."

"Okay, so we're good," I say, wiping the fake sweat from my forehead.

"Am I allowed to kiss you now?"

With the playful mood already between us, I press my finger to my chin, appearing to ponder his question. "I don't know."

He steals my wine glass from my hand and places it beside his. "You don't know?" he asks.

"You're kind of a bad kisser," I joke, but with a poor attempt at being serious.

He presses his hand against his chest. "Am I, now?"

"Kinda," I say, sounding even less serious than I did a second ago.

Jackson moves forward, trapping me beneath him as I fall deeper into the plushness of his couch. He's hovering over me, and the view from this angle is generating a fire within my veins. Muscles emerge on his arms that I hadn't noticed, and with the collar of his shirt unbuttoned a bit; I'm able to see a lot more of those muscles rippling down the center of his body.

"You think we're moving too fast?" he asks. "I know you're still on the rebound and all." His lips quirk to one side, revealing a sinuous smirk I can't resist.

"I'm not on the rebound. I'm being revived."

"That is the hottest thing anyone has ever said to me," he murmurs.

His proximity is so close, I can almost taste his lips. "Did you know how fast a heart beats right before a kiss?" His words fall warmly against my mouth as I try to think a clear thought while in this position.

"Do *you* know?" I throw the question back.

"I've never tested it out," he says, his brazen smile reappearing.

"Are you stalling?" I ask him.

"Just enjoying the moment," he whispers before pressing his lips to mine. My heart beats heavily against my compressed chest, and I know he can feel what he's doing to me. His lips are so soft against mine, but his movements are meticulous, as if he knows where each nerve ending in my lips begins and ends as he connects the dots. His mouth opens slightly, and I follow in motion, feeling his tongue stroke against mine. I feel his entire body melting into mine, and his hands gently graze the side of my face as his fingers weave through the loose strands of my hair. An unstoppable soft hum vibrates through my throat, and in turn, his grip tightens.

Our bodies tangle as he maneuvers his legs to the ground, lifting me up with him, where I remain wrapped around him.

Where we're going, what we're doing, and how it's going to turn out doesn't faze me in the slightest because he has stolen a beat of my heart with every kiss. I can't imagine anything better than this, but something is telling me the best is yet to come. His lips move down my neck, sending a warm, striking shock down the lengths of my arms and across my chest.

Without an initial tour of his entire apartment, I'm not surprised to find a king-sized bed in the center of an impeccably decorated room that's coated with hues of blues, grays, and white. I'm even less surprised when I fall heavily against his cloud-like mattress. He climbs back over me, repossessing my lips as the bed covers float around us like a storm of feathers.

"I need you. I've needed you in my life for so long."

A fierceness grows inside me, and I tie my legs around his waist, pulling him down closer as I work at the buttons on his shirt—one by one—while sliding my fingers gently down the center of his chest. "I didn't think you existed," I tell him, breathlessly.

"I'm right here." He pulls at my dress, slowly drawing it over my head before his lips become more familiar with my collarbone, then the lacy exterior of my bra. His hands meet in the middle of my back, and I feel the release of my bra's clasp with the slightest flick of his fingers.

"I've never been with a doctor," I mutter as my back arches toward him, craving more of his teasing touches.

"I'm glad to hear that," he says, his lips vibrating against the top of my breast.

My restless hands drag down the sides of his solid core, offering me nothing to hold on to, which doesn't make much of a difference when he takes my hands within his and presses them into the pillow above my head. He has completely taken control of my body and every one of my senses. He gently moves the tips of his fingers inside of the hem of my panties before sliding them down my legs, allowing the silk fabric to feather against me at a torturously slow pace.

My eyes close in an effort to be patient as I hear a rustling from his drawer. I want to move my hands and help him with his boxer briefs, but I'm obeying the position he left me in.

The world around me is spinning and silent as he removes the last article of clothing that separates us. He slides on the condom and I peer down to steal a glimpse of this amazing man now that we are both bare and exposed. He is as flawless outside as he is inside.

With Jackson's smooth body pressing against mine, the friction and synced motions between us bring about sensations I've never experienced, inviting the understanding of the difference between simply being with a man versus being passionately intertwined in an endless symphony of desire. I try to contain the sounds aching to roar from my throat, but with the beads of sweat forming between us and the gasps of air bringing in little to nothing, I fall helplessly to the stranger of consummation.

Still struggling to pull in a breath of air, I feel as if I'm drowning in a pool of seduction. The release of emotions and what I had thought to be permanent stress makes me feel like a limp rag doll as his body comfortably rests against mine. "Well, did I revive you?" he murmurs weakly into my ear.

"I think you may have given me a new understanding of the word," I reply.

Jackson props himself up on his side as he twirls his fingers through a loose, tangled strand of my hair. "Where have you been?" he asks.

"Making a mess of my life." It wasn't meant to be funny, but I can't help the laughter that follows my statement. I'm good at making messes, I guess.

"I've always been under the impression that the bond between two people is something that grows over time, but I've been wrong. I think it all starts with a connection and grows into something more than I can comprehend at this moment."

"You're a brilliant man," I tell him. I love that he's unashamed to admit his worldly assumptions have been inaccurate due to inexperience.

"Thank you." He looks surprised to hear my simplistic response to his understanding of life, but I have nothing to match it with because I agree. "Emma, I want to spend more time with you, and I need you to know that I want to be careful not to rush into anything. I want our relationship to be separate and distinct from the one you had with Mike. I don't even want you to compare us and keep thinking about how much better I am for you. I just want you to think about me as a new chapter in your life." He interrupts his explanation with a short, soft kiss, and though I open my mouth to reply, he places his finger down gently on my lips. "However, I can't pretend that staying away from each other 'to let time heal' is going to fix whatever pain we've both been through."

I would only disagree if I were to follow those unsaid rules of dating, but I've never been one to follow rules. "Jackson, I've only felt *this* type of comfort and contentment during the times I've been with you, and I don't need time to figure that out," I tell him.

"So, we're on the same page?" he asks.

I squint my eyes, shamefully knowing what I'm about to say after just two dates with this man, but I'm done wasting precious moments in my life. "Will you laugh at me if I ask you to be my boyfriend?"

"Only if you don't laugh when I ask you to wear my high school ring."

I wasn't expecting the joke, so I teasingly slap his bare chest, causing him to flinch and cover himself from further damage. "You have a high school ring?" I laugh at the thought. He must have been the guy all the girls drooled over, begging to wear his ring.

"No, it just sounded like the right thing to say in response."

"We're not being ridiculous, right? After all, we have only known each other for less than a week." I don't feel like I need more reassurance, but I want to hear it again.

"What's the worst that can happen?" he asks.

"A couple of broken hearts," I reply.

"We'd survive. You come from a line of survivors, and I've been through my own form of hell. I say we just live how we want and throw the rulebook out the window."

"Damn rules," I tell him.

"I think my mom and sister will be happy to hear I have a girlfriend."

"I think my mom and grandmother will start planning a wedding," I reply with amusement.

He doesn't respond to the craziness that's likely to be true, but I don't think he cares as he kisses me again.

"Will you sleep over?" he asks.

"I suppose I could do that."

"I figured since you're already in your pajamas..."

"I'm naked," I tell him.

"I know." He wraps himself around me, embracing my body with his. "I like this."

Now settled down without intention of moving, he grabs the

remote and turns the TV on, which immediately brings up the comedy channel. I would have to watch comedy before bed too if I saw what he sees every day.

I fall asleep in the crook of his arm and chest, inhaling the fresh soap scent on his skin as if it were aromatherapy.

Without knowing what time it is, based on the darkness outside his window, I'm startled when Jackson's phone rings on the nightstand. It shouldn't come as a surprise since he's a doctor, and I'm sure he's on call at times, but my heart pounds with curiosity and a nervousness I shouldn't feel from assumptions.

I look around for a clock, but the only one is across the room on his cable box, and it's blurry from all the way over here. "Beck," he answers.

He rubs his hand over his eyes, pressing his thumb against his temple. Jackson looks over to his side, and I look too, finding an alarm clock showing that it's two in the morning. "Yes, stabilize her, and I'll be there in twenty." He looks over at me with an expression I can't read, but it makes me more nervous. "No, she does not have a DNR on record, so continue efforts."

The moment Jackson disconnects his call, he's out of bed, grabbing his boxer briefs and slipping into his bathroom for a quick second. "Take a deep breath," he tells me as he returns.

"I can't. It's my grandmother, isn't it?"

"You're coming with me, but I need you to breathe because I haven't heard you take a breath in at least thirty-seconds."

"What is it, Jackson?" There's panic among my breaths, but the panic is louder than the minimal air escaping my lungs.

"She wanted to go for an unassisted walk and fell. It sounds like she may have dislodged the pacemaker, but I won't know for sure until I get there."

"Is she alive?" I cry out.

"They're keeping her alive."

Jackson is dressed in a clean pair of scrubs within a minute, and I'm still sitting in his bed, wrapped in a sheet. Since I'm in shock and haven't found a way to move, he helps me dress. "Come on," he says.

I'm shaking so hard, I'm having trouble standing, but Jackson takes my hand tightly within his, holding me up with his other hand as we make it to the front door. He leaves me to lean against the wall for a moment as he grabs my bag, diary, and his bag, then returns to my side, helping me out as if I'm completely broken.

"Jackson." I keep sputtering his name with nothing to follow. He doesn't have answers, but I want them. "I need her to be okay. I'm not ready to say goodbye."

"I know, Emma," he says as the elevator closes us inside. With the bags draped over his shoulders, he faces me and smooths my hair out, pulling it together behind my shoulders. His knuckles then tend to my falling tears and his hands cup around my cheeks, forcing me to look up at him through the blurriness. "I will do whatever I can for her."

"I know," I mumble through a weak moan.

The doors to the elevator open, and I hardly feel my feet touch the ground as Jackson guides me over to the passenger door of his car. "I thought the pacemaker was put in to regulate her arrhythmia if it happened. How could it cause her heart to stop if it's not working?"

"I don't want to give you any answers until I have them. He leans in quickly and places a kiss on my cheek before closing the door."

We drive much faster through the city than I've ever driven before, and we whip into the parking lot with available spaces up front. I jump out of the car as fast as he does, even though I know I'll be stopped at some point since I won't be allowed in there again. More waiting than I can stand. *I have to call Mom too.*

The elevator brings us to the ICU floor, and Jackson stops briefly, gazing at me with pain encircling his eyes. "I'm so sorry, but I can't let you in there. It's protocol." He hands me my bag and opens the door to the waiting room.

I nod through my quivering chin and walk into the empty space I've become all too familiar with this week.

After placing my bag down, I pull out my phone and dial mom's number.

She's groggy and sounds confused when she answers the phone. "Mom," I say softly, trying not to startle her more than I probably already have. "Grams fell, and I need you to come down to the hospital."

"What?" she shouts. "Why didn't they call me? Did they call me? Did I miss a call? When did this happen? Emma, is she okay?"

"I don't know, Mom. I just need you to get down here, okay? Please drive carefully...please."

She hangs up the phone without a goodbye, and I know she'll be driving like a maniac down the highway. I'll be worried sick until she gets here—I don't want anything to happen to her.

My mind is spinning, and I can't think of any way to calm myself down other than pacing the room a hundred times before my knees start to ache. I know Jackson will tell me something as soon as he knows, but I'm not sure how long it will be before that happens.

I finally drop down into one of the chairs. My foot catches on the handle of my bag, and it falls over, spilling Grams's diary out onto the floor. As I lean down to pick it up, I contemplate whether I can stand to read it right at the moment. Her story doesn't make me feel better, it only reminds me of how much she has survived though, and how ridiculous it would be for her to die from her heart of steel after everything she has experienced.

Will she escape death a second time? I curl into my seat, holding onto hope as I impulsively reopen the diary.

CHAPTER NINETEEN

AMELIA

MAY 1943 - DAY 521

I had been shaking since I woke up that morning. Unable to focus on my job, I was merely asking the first question on my list to each patient in line, all of whom were seemingly melting in April's abnormal heat. The elderly were dropping to the ground quicker than normal, resulting in at least fifty bodies needing to be dragged away by their feet. There was no sympathy or sense of emotion when it came to the Nazis. The Jews were no more than rodents in their mind's eye. Charlie was the exception, but he left me wondering if there were any other exceptions. It was hard to see who was truly hateful in their soul because those soldiers were forced to be the way they were. I believe there were just as many who did not want to be there as the ones who truly hated us.

Nevertheless, I knew better than to test my luck with any one of them, which is why I had done nothing except the job I was assigned to do more than a year earlier. I will forever wonder why I was on the list for transition—why they would want to kill a healthy, hard worker. I guess my luck, if you would call it that, ran out.

Lice were becoming a pandemic in the camp, and they had begun shaving every person from head to toe. I could only assume the little parasites hadn't hit our barrack yet because as of that time, no one had come down with symptoms. Whenever possible, I kept my distance when lice-infected people was near, knowing that the bugs could easily travel from one body to another, but I never had any real protection to wear. Typhus was also quickly spreading through the camp, causing more and more prisoners to perish while waiting for medical treatment, because there *was* no medical treatment available, or at least there wasn't any available to us. It had become easier and easier to spot those who were infected—the little red bumps, the high fevers, vomiting, and some literally dropping dead.

The lines were on the shorter end that day, and I feared what Charlie had mentioned the night before. They must have been transporting large herds of Jews to the death camp.

I promised myself I would not become scared of whatever the outcome would be that night, but I couldn't help wondering what it would feel like to have a gun pointed at my head, or worse, have a rope tied around my neck as I hung from the post on the execution field. I had seen too many of us hanged, and I concluded that being shot would be a blessing in comparison. It took up to five minutes for some to die from strangulation, and I couldn't imagine what those final moments would be like, what thoughts I would have while thrashing and kicking as my neck slowly and painfully broke. I had nightmares about it, and had woken up in a sweat, clutching my neck with fear of finding the rope.

The thought of being gassed sounded easier than the other two options, and if I had to choose a way of death, I would go with fast and painless, but none of us had the privilege of choosing how we preferred to go. There were no rules. It was whatever the Nazis decided it would be.

After the sun had completely set and I headed back to my barrack for distribution of the daily ration, I passed by Charlie, who was standing guard outside my block. He eyeballed me as I headed inside, but I didn't make it too far before I was grabbed from behind and dragged away. The bullish way in which I had to be handled was never okay. It hurt me, not physically, but emotionally. Knowing others were being dealt with in the same fashion, but with hate and malice, scared and saddened me.

There was a sense of urgency, and Charlie's fist shook against the back of my shoulder as he continued to pull me along. I knew better than to ask questions, so I kept quiet until we reached a building I hadn't been invited or dragged into before. I went where I was told unless Charlie brought me there.

We took a set of stairs that led underground, and Charlie lit up the area with his dull flashlight as we came upon dozens of crated items. I couldn't quite make out what was inside the crates, but as I moved in closer, I found they were filled and sorted into categories of various items such as glasses, hair, false teeth, gold teeth, jewelry, shoes, and clothes.

"What is all of this?" I asked.

"Not now," Charlie responded with haste. He sounded angry, or maybe he was just nervous like I was. He was usually quite composed, but not that night.

"No, I want to know what this is." I knew what it was, but I needed to hear it out loud.

"Belongings of the deceased," he snapped through quick breaths.

"Pardon me? They're keeping them here and organizing them into crates?"

"Yes, Amelia." His answer had a finality to it, and I took the suggestive tone as a hint to stop asking questions. I had never been afraid to test my limits with Charlie before, but with both our lives at stake, it was different.

"A potato sack?" I asked, watching as he took two and threw them over his shoulder.

"Yes," he said without offering any further indication of why they were needed. A year prior to that day, I would have been afraid. I may not have been able to ignore the feeling of distrust, but I had to believe Charlie knew what he was doing. "I need you to stay here while I find a way to get Lucie."

"How?" I asked him, but I should have truly stopped with the questions.

"Amelia, please trust me. I will be back within ten minutes."

I could no longer hide the fear on my face. How could I? I had little to no information on how it was going to work, and I assumed we would not be taking the route the other Jews had taken when trying to escape. It was clear that Charlie had other plans.

"Okay," I said in no more than a whisper.

He walked toward me with his flashlight pointed at the walls in the back of the room, offering enough glow for us to see each other in the unlit, damp room that smelled of human remains—a scent I had sadly become accustomed to. However, the moisture added another degree of putrid odor that couldn't be blocked out, even when only breathing through my mouth.

"Hurry back, please," I begged. I wasn't scared of the dark like I once was, but I had an uneasy feeling down there.

Charlie kissed me gently and briefly caressed my cheek before storming back up the stairs without the potato sacks, which he left in a small pile at the base of the steps.

Ten minutes felt like an eternity in the enclosed obscurity while I imagined the souls that may have been floating above the surrounding crates. I figured they were likely furious and wanted their belongings back. Mama had always told me ghosts were just a figment of our imagination, and while I would agree with her for the sake of agreeing, I didn't exactly take her stance. I believe in ghosts, and that belief helped me through my time there as I envisioned an angry and hostile army of Jewish spirits who had a vengeance for their murders.

It also helped to think Mama and Papa were watching over me, keeping me alive by a miracle that could only be explained by the powers above. Those thoughts contradicted why I asked God for a reason as to why I was being punished so brutally. However, I still believed there was a purpose for everything, and if it was some horrible lesson I was supposed to learn in my life, I hoped I would at least come out on the other side with some wisdom on how to survive in a world filled with so much hate. I would look forward to sharing the information with my family, who would be waiting for me at the gates of heaven.

Mama may not have believed in ghosts, but she did tell me that no matter what happened in our world, if she left earth before Jakob or I did, she would be right there waiting for us in heaven. The faith I had that she was right made the thought of dying more acceptable. I wondered if she had a premonition about what happened to us all, and if that's why she said what she did, but I may never know.

The door above opened and closed, and I took steps backward until I hit a crate, wanting to hide in a corner in case it wasn't Charlie, but as a flashlight's glow made an appearance toward the ceiling, I quickly found Charlie's concerned grimace below the light. He was holding Lucie snuggly in his arm, and I wondered how he could take her without question, but I knew those questions would not be answered until later—if there was a later.

I took Lucie out of Charlie's grip, and she clung to me as she did any time I snuck in to see her. Lucie was sick a lot over the last few months. The nurses mentioned it was because she had not been breastfed, but Mama said she was unable to do so with me, and I was just fine. I couldn't understand how they could blame breast milk for illnesses when Lucie had been surrounded by bacteria and deadly germs from the day she was born. It's a wonder she had been as healthy as she was.

I also wondered why they chose to keep Lucie alive without Leah. Leah could have cared for her, rather than utilizing a German nurse's time. It was hate. That's the only reason to separate a newborn from her mother.

"We're going to be okay, Lucie," I cooed while bouncing her around in my arms. She squeezed her hands around my neck and buried her face in my chest.

"She's scared," I told Charlie.

"As she should be," he replied through a frustrated huff. "Amelia, we aren't safe yet."

"I know we're not safe, Charlie. I'm trying to be brave though, and you're making it very difficult for me." It was the first time I had been that angry with Charlie. I knew he was acting out of fear, but it was only making things harder. What if those had been our last moments together? We had to consider that possibility, but it didn't seem as though Charlie was willing to, which made me believe we would be okay. It was all outlandish, but the only other option was death. Either way, I would try to survive.

"Put Lucie into this bag," Charlie said, handing me one of the sacks.

"Inside?" I questioned.

"Yes, put her inside."

"Will she be able to breathe in there?" I asked him, figuring he probably tested it out.

"I will make sure there is airflow," he said with a furrow between his brows, making it known he had already considered the thought.

I took the bag from Charlie's hand and carefully slid Lucie inside. "It's okay, baby girl, we're going to go get some good food and find shelter where we can be together."

"Amelia," Charlie snapped. "Please."

"Why are you being like this?" I asked him, feeling the animosity wrench through me.

"I'm scared to death, Amelia. I have your life, and Lucie's to care for right now, and I would never forgive myself if I were the cause of something happening to either of you. Do you understand?"

"And what about yourself?" I argued in return.

"I don't care about myself, Amelia. I could be here or be gone, and it wouldn't matter in a week." *Because I would be gone too.* "But if something happens to you when I could have prevented it, I will have to live with that. I will have to live without you."

Without another word, I take the other sack from Charlie's hand. "Am I going in here?"

"Please," he muttered.

The bag had sharp, wispy threads that scratched my skin as I slipped it up around me and cowered into a ball. "If you swing Lucie a bit, she'll likely fall asleep," I told Charlie. I had spent hours watching the nurse care for her after Leah was killed. The only way to urge Lucie to sleep was by gently swinging her from side to side.

"Okay," Charlie replied.

I was cloaked entirely by the bag and lifted off the ground, accompanied by the sound of a grunt. Granted, between Lucie and I, we probably weighed less than a hundred pounds, but carrying bodies was no easy feat for even a strong man with two arms, never mind a man with a missing arm. Personally, I had tried many times to assist in dragging bodies out of the medical line so others could pass by, but I never made it more than a couple of inches with them.

The feeling of swinging in midair was unnatural and unsettling. It was hard to breathe and very hot and humid inside. The scent of old potatoes, along with the unsteady motion, did not agree with my stomach, but I tried my best to focus on something else, knowing I didn't have the option of vomiting.

The walk seemed to carry on for miles, even though it was probably less than five minutes before the slightly muted sounds of Charlie's voice filtered in through the bag. "Where are you going so late at night?" another voice asked.

"I need to get a head start for my doctor's appointment. It's first thing in the morning," Charlie said, his voice deepening to depict a more serious tone with the other soldier.

"Oh, you're the soldier who had his arm amputated," the soldier said.

"That's correct."

"And, what's in the bags?"

Charlie did nothing to make friends there, and it seemed they felt the same about him until he arrived back as a war hero with a missing limb. I wasn't sure what was so fascinating about losing an arm during the war, but they appeared enamored with his heroic ability to survive. It shouldn't have surprised me. Casualties and murder were obviously intriguing to most of them.

"I was asked to bring leftover clothing to the hospital for some recovering soldiers who have nothing to leave with."

"Ah, yes," the other soldier said. "Did you take some shoes, as well?"

"Of course." Charlie's voice was starting to sound garbled, and the bag was shaking haphazardly, making a show of his nerves that hopefully only Lucie and I noticed. My body was beginning to ache and tremble too, fearful of Lucie making a sound or crying, but by another instance of luck, I heard the metal gate open. It was truly the most beautiful sound I had ever heard. The squealing metal and whining of hinges tickled my ears the same way an orchestrated arrangement would.

"We'll see you back here tomorrow, soldier. Is there transportation arranged for you?"

"Yes, it has all been arranged outside of the headquarters. Thank you, sir." *Sir*. I assumed he must have been a higher-ranking soldier than Charlie. However, I felt it was odd to have a higher rank on guard at that time of night.

Footsteps continued, and we all remained silent for quite a

while. I was scared to say anything without being able to take in the surroundings, but I heard Charlie's footsteps thump along the stone, which told me we were on a road of some sort. I knew he would place us down the moment he could, but I wasn't familiar with the outside area, and therefore, wasn't sure where or how far away safety would be.

I was finally rested down gently onto a hard surface, but I heard Charlie mumble, "Don't move." I stayed as still as possible, hoping Lucie was doing the same.

The sound of a car door opening made my pulse quicken. I wondered if we were getting inside of a car with a driver or if Charlie would be the one driving. I didn't think it could be so easy. After all that time, we seamlessly walked through the secured gates toward our escape. There was only one problem I hadn't considered...if Charlie didn't return, it would only be a matter of time before they'd be after him.

I was lifted back up and placed on top of a soft surface. I still didn't move, but after the soft click of a door closing, followed by a second door opening and closing, my hope was becoming a reality. The engine roared to life, and we began to move. "Amelia," Charlie called out eagerly, "you can pull the bag down." Though I was still stricken with fear, I did as he said, finding myself in the backseat next to the other potato sack filled with Lucie. I helped her out of hers as well, finding she was asleep, as I had assumed.

"Charlie, you did it!" I told him, quietly but excitedly, grabbing the back of his seat. "Whose car is this?"

"It doesn't matter," he said.

"Where do we go now?" I asked while rocking Lucie within my arms.

"We need to get out of this country, Amelia. We're not safe."

"For now, at this moment, we are," I told him. I wrapped my arm around his neck from behind and kissed his cheek. He didn't respond; instead, he peered into the rearview mirror with an empty look taken up the vicinity of wide eyes.

"Is something else wrong?" I asked.

"I don't know if anyone saw me steal this car," he said.

"How did you get it started?" I knew we wouldn't have any mode of transportation, so I wasn't surprised by the situation, but by the looks of the dark interior finish and unfamiliar gadgets on the dashboard, the vehicle was incredibly lavish.

"My father and I used to work on cars together. He was a mechanic at a gas station. I hot-wired it." With a thickness in my throat, I swallowed hard as I concluded that we were not only escaping but committing other serious crimes as well. Not that we had much choice, but I was the girl who never missed a class in school, who always met my curfew five minutes early. Crime was never in my future, but there I was, committing several of them at once.

Within minutes after we had taken off from wherever the car was parked, the sound of a handheld, crank-siren echoed in the distance. "Charlie, is that because of us?"

"I don't know," he said in a choked grunt.

I held Lucie a little tighter as the eerie sound grew louder. "Pull down a side street," I told him. It was hardly worth mentioning, as he had already pulled down several side streets, but talking when I was nervous made me feel as though I was helping. "What should we do?"

"We're going to have to run," he said.

"Run to where?"

"I don't know, Amelia." Charlie was visibly upset, as was I. However, he was the one with the plan, and I was clueless as to how we would escape the trouble that may be coming closer to us.

"When I tell you to get out, you need to run like mad. Do you understand?"

"Of course," I told him, knowing I was unable to run as fast as I used to. I was beyond the stage of malnutrition and had little muscle left in my body. My lungs constantly felt as though they would collapse after walking from one block to the other, never mind running an unknown distance to safety.

It sounded as if the siren had died down for the moment, but if it was us they were looking for, I was sure they wouldn't give up their search too easily. "I need you to see if there's a map under the seat," Charlie said.

I leaned down and reached under the seats, finding an attaché case. It was a bit of a struggle to pull out, but once freed, I was pleased to find there were no locks on the clasps. I pulled the case open and found a stack of papers and a folded map. "There is one," I said. "A map."

If Charlie was unsure of our direction, I was not going to be of much help without familiarizing myself with our location. I unfolded the map, searching for Theresienstadt. Thankfully, I found it quickly, though it was hard to see much with only the smattering of gas lamps we were passing by. "Where are we going?" I asked.

"Zurich," he said.

"Charlie, that will take us almost a full day of driving if we don't stop, and we're in a stolen car," I reminded him.

"I know, Amelia, but what other choice do we have?"

"We need to find a different car," I told him.

"I agree. I'm just not fond of theft," he said.

"You won't be fond of prison or execution either," I argued.

Charlie continued peering into the mirror with a frightened look in his eyes as we continued heading away from the more populated area.

After we had driven for hours, the tank of gas was nearing empty, and it was hard to tell how far away from the Austrian border we were. "We're going to have to start walking," Charlie said.

"We should drive until the car runs out of gas," I told him.

"I just don't want to get too close to the border with this car."

I peered down at Lucie, who was still sound asleep, and began to imagine how hard things were about to become. It wasn't long before an increased frequency of cars started to pass by us, and we knew that was our cue to get rid of the evidence, never mind running out of gas. Charlie pulled off into a field of tall grass that nearly covered the car, though I suspected it would still be obvious in the daylight. However, I had hoped we would be long gone by then.

With Lucie cradled in my arms, I shimmied out of the back door and into the tangled grass. Charlie's hand looped gently around mine as he helped us climb up to the main road, where a pair of headlights unexpectedly caught us as we crossed the road. Without a word exchanged, we began to run, heading into the dense woods.

We hadn't gotten far when a man began to shout in the distance. "Hey! You, there!"

Charlie grabbed me and pulled us along faster as we moved further into the woods. We ran until we couldn't run any further. My legs collapsed, and Charlie tried to lift me back up, but I couldn't stand any longer, especially while carrying Lucie.

There was no path within the woods, and I had hope that with the darkness covering our trails, it would be difficult for anyone to find us. The possibility of the passing car being a Nazi who may have been aware of our escape wasn't as likely as we imagined it to be, but we couldn't take any chances.

"Hey!" a voice shouted again.

"Dammit," Charlie whispered. "He's after us." Charlie dragged us toward a wide tree, pinning our backs to it as he towered over us. "Don't say a word." I knew not to speak.

Lucie didn't understand, though, and a soft cry escaped her lips. It was the first noise I had heard from her since we left the camp. "Shh," I tried to soothe her. "Hush now."

I bounced her gently on my lap, and Charlie combed his fingers softly through her fine hair. "Shh," he repeated after me. "It's okay, baby girl. We're going to take good care of you. I promise."

"Where did you go now?" the voice sounded again, but with so many trees for the sound to bounce off of, it was hard to pinpoint a source of direction.

Lucie's cries grew louder as she reached for my neck. She must be hungry or have a wet bottom, so I carefully cupped my hand around her mouth, avoiding her nose. "Shhh, shhh." Our efforts were relentless.

"You're a soldier," the man said. "And you have a prisoner. Is that a stolen car you got there, too?"

I looked into Charlie's eyes, and he looked into mine. I don't know if we were thinking the same thought, but one thing was certain...the man didn't want to give up, and daylight would be coming soon.

CHAPTER TWENTY

EMMA

*A*s I finish the last word, my heartache continues to grow for Grams, both for what she endured back then and for what she is going through right now. At least I know she somehow survived that ordeal all those years ago, and I'm eager to find out how.

I hear feet storming through the hallway amid breathless gasps, and I can only imagine the sounds belong to Mom. The running stops—probably when they direct her to this cave they refer to as a waiting room.

Just as I predicted, the door opens, and I slip the diary back into my bag to avoid questions since Grams asked me to keep this to myself, which I'm starting to understand why.

Mom falls into me without a word, and her body trembles as she bursts into tears. "I'm not sure how much more I can take," she says.

"We're going to make it through this," I tell her, trying to sound as positive as I can. "Grams doesn't give up." I know this now.

"How did you get here so fast? Where were you when you got the news? Please tell me you weren't at Mike's house."

I take in a slow, deep breath, needing a moment to switch gears from death and morbidity to explaining how I've suddenly fallen into a committed relationship with my grandmother's doctor over the past two days. "I was with Jackson," I tell her.

Of course, her face registers a look of surprise as she glances down at her watch to confirm the time. Since she was, in fact, woken from a dead sleep in the middle of the night, and I was with Jackson when that happened, it only takes a moment for her to put two and two together.

"Are you two—" She puts her hands together and tries to smile, but her lips quiver instead. There's no hiding how scared she is—I understand. "At least something good is happening now with all this other horrible stuff going on with Grams," Mom says, trying to sound upbeat. She looks away for a second and then back at me, her eyes burning with curiosity. "Were you..." she stops short of finishing the question and says, "Never mind, it's not my place." There isn't much Mom won't ask me, but for some reason, she is respecting my privacy tonight. She already has too much on her mind while worrying about Grams, so I assume that's why.

Mom repositions herself in the seat beside me and places her hands over her heart. "Where were the nurses when she got up?"

"I don't know, Mom."

"Someone should have been with her."

"I don't know how that works," I tell her.

"Well, I'll have a word with whoever is in charge."

That's not what I would be doing now. "We want them to help us with Grams. You can't start threatening and scolding them. Have you talked to Annie?"

"She should be here any moment." Mom picks up her phone, checking for missed calls or text messages, but her phone is always on the loudest volume, so I don't see how it would be possible to miss anything. "How long before we'll hear something?" she asks.

"I really don't know any more than you do," I tell her.

Annie quietly makes her way into the room. Her rosy cheeks are stained with tears, and her makeup-less face gives the appearance that she's closer to her actual age than she typically looks. "How did you hear about her first?" Annie asks immediately.

"Oh, she just happened to be at the hospital checking in on Mom when it occurred," Mom says to Annie.

For the fact that Annie doesn't question the time of night I was apparently checking on Grams, I'll assume she's as exhausted as Mom.

I am impressed that Mom isn't pressing the matter. She likes to find distractions when she's upset, so this is big. Maybe she doesn't want to jinx it. I'm sure under normal circumstances, she wouldn't be able to contain herself, and the information she thinks she has would have been blurted out to Annie by now. Mom and Annie are like two peas in a pod. Annie never had children, so I have been her sole focus just as I have been Mom's. Three women, including Grams, have simultaneously lived vicariously through my life since I was old enough to be considered a prime age for love, and all the other exciting stuff that young women are supposed to experience. They all think I should be focused on marriage, having children, and keeping the perfect home. Yet, here I am, the ultimate disappointment who has preferred her career over everything else, including a normal relationship with a man. Jackson may be a game changer, but I still don't see a reason to rush my life away.

With the thought of Jackson lingering through my overstressed mind, the door opens, revealing his scrub-clad body and a look of exhaustion. We all stand up, waiting for his life-or-death answer to our burning question.

"I was able to revive her. My assumptions about the pacemaker dislodging when she fell forward were accurate. It didn't cause her harm, but it wasn't doing what it was supposed to. Her blood pressure elevated from the fall and her heart was racing at a fast pace, so the arrhythmia caught up to her, which caused her heart to panic after losing a sense of direction."

"Is she going to be okay?" I blurt out.

"Before we re-attached the pacemaker, we did some more in-depth scans of her heart. During a CT scan and an angiogram, we noticed that her aortic valve is very narrow. Even though the stroke *was* caused by the atrial fibrillation, we now know that she is also dealing with a restricted and narrowed valve. The narrowing means that it's harder for the blood to get through the valve. This may have been a contributing factor to her falling tonight, too. I believe she may have blacked out when she stood up due to a lack of blood supply getting through the valve and to the brain." The information rolling off Jackson's tongue is jumbling in my head—it's a lot to take in. I know there is a reason for all the information, and I'm scared of the outcome. "The bright side of the story is, we spotted the narrowed valve because of the accident. It would have been spotted eventually, but with every-thing that has happened to her in the past few days, the most important thing was to stabilize her and then see what else was going on—but now we know."

"What does all of this mean?" Mom pleads. The medical jargon is confusing, and I'm trying to understand it all too, but I can assume it all means that there's a bigger problem with Grams's heart, and it isn't being fixed by the pacemaker.

"It could mean more surgery—an aortic valve replacement, to be exact," he says.

"Is it risky?" Annie asks as she trembles while holding onto Mom's arm.

Jackson takes a seat across from us and folds his hands over his knees as he leans forward. This is his way of talking to us calmly to explain why there isn't a good outcome to this. I can feel it. I can see it in his eyes. "It is, and I have to tell you my profes-sional opinion: I don't recommend it at her age or in her condition. If she were ten years younger, I would say to go for it, but she is already weak and frail. I just feel it may be too risky."

"But I thought the pacemaker would fix her heart?" Mom asks. She must know the answer couldn't be so simple, but I'm also sure she's in shock, as it appears Annie is too.

"It fixed part of the problem," Jackson continues. "Her heart will continue to beat at a normal pace; however, the narrowing of that valve causes oxygen deprivation, which could eventually lead to a heart attack. Now, I'm not saying it will, but it *could*."

"Eventually?" I ask.

"Ninety-two years old is quite a feat," he says, redirecting his attention onto me while revealing a look of grief in his eyes.

"It's not enough time," I tell him.

"She can either live out her life at home, or we can find a special care facility for her, but after the short time I've known Amelia, I'm assuming the first option would be best."

"How long does she have, Jackson?" I ask.

Jackson pauses a moment. His Adam's apple slides up and down his throat, and his chest rises as if it's taking a lot of will to muster the answer. "It's hard to say. She could have two more years, or something could happen tomorrow. I don't know how long it took her aortic valve to reach the state it's in, so I don't know how fast the narrowing is progressing. If it's slow, then that will be good for her." He pauses again, needing to take another breath. I've made this harder on him. There's more at stake than just an everyday patient now. I can see it and hear it through his struggling words. He doesn't want to hurt me. "I guess what I'm saying is...just relish the time and help her enjoy life for as long as you can. That's really what everybody should do, anyway. We'll keep her on the heart meds and blood thinners, and that, along with the pacemaker, should prevent her from having another stroke."

Mom and Annie wrap their arms around me, both falling apart

as they squeeze tightly. I feel helpless as I stare into Jackson's caring eyes as he mouths the words, "I'm so sorry."

"When can we see her?" Mom cries out.

"She's resting comfortably right now, so I suggest coming back first thing in the morning."

They both nod as tears roll down their cheeks at the same time. I've never been as emotional as the two of them, but something inside of me is feeding my strength. I know I need to be strong for them. I'm all they have.

Mom and Annie nudge me forward. "Come on," Mom says, "let's get home so we can get a little sleep."

"I think I'm going to stay here," I tell her.

"Emma, don't be ridiculous. You need some sleep, and we both know you won't be getting any rest in these chairs."

"Mom, I'm fine, okay?"

"Okay. Well, call me if there is any change," she says, placing a kiss on my forehead. "Please don't wait. I don't care what time it is."

"I promise," I tell her.

"I'm going to stay with you tonight," Annie tells Mom on the way out.

Jackson and I are left alone in the waiting room, and he pulls me up from my seat and onto his lap, offering me the kind of hug I've desperately needed for the past couple of hours. "Are your mom and aunt going to be okay tonight?"

I sniffle and peer up at Jackson through a blur of contained tears. "Yeah," I croak. "Annie stays with my mom a lot anyway because my Uncle Aaron goes on frequent fishing trips with a bunch of his retired-police friends. Plus, Mom and Annie take care of each other when I'm not around too, which is nice."

"Good," Jackson says. "What about you?"

I force my lips into a fake smile and shake my head. "No, I'm not okay."

"I would do the surgery, but I don't think she's strong enough

228

to make it through an open-heart procedure, and she isn't a candidate for the other methods at this time."

"I'm sure she would agree. I don't see her wanting to go for any further surgeries."

"She has certainly suffered enough for one lifetime," Jackson says.

As he pulls away just a bit to lean back into the chair, I replace his embrace with my arms, wrapping them around my chest to hold myself from the shiver running through my body. "She's also had an amazing life too," I feel the need to say.

"With you being a part of it, anyone's life would be incredible." I rest the side of my face into his chest, feeling safer and comforted by his warmth.

"I need to find him before it's too late," I say. Though the words are quiet and under my breath, I'm sure of my statement.

"Find him?" Jackson questions.

"I need to find Charlie, or at least see if he's still alive. I need to do it for her. I'm not ready to let go of her yet, either, especially after learning everything from her diary. I feel like I just met her for the first time."

Jackson places his hands on my shoulders and glances down at me with determination written across his face. "I have Friday off. I can help you if you want," he says. "For now, though, come with me." I don't even know what day of the week it is right now. I want to start looking for Charlie this very second, but I can hardly see straight.

Jackson takes my hand, leading me out of the waiting room and down the hall to where he pushes open a door that leads into a stairwell. "Where are we going?"

"We need sleep," he says.

I agree with him there, but *where* we are going to sleep is what I'm wondering. We hike up a couple flights of stairs that lead to a different wing of the hospital. This place keeps getting bigger and bigger, I swear. Jackson swipes his badge along one of the security boxes and opens the door into a lobby-like area. "Where are we?"

"When we have double shifts that overlap at night, we take naps. Sometimes I just sleep here when my shift runs longer than it should, and I have to be back early in the morning." The lobby area leads down a hall with several doors. Some are open and some are closed. I assume the closed ones are occupied, as we walk into one of the open ones. It looks like a small hotel room inside. "It's nice that you have a place to stay here."

"We're lucky to have a space like this. Most hospitals don't offer such high-class quarters," he says with a tired smile.

I don't think twice before dropping my bag against the wall, kicking my shoes off, and climbing into the inviting bed. He follows, but removes his shirt before pulling the sheets over us. Jackson wraps his heavy arm around me, and the comfort of being held by him soothes my worries into the back of my mind, even if only temporarily.

Jackson had to be up at six, and without the comfort of his body taking up the space beside me, I wasn't hard to rouse. He told me I could stay here for a while longer and sleep, but I thought it might be awkward if I walked out of here alone and ran into any of the other medical staff, so I decide to head back down to the despised waiting room.

I'm ready to begin my research on Charlie, but I'm also nervous for what I might find. Would this complicate Grams's life or give her the sense of peace she may have been looking for half of her life?

I pull my laptop and the diary out of my bag because I still can't remember if Charlie's last name was mentioned, so I'll have to start there.

After skimming through the first few entries I read, I come

across the name Charlie Crane. I can only imagine how many Charlie Cranes there are in the world.

I open my browser and type in his name, followed by *World War II soldier*. My throat tightens as the swirling icon spins over a blank page.

I'm not surprised when several pages of articles pop up, but nothing with Charlie's name in the headline. I delete the *World War II soldier* part and just search broadly for his name, but I'm greeted with even more pages of Charlie Cranes. I need to know what country he's living in, or lived in, for that matter.

Out of frustration from not knowing where to start, I search for Grams's name to see what information comes up about her. There's very little, but her name is on a list of survivors documented at Ellis Island in 1944, which means there is still a year between the time she escaped and when she made it to the United States. I have no idea what happened during that time.

A blur of blue scrubs moves past the window, stealing my attention away from the screen. The door then opens, and Jackson pops his head inside. How does he look so good after getting so little sleep? I probably look like a zombie right now. "She's awake if you want to go on down there," he tells me.

I hop up from my seat, slapping my laptop shut and tossing it into my bag, along with the diary. "Is she groggy?"

"Not really," he says. "I want to warn you that her face is pretty bruised up, though. I don't want you to be surprised when you see her."

"Did she need stitches or anything?" I ask.

He shakes his head and presses a slight smile to one corner of his lips. "No. Luckily, they're just superficial bruises."

"At least that's one good thing," I sigh.

"Hey," he says, walking into the waiting room. He pulls me in for a hug and runs his hand over the back of my head. "She's alive, and that's a good thing." He's completely right. How quickly I've forgotten about my distress from last night is proof that exhaustion is starting to get the best of me, as well.

"You're right," I agree.

He takes my free hand and pulls it up to his lips, kissing my knuckles gently. "It's going to be okay."

Jackson stands back up and guides me over to the door, holding it open for me to walk through. "I'll be down there in just a few," he says. "I have another patient to check on first."

I make my way through the hall to Grams's room, anxiously stepping inside as I try my best not to wince at the blue and purple splotches covering her face. This kills me. Weeks ago, she was still walking every day, managing her life just fine, and now, out of nowhere, or so it seems, she could be slowly dying. I can't help but wonder if she was ignoring symptoms, or just failing to mention them to us. She's done it before because *"she doesn't need help,"* as she likes to remind us.

"Good morning, Grams," I say, upping the level of perkiness I tend to use.

"Oh, Emma," she says, sounding annoyed. "I don't know what I was thinking."

I pull up a chair and sit beside her. "You were thinking you've had enough of this bed along with all the help you need and wanted to take a midnight stroll to see if this hospital has a bar downstairs. Am I right?"

A choked laugh catches in her throat. "Oh, my girl sure does know me." A world without her won't be okay. She's like a second mother to me. This woman hasn't missed one important moment in my life, and she sat beside Mom as she raised me, always having a thing or two to say about the matter. I couldn't have asked for a better family than the one I have.

"Are you in a lot of pain?" I place my hand carefully on hers, scared to do anything that could hurt her more.

"Eh, I've fallen before. I mean, falling face first on this floor wasn't the highlight of my life, but what are you going to do?"

"Never a dull moment with you, Grams," I tell her.

"So, I hear I'm dying," she says with an exasperated sigh.

Recoiling from her words and the shock that she already knows too much, my mouth falls agape. I have no idea what to say, besides, "Don't think that way. You could still have years left. You just have to be careful and follow the doctor's orders." It's so hard to swallow my words because I feel like I'm not telling her the whole story.

"I knew it was coming," she says.

"What? How?"

"If you search online for shortness of breath, tightness, and pain in the chest, plus fatigue, it gives you the answer right there. The only solution is surgery, and it's too risky at my age. I figured I had a few good months left in me." Wow, I guess when you've lived ninety-two years, through just about everything, you don't need someone to tell you anything.

"Grams, you should have been a doctor," I tell her.

"With the amount of knowledge I gained while working at the sick bay, I probably could have been, but I wanted nothing to do with the medical field once I was free. I had seen enough scars to last me the rest of my life."

I brush her hair off her forehead, careful to avoid any of the bruises. "Grams, where did Charlie live? I mean, the last time you heard from him." I'm determined to find this man now.

"The last time I heard from him?" she asks through more struggling laughter. "Oh, Emma, it's been seventy-four years since I heard from him last."

"You—he, I don't understand."

"Honey, I don't know if he's dead or not. I want to think he's not because I've now been revived twice, and he hasn't been there along with the others who are waiting for me. I know it sounds ridiculous, but in my heart, I feel like Charlie is still alive somewhere."

"In the United States or another country?"

"I have no idea, Emma. Anything could have happened since I saw him last."

"Well, what happened?"

Grams stares at me with angelic eyes, as if she were gazing right through me. Her head gently shakes from side to side before she begins to speak. "I can't," she says. "If you want to know, you will have to read it for yourself." I want to tell her that talking about things sometimes helps, but I will never be able to understand what she's gone through. "Anyway." She nestles her head into her pillow and shrugs her shoulders a bit. "How is Jackson?"

"Grams, he's fine," I say shortly, hoping to change the subject back to Charlie. We're not doing "that" now.

"He said he would be back in just a few minutes, but I have a strange suspicion you already knew that." Even with the bruises lining her swollen cheeks, she can still wink at me.

"Grams," I say again.

"Oh, Emma, my goodness, I was your age once. I know what young people do."

How do I belong to this family? I'm going to turn into her someday and embarrass my children without a care in the world. "That's great," I tell her.

"So, do you think you could grow to love him?" How can I look at her like this and get irritated? She knows that, and she's using it against me.

"We only started seeing each other a few days ago," I remind her.

"Love will grow, sweet girl. Just give it time and be good to each other."

I'm beyond thankful that Jackson walks in when he does, interrupting this uncomfortable discussion of my personal life. I do need to figure this out for myself. It's new and exciting, but I don't want to get hurt again, either. Yet, I *was* sort of quick to ask this man to be my boyfriend last night. I'll chalk that insanity up to pillow talk, sleep deprivation, and distress. That's what it must be.

"Hey, Amelia, did they bring in your breakfast yet?" Jackson asks her.

"Not yet, but it's okay, I can wait a bit," she says. Grams twists her head to look over at Jackson as he's reviewing her cardiogram report. "So, when are you two getting married? I need a great-grandchild, you know." Before I have a chance to intervene and stop whatever will come out of her mouth next, she continues, "I suppose with the short timeline you've left me with, that may not be possible, but there is enough time for a wedding."

Jackson takes the outpouring of suggestions quite well. Thank goodness, he's understanding. The small smile on his face and the nod he gives as he continues reviewing the report, says it all. "You know, Amelia," Jackson says as he places the report down, "most of my patients who have gone through what you have in the past week aren't as talkative as you are. You are just full of energy, aren't you?" Jackson has his doctor smile on—the one that probably calms his patients and makes them feel comfortable under his care.

"Grams, Jackson and I just met a week ago," I remind her again. Not like she didn't hear me the first time, but maybe it'll sink in this time. Doubtful, though.

"Yes, but you only live once, although you may die twice...if you're me," she says.

I close my eyes and drop my head into my hand. I believe I hear a snicker from the peanut gallery on the other side of the room while Grams is just roaring up to keep going.

"You know, it's possible to fall in love in a night," she says.

"That's not what everyone else says," I argue.

"Everyone else is wrong, or they've never fallen in love at first sight." I don't think she understands exactly how I'm feeling right now. If she did, she'd know how uncomfortable I am with the fact that I just stepped out of one relationship and right into another. I'm not complaining per se, but it doesn't sound good out loud.

"Grams, we're not getting married in the next few months," I tell her, assuming Jackson is silently agreeing with me.

"Fine," she says, folding her hands over her chest. "If you want to question my lifelong research and experiences, that's fine, but I bet you one thing—"

"What's that?" I ask, looking over at Jackson, who's suddenly intrigued by whatever Grams is about to say.

"By the time you are finished reading my diary, you will have realized two things," she begins.

"Okay...?" I question.

"First: Love has a way of sneaking into your heart and taking you hostage for an entire lifetime. Second: If you're lucky enough to hold onto love, you won't have to experience the pain of having your body captivated by a soul that may or may not still be alive."

I pull in a shuddering breath as I wrap my hand around the front of my neck, still unable to shake away the tightness. "I understand," is all I can say. I won't question the meaning of her life. I can't.

"Jackson," Grams says. "I need you to marry my granddaughter."

I'm mortified. You can't put a man in a position like this just days after meeting a woman, especially a man who just went through a divorce less than a year ago. "Grams, please stop."

"Amelia," Jackson says her name without so much as a hitch in his deep, soothing voice. "If by the end of your diary, Emma tells me she can't spend a day without me, in fear of suffering from the unknown for the rest of her life, I will do what I can to arrange the fastest marriage known to man. However, she has to tell me this herself."

Are they *both* crazy? Who does this? People don't get married after meeting someone a handful of times. They don't talk about marriage. In fact, some people would become physically ill thinking about the idea after a horrible six-year relationship.

"People do it all the time on TV," Grams argues with my silent thoughts.

"Jackson, may I speak to you for a moment," I articulate, standing from the chair and taking his arm so I can pull him into the hall.

"Do you know what you just agreed to with a dying woman?" Jackson looks down for a minute as if I were scolding him and he's ashamed, but when his face lifts, he's chuckling—this hoarse little laugh he does when he's teasing me. "You can't play games like that with her, Jackson. She's serious."

"Emma," he says with a stone-walled expression. "If you truly feel that way when you're done reading her diary, then I would agree to marry you. If you were certain after only knowing me for a short time that I'm undoubtedly the one person in this world you can't live without, I would be a fool to walk away."

The first time he agreed with Grams, it just made me uncomfortable, but this time, he's taken my breath away. "You just went through a divorce," I remind him.

"What's your point?"

I don't have an answer. "I suppose I don't have one."

"The two of us are both single for a reason, and it wasn't because we found this kind of love she's talking about with someone else."

"A week. We've known each other a week," I tell him.

"And I can't stop thinking about you. I want to spend every minute with you. Your laugh makes me smile. Your smile makes my heart do these strange flip-flops in my chest, and I could probably sit and talk to you for a week straight without needing a breather."

His words are wooing everything inside of me, but there are other parts of this he isn't considering. "Did you know that I like sardines? Hmm?"

"That's gross, but it doesn't change anything."

I narrow my eyes at him, determined to throw him off his sureness. "I eat them out of a can sometimes," I tell him.

"Still, gross, but I'll sit next to you and admire your can-peeling technique."

"Whenever I get a migraine, I vomit," I continue.

"I'm a doctor. I've been vomited on more times than I can remember. I can hold your hair back."

"I have a horrible singing voice and I like to sing loudly on long car trips. Oh, and I know all the words to every popular song there is."

"That's so funny," he says, leaning up against the wall as he crosses his arms over his chest. "I do the same exact thing."

I find myself looking from side to side, trying to think of another terrible habit I have. "I own fifty pairs of shoes."

"I'd be interested to know what you need them for, each individually, of course."

"Ugh, forget it. You are infuriating," I tell him. "Oh, I know, I like to pick little fights a lot."

"Noted, but that can make a relationship stronger," he rebuts with a grin. "Plus, you're adorable when you get mad. Your nose scrunches up, and your voice squeaks."

"I can't handle you right now," I argue.

He lowers his arms and wraps one of them around my back, pulling me into him as he places a quick kiss on my lips. "I'll see you a little later, crazy."

"Me? I'm crazy?"

"Just a little." He pinches my chin between his fingers and jiggles my face from side to side.

I slowly fall prisoner to the walk of shame back into Grams's room, finding her beaming, of course. "I just knew it. It's a talent I have."

"Grams," I say, trying to hold on to the angered inflection in my voice.

"Emma, please sit down and continue reading to me. The

faster you get through the book, the faster I can move on with my life." I have a sad feeling I know what she means by that, and I'd like to think that's not how this is going to go.

"Don't say that," I tell her.

"Oh, I'm not going anywhere until you marry that man. Don't worry."

I roll my eyes and grab the diary from my bag. "I left off at the part where you were country hopping," I tell her before opening the book.

"Oh, and that was quite a trip."

CHAPTER TWENTY-ONE

AMELIA

MAY 1943 - DAY 522

$\mathcal{I}$ knew we weren't safe. I figured the worst was about to happen, and the progression of fear turning into terror consumed me as I held Lucie tightly, finally calming her into a peaceful state that quieted her cries.

However, the glow of a flashlight continued to bounce from tree to tree, hovering just a few feet above our heads. I prayed, but had little faith left after the past year. I would always look to God with questions that would go unanswered, and I often begged him for mercy, but I wasn't sure he could hear. Though, I'm sure Mama would have rolled over in her grave if she heard my thoughts.

Charlie caressed the side of my face as he stood over us, knowing full well that if we were caught, there wasn't anything he could do for us.

It was only minutes before the footsteps came too close. There was no way the man didn't know precisely where we were. I figured he was taunting us, making us believe we had gotten away from him, but that was probably what his type did to people like us. Torment was a game. We could no longer move to another tree since the twigs and branches below us would crackle and crunch. As far as I was concerned, we were already cornered.

Just a year earlier, I would close my eyes in the face of horror, but at that moment, with Lucie in my arms, I decided to look evil in the eye with hope of intimidating the enemy. I used to react when facing danger—my heart would beat fast and hard against my sternum, pulsating in my ears. Sweat would run down the back of my neck, I'd become short of breath, and a knot would form in the pit of my stomach. However, during my time in the prison camp, fear gradually became a muted sensation as I fought against becoming a victim of the deadly solution that was quickly eradicating my race. I was convinced that I couldn't be a victim if I fought back, and since living in fear was allowing Hitler to win, bravery was my only defense.

As I expected, the light found us, bearing its dreadful glow onto the tops of our heads. "What are you running from?" the man asked.

"We aren't running," Charlie lied.

The man laughed and straightened his posture to re-light a cigar he had been smoking. "It's obvious you're running from something."

"No, we're not," Charlie said, muttering into the sleeve of his jacket.

"Well, most people don't dump a luxury car that looks as if it belongs to the SS, then run into the woods just two miles from the Austrian border."

"Who are you to care?" Charlie retorted.

"Absolutely no one, but I live about two hundred yards behind you, and I think I have a right to know who is passing through my property tonight."

The man waved at each of us with his flashlight, making it impossible for us to see what he looked like or what he was wearing. "We don't mean any trouble, sir," I said.

"Now, if you tell me the truth, I'll offer you a roof to sleep under tonight. My wife and I like to keep a low profile though, so you'll need to answer my questions first."

Charlie looked down at me and curled his arm around my shoulders. "My wife and daughter weren't safe where we were living, and I needed to get us out of there for a while until things settle down."

"The stolen car?" he asked.

"I had no other way to get us out of there."

"There?" he continued to press the subject.

"We were living just outside of Terezín."

"Just outside, huh?" the man asked.

Lucie whimpered from behind the shield I was creating, so I lifted her up and perched her on my thigh. "Shh, baby girl." Her head fell limply against my chest, and her hands gripped the material of my dress.

"She's quite small," the man said. "How old is your daughter?"

"Just over a year," I answered quickly, without giving Charlie the option of saying something wrong. I wouldn't expect him to remember when she was born, considering he left just weeks after.

"She looks much younger than that," the man said. She had been suffering from malnutrition for a year. But if I said that, he would have known we were prisoners of a camp.

"She's just small like her mama," Charlie said while placing a kiss on my cheek. The lying created waves of undeserved happiness. Listening to him speak of us as a family was something I had stopped dreaming about a year earlier when he was deployed. Hearing those words come out of Charlie's mouth at that moment, though, reignited the hope of fulfilling that dream one day—a child I could call my own, a man who loved me, a house near a field of flowers, dresses that felt like pure cotton against my skin, and delicious foods that would melt as it touched my tongue.

243

All those thoughts had become lost within the decimation of my world, but I still held out hope.

"Come on," he said. "That child is visibly starving." I looked at Charlie, and he helped me up with Lucie. We didn't know the man, but he seemed to be safe for that moment. "The house is just up ahead. I'll meet you there if you want. My car is still on the side of the road."

"Sure, we'll find our way over there," Charlie said. Since the man left us in the woods to run if we pleased, it offered another inkling of hope that the stranger could be trusted. It was hard to tell who was on what side, who believed what, and who hated whom. Throughout the prior year, I had learned to believe that almost everyone hated me, other than Charlie. Out of desperation, the other Jews had even begun to turn on each other in the camp. It was survival of the fittest.

"Do you think this is okay?" I asked Charlie once the stranger was out of hearing range.

"It's either this or trying to find a way through customs tonight."

"How are we ever going to get through customs?" I asked, having not considered that part of our journey until then. I'm not sure why it hadn't crossed my mind, but I was more concerned with what we left behind than what was ahead.

"Either we find a way around customs, or we find a way through it." Charlie's hand reached toward his pocket where his pistol was, and without a word, I knew what he was thinking. Stealing a car was bad enough, but taking a life was more than I could contemplate at that time. I knew there may not have been a choice in the matter, but it didn't make it easier to accept. I didn't want to be like one of them, like the person who killed Mama, or the people responsible for Papa and Jakob dying.

"Amelia, I'm trying to save us. I promise you, that's all I'm trying to do."

"Charlie, you don't need to explain yourself. You have proven your feelings more than enough times. I know your intentions are good and pure." He looked at me for a moment, and I could almost read each thought swimming through his eyes. I wished he had shared every one of them with me, but Charlie was a man of few words. I cherished every word he offered, but I wanted more. He tugged at my arm, pulling it away from Lucie, and ripped the Jude patch from the sleeve of my jacket. I hadn't thought to do that, so it was wise that he did.

"Take off your coat," Charlie demanded. Puzzled at his stern request, I removed the layer of clothing, and he quickly tore the Jude star off my dress, too. *How could I have forgotten?* Our clothes, filthy appearance, and state of malnutrition hinted that Lucie and I were from Terezín, but that star would have confirmed who we were. No one could know that truth. As we moved forward, a gas lamp shined through the trees, serving as a guide, welcoming us to the man's house. Lucie was wide awake at that time and taking in her surroundings, babbling as if she were trying to communicate with us. "I know, baby. Everything's going to be all right, sweet girl," I assured her.

Once we arrived at the house, I found the outside to be odd. The area was covered with trees, which shaded the windows, and there wasn't a path that led to the front door. It was a log cabin, fully covered in vines, nearly camouflaged against the wooded area. It seemed as if the man was also hiding.

The moment we stepped onto the cement block leading to the front door, the gas lamp went off, the door opened, and we were hurried inside of the candlelit house.

Each interior wall was as it was outside, but without the vines. Dark paneling and matching floors held the glow from a small fire in a metal pit along the far wall. There were old, tattered chairs strewn around what looked to be a handmade, wooden table, but beyond that, there was emptiness.

After the man let us in, he disappeared into another room without a word, leaving the three of us standing like statues in front of the closed door. There was a lot of commotion between the man and a woman, who I assumed to be his wife, but it was hard to tell what they were saying. We waited several minutes before they joined us in what appeared to be their main living area, and it was instantaneously obvious how they felt about our presence.

With enough light, I could see that the man was older—maybe around Papa's age, and the woman looked to be around Mama's age. She was wearing an old, worn dress, and he was cloaked similarly in gray slacks and a white cotton shirt. "Your baby, she's hungry?" the woman asked. She had a strong Swedish accent, and I wondered why she would be there in Czechoslovakia if she were from Sweden.

"Yes, Madame," I replied. "She is, but our intentions were not to beg for food."

"Oh, hush," she said. "Louis already explained your situation to me."

I felt very uneasy even though things seemed to be okay, but I couldn't help wondering what Louis explained to her? I dreaded that it was only a matter of time before they would figure out the truth. Lucie and I were extremely dirty and smelled vile.

"Come," she summoned us toward her with an inviting nod before gently placing her hand on my back as she led us into her small kitchen. There was a fresh loaf of bread on the counter and a basket of fruits hanging from beneath one of the cupboards. My mouth filled with saliva, dreaming of what it would be like to taste something so tart again.

I became more curious about their story and why they were in the middle of the woods alone, but I wasn't there to pry, and Mama always told me it was rude to ask too many questions when invited into someone's home. Plus, if I didn't want them asking about *me*, I should offer them the same courtesy.

"I'm Svaya," she offered.

"I'm Amelia, this is Lucie and—my husband, Charlie," I replied.

She leaned forward and smiled at Lucie. "May I?" She held her arms out, wanting to hold the little girl I didn't want to release after being freed from that hell. However, after a moment of hesitation, I reminded myself how unbearably tired and weak my arms felt from holding her so long. I handed Lucie to Svaya, watching a smitten appearance take over her forlorn features. Lucie cooed as Svaya tickled her tummy. She even giggled, and it was the first time I ever heard that sweet sound from her. I felt thankful that Lucie would never remember what she was born into.

With my sweet girl in one arm, Svaya tended to the loaf of bread and sliced up some fruit as if she had heard my thoughts. Drool pooled in the corners of my mouth as she placed the food down on a plate. She sat on one of the carved chairs, and I situated myself on the other as she fed Lucie small pieces of the fruit and bread. I took bigger bites but made sure to leave enough for Charlie.

After a few moments, the men joined us, both quiet and reserved as if they shared uncomfortable words. "Charlie, I saved some for you," I told him.

"Amelia, eat," he said, sternly. "I want you and Lucie to have it."

"That's nonsense. There's plenty for all of you," Svaya said. She stood with Lucie and sliced up more of the food as Charlie rubbed my back. "What happened to your arm, young man?"

"I was deployed over to Prague for a year. I was too close to a mine field when one of our men mistakenly assumed there was a clear path. I was one of the lucky ones." I had yet to ask Charlie what happened because I couldn't handle the thought of what took place. It was selfish to be ignorant, but my mind was too bogged down and weak to take in more than I already had to handle. I stopped chewing the fruits as his words sank in, and images flashed through my mind. *He must have been terrified.*

247

"Goodness. I'm glad you survived," she said. "You're a hero."

"No, madame. I was just doing what I was told to do."

"I see," she said, appearing to understand that Charlie was not one of *those* soldiers.

"Can I take your coats?" Louis offered.

I was becoming quite warm from the fire, so I complied without hesitation. "Please," I said gratefully, as I shrugged the coat off my shoulders and handed it to Louis. "Thank you for your kindness."

As he took the coat, he stared at my malnourished appearance with shock. "You're a—a Jew," he said with distaste as he took a step back. The transition was immediate as he eyed me differently than he had a moment earlier.

"I told you she was a Jew, Louis," Svaya said.

"How can that be?" Louis asked. "You're a soldier." He pointed at Charlie as if he were also the enemy, just from association with my kind. "You're helping them escape, aren't you?" They figured everything out, just as I feared they would.

Charlie looked between the two strangers, noticeably unsure of how to respond. "Love is stronger than hate," he said simply.

"Surely, you aren't married, then," Svaya said as she handed Lucie back to me.

"What does it matter?" Charlie argued. "I love her, and if she could be my wife, she would be. There's no difference in my mind."

My heart felt so full of love at that moment that I felt the unfamiliar sensation of joyful tears pricking at my eyelids, but I kept them hidden inside as I had grown accustomed to doing. I agreed with Charlie. It didn't matter who he was. It only mattered what he was inside, and that he was a man who would risk his life to protect a little girl and me—two people he didn't need to be concerned with.

Louis grabbed Svaya by the arm and pulled her into a room down the short hallway.

"We need to leave," Charlie said.

"And go where?" I argued, wanting to see what they would say after discussing the situation.

Charlie didn't have an answer. Instead, he wrapped his arm around me and kissed my forehead. "I'm sorry I hadn't asked you what happened to your arm," I blurted out.

"There wasn't much time to ask questions," he said.

"It should have been the first question I asked you, but I was scared to hear the truth. I'm still afraid to see the damage, which is ridiculous after everything I've already seen."

"It isn't ridiculous," he rebutted. "It's what happens when you care about someone. It hurts you to see that person in pain. It's how I have felt about you for so long, Amelia. It's why I need to keep you safe. I need you to be free, happy, and out of agony. It's all I care about."

I took his hand and placed it on my chest. "Inside here, there's happiness. You may not be able to see it, but it's there, and it's because of you." My heart was beating fast, partly from panic and partly due to the realization that Charlie loved me so much, he was willing to risk his life for me.

"Your heart is pounding, Amelia," he said.

"It's because of you." He leaned down and softly touched his lips to mine.

"I love you, my Amelia."

I pressed his hand a little firmer against my chest. "I'm happy you can feel my heart."

"I can," he said with a small smile. "Someday, I'll make you feel safe, and you will be able to tell me how you feel with words." I wasn't sure if that would ever be the case, so I didn't respond.

Svaya and Louis returned—his arm was around his wife's shoulders as she peered down to her clasped fingers. "You can stay here tonight, but you need to be gone in the morning. We've hidden out here for too long to risk having a Jew in our home." I couldn't imagine what they were hiding from, but I accepted their offer without argument. I understood it was a risk for them to have us in their home, and I appreciated the one night.

"I've set up some blankets for you three in the extra bedroom. We'll keep the fire going a bit longer so you stay warm."

"Thank you, again, for your kind hospitality," I said.

She nodded. "Follow me, and I'll show you to the room." I walked past Charlie, leaving him behind with Louis. The only thing I heard as I entered the spare room was, "I told you to be honest with me, son. You're a soldier. You should know better than to help a Jew at a time like this. You're risking your life for her."

"I'm aware, sir," he said, quickly ending the discussion as he made his way down the hall to find Lucie and me.

"We are just across the hall," Svaya said before closing us into the empty room with the blankets and a small oil lamp in the corner. I fluffed the couple of blankets she gave us and made an area for the three of us to sleep on. I wasn't sure Lucie would sleep well after napping so much on the way there, but she looked tired, so I was hopeful that she would rest along with us.

The door reopened, and Louis stuck his head inside. "Be gone before sunrise," he said.

"Of course," Charlie complied, tipping his head in agreement. We needed to leave early anyway so we could find a way around that checkpoint—a plan that seemed impossible. Though, it was clearer than ever that we had no other choice.

CHAPTER TWENTY-TWO

EMMA

*W*hen I finish this entry of Grams's diary, I'm a bit surprised when I look up to see she's still awake, considering she's been asleep each time I've read to her before. "You're still awake?" I mention with a smile.

"Well, of course," Grams says. "You're getting close to the end."

I notice that there are only a few pages left in the diary, which makes me sad because I don't want their story to end.

"Grams, I want to help you find Charlie," I tell her.

"Sweetie, I know we have technological resources now that can do incredible things, but I'm not very confident that you'll be able to find him."

"If I did, would you be happy?"

Grams grabs my hands firmly. "Emma Hill, if you find that man for me, I will forever be grateful. However, if you can't find him, I will still die knowing how lucky I am to have such an incredibly loving granddaughter."

"I'm going to find him, whether he's dead or alive," I tell her.

"Emma," Grams says. "If you happen to read the last couple of entries without me..." Her hands loosen from around mine, and she places them over her heart. "Try not to be upset about the secrets I have held inside all these years. I had my reasons, and they were out of love and protection."

"Secrets, Grams?"

Her lips turn down into a grimace I've never seen on her face before.

"I feel as though my life was built on lies, and the last thing I wanted to do was teach your mom, aunt, and of course, you, that lying is the only way to get through life. It may have been the only way back then, but honesty is what sets us free, Emma. Maybe if I had been honest sooner, I would have been freed from this emotional pain that I may die with."

"Grams, you can talk to me," I say, climbing into the bed with her. I lay my head on her shoulder and wrap my arm around her chest. "Please, tell me."

She drapes her arms around my shoulders and sighs. "I just—it will hurt those people it involves." I'm already hurting, and I can't imagine what she's holding back.

I rest beside her in silence as my brain pieces together the scattered parts of the puzzle. I'm not sure I'd be able to hold on to a secret for so long. I've been an open book most of my life, and secrets, even the small ones, hurt to keep inside. "I think we're running out of time, Emma. If you think you can find Charlie for me, I would be very grateful."

"I won't stop until I find him," I tell her.

"Go," she says, turning her head to kiss me on the cheek. "Be my hero."

I kiss her on the forehead and slide out of the bed. "Mom sent me a text and told me she's on her way with Annie." I'm not sure visiting hours have even begun yet, but Jackson obviously has a little pull with that. "I love you, Grams."

"You'll always be my sweetheart, Emma. Thank you."

I relocate myself back into the waiting room and plug my

laptop in. If I have to go through the records of every single Charlie Crane in this world, I will.

Before I'm through the second page of Charlie Cranes, Mom and Annie walk in, forcing me to pause my search. "Did you really sleep here all night?" Mom asks.

"Yes," I say, leaving it simple and without the details of which room I slept in.

"How is she?" Annie asks.

"She seems okay," I tell them. "I left her because she wanted to rest a bit before you got here."

"Can we go in?" Mom asks.

I look down at my phone, seeing it's nine o'clock. I'm not sure when visiting hours are, but I assume it would be around now. "I'm sure it's fine."

"You have your head buried in that laptop every time I see you. What in the world are you working so hard on?" Mom asks.

"I have lots of projects to get through. I've managed to reschedule most of my clients for the next week to give myself a little breathing space, but even that takes time."

With everything going on, it's my number one priority to find Charlie. It would be so much easier to know what happened at the end of their story, but Grams doesn't seem like she's about to speak a word of it no matter how many times I ask. I wonder what she is so afraid to tell me.

"Okay, well, we'll be with her if you need anything," Annie says. The two of them look like the world is sitting on their shoulders, and I wish I could take some of their stress away, but I'm scared to say too much. I feel guilty about keeping this secret from them as it is. After all, they are her daughters, and they have even more of a right to know than I do.

For a reason I don't understand, I feel like Grams is passing the torch to me, and that I will have to keep and protect her secret after she's gone. However, if I'm able to find Charlie, I may be relieved of that burden since I think it would offer Grams the strength to tell all of us the truth. Charlie is the other half of her story. She needs him so she can reveal whatever these secrets are and finally be free.

On the fifth page of my search, my focus locks on the headline: "Charlie Crane, former German soldier with an untold story of love and war, interviewed on NBC New York."

A cool wave of sweat beads up on my forehead as I click the link. *Please, let this be him.* I scour the page for a date first, finding that the interview is from four years ago. *Oh my gosh, this could be Grams's Charlie.*

I scroll down a bit, finding the subtitle to be: *Seventy Years: The Personal Aftermath of World War II.*

A still picture of Charlie stares back at me, and I wish Grams had a picture of him so I could find the similarities. In the picture, the man has a full head of white hair, perfectly combed to one side. His eyes are a watery light blue, and his face is lined with many small wrinkles, each one likely telling a story of his life. I zoom in on my screen to get a better look, and I notice what looks like faint scars lining both sides of his face. I remember Grams mentioning the way his face looked when he returned from war. The scars don't look as bad as what Grams described, but seventy years of aging would likely soften scars such as those.

I hold my breath as I click play, but at the same time, Jackson walks in. "How are you doing?" I click pause. "You look like you've seen a ghost. Are you all right?" He lets the door close behind him and takes the seat next to me. "Emma?"

"I think I may have found Charlie."

He peeks over at my screen. "Charlie Crane, is that his full name?"

"*Yes.*"

"*Seventy Years: The Personal Aftermath of World War II.* Maybe it *is* him. Click *play*," he says.

I hit the button again, feeling my heart skip a beat as it takes a moment for the feed to load.

Today, we have with us, Charlie Crane, an eighty-nine-year-old gentleman who has lived in Staten Island for the past sixty years. Charlie is one of the most well-known and adored residents of his neighborhood. After hearing bits and pieces of his story from his neighbors and friends, we reached out to Charlie with the hope that he might share a part of his story and his past with us. We were quite honored when he agreed to do so. Charlie is a veteran of World War II and has a story that most of us can't fathom. We're incredibly grateful and humbled to introduce to you...Charlie Crane.

The video zooms out, showing not only the interviewer but the man in a chair across from her, as well.

A smile is etched unevenly across the man's face, as if he were unsure and nervous to be sitting through the interview. He's dressed in a crisp-looking pair of gray slacks and a starched white shirt that's neatly tucked into his pants. A man of his age must care a lot about his image to be so neatly dressed, but it's admirable.

"Charlie, thank you so much for being here today," the interviewer says.

"Thank you for having me," Charlie responds.

This man has two arms, which makes my shoulders slump with disappointment. Charlie was left with one arm. "It's not him," I tell Jackson.

"Why do you say that?" he asks.

"He has two arms."

"Just hold on for a minute. Let's keep watching."

"Now, Charlie, we've heard from some of your friends and neighbors that you have quite the story about how you ended up here in the United States. We'd love to hear more," she encourages.

Charlie straightens his posture in the chair with a sense of discomfort before he begins to speak.

"*Certainly, of course. I may sound like a foolish man, but—well, it was all for love.*"

The interviewer purses her lips with curiosity and tilts her head to the side.

"*Hmm. So, you're saying it wasn't for a chance at a better life, which is why so many people emigrated here during that time?*"

Charlie shakes his head a bit, lifts his right hand from his lap, and scratches at his chin before relaxing back into the chair.

"*For me, a better life was only about the love I had for one woman,*" he says.

"*And did you end up finding this woman?*" The interviewer asks.

"*I did,*" Charlie answers immediately, bowing his head briefly.

I look over at Jackson with bewilderment. "I need to know if this is him," I say.

"Shh, keep watching," he tells me.

The interviewer clasps her hands together over her skirted lap before continuing.

"*So, was it the classic happily ever after you were hoping for?*"

Charlie doesn't take much time to respond. It was as if he had pre-planned the answers to the questions she would be asking.

"*It was a happily ever after,*" he says.

My knee has been shaking for minutes, but it stops as I look back over at Jackson to gauge his reaction. He doesn't say anything; he just continues watching.

"*Are you two still together now?*" she asks.

. . .

"Oh my goodness, no. We were never together again after we arrived here in the states."

The woman chuckles nervously, making me wonder if maybe she didn't have the answers to these questions before the interview.

"I'm not sure I understand, Charlie. How do you explain your happy ending if you didn't end up with the love of your life?"

I notice Charlie fidgeting more in his seat. His right hand is tapping against his knee, and then he tugs at the collar of his shirt with the same hand.

"His left hand hasn't moved an inch," Jackson says. "It's prosthetic."

"What? How do you know that?"

Jackson cocks his head to the side. "I'm a doctor. Give me a little credit, will you?" Fair point. "When the human body is under stress, you don't just have three out of four limbs moving around. He's bounced both his knees several times and has been tapping his right hand throughout the interview. His left hand and arm haven't moved once."

"But his story—"

"Love isn't necessarily about being with that person. It's about knowing that she's safe and happy. My one and only love was both of those things, and it gave me the peace I needed to go on with my life," Charlie says.

"Wow," the interviewer replies, fanning herself a bit with her papers. *"If only there were more men like you, this world might be a better place."*

Charlie leans forward, resting his good arm on his knee. *"You know, love was different back then,"* he continues, seeming more comfortable in his skin for the moment. *"Finding safety and peace out of harm's way was the ultimate act of love for the ones you cared about.*

Making sure your family had food to eat and shelter from the enemy meant that you were a decent human being. We lived through a scary time, and we had a hard road, escaping from the horrors of war in Czechoslovakia. It certainly wasn't an easy feat to stay alive and end up the way we did."

The interviewer places her fist beneath her chin. *"Do you know where this woman you loved so deeply, is today?"*

"Love," Charlie corrects her. *"And, I'd rather not say."*

"Understandable," the woman continues. *"So, Charlie, the most intriguing part of your story is that you were once referred to as a Nazi, and this woman is Jewish. Am I correct?"*

"Yes, you're correct," Charlie states, simply, before swallowing hard, then bouncing his knees again.

It's him. "It's him!"

"It definitely is," Jackson says.

"How in the world did you manage to get away with that?" the interviewer asks.

"With all due respect, some secrets are worth keeping as secrets," Charlie answers.

"She's alive because of you, isn't she?" the woman continues.

.   .   .

Charlie stands from his seat and pulls the microphone off with his right hand as his left hand dangles by his side. *"I apologize. I can't continue."* Charlie quickly walks away from the cameras and off the set, leaving the interviewer stunned and visibly shaken as she tries to clean up the mess that must have been filmed live.

"Do you think he's still alive?" I ask Jackson.

"There's only one way to find out." Jackson takes my laptop from my hands and types Charlie's name into the search engine, followed by Staten Island. "He must be what, nine-three now?"

"I think he was a year older than my grandmother, so yes, I believe so."

Two Charlie Cranes come up as residents in Staten Island. One is only forty-two, and it says the other is ninety-three. Jackson points to the second one. "That has to be him. Can I have your phone?"

I'm shaking as I reach for my phone in the front of my bag and hand it to Jackson, watching him with a frozen stare as he dials the number on the screen.

It's hard to contain my emotions as I hear the muted sound of a ringtone.

"Hello, is this Charlie Crane?" Jackson asks. Everything stops, and it's as if time stands still for a moment. I can't breathe. I can't blink. I can't move. I can't think. I'm just hoping for the response I'm praying for.

"My name is Jackson Beck. I'm a doctor at Mass General Hospital in Boston, Massachusetts. Are you familiar with a woman by the name of Amelia Baylin?" Jackson looks at me and places his hand over his mouth as he waits for the response. "I have her granddaughter here with me, and she's been looking for you. Do you mind if I hand the phone over to her?"

Jackson nods his head at me to let me know that Charlie has agreed. I'm not sure I'll know what to say, and I stifle a sob, still finding it difficult to breathe. Nevertheless, I try pulling in a deep inhale to compose myself before I take the phone from Jackson. I press the display up to my ear and blow out the pent-up air I've been holding in. "Charlie?" I question, my voice quavering. "My name is Emma."

"Emma," he says as if it's a revelation. "Emma, is your grandmother still alive? My God, is she okay?"

"She—she's alive, but she's not well. Her heart is failing—she's had two strokes. Charlie, sir, she's been asking for you. I've read most of her diary per her request, and I wanted to find you—to see if you are able to come and see her."

A long, silent pause makes me look down at my phone, checking to see if we were disconnected. "Charlie?"

"Oh, Emma, it's just been so long, and—"

"Please, it would mean the world to her."

"Oh, sweetheart, you don't need to beg me. You didn't even need to ask. Of course, I'll come. I'll be on the first train out tomorrow morning."

"You will?" I stand up, reaching my arm across my chest—my body feels like it's caving in on itself with relief and happiness—feelings I can't even put into words. "Really?"

"Where shall I find you?" he asks. "You're in Boston, correct?"

"Yes, she's at Mass General, here in Boston."

"I'll find my way, and I will be there tomorrow."

"Charlie?"

"What is it, sweetheart?"

"Have you known where my grandmother is living?"

"Yes, dear, I have."

"Why didn't you ever reach out?"

A heavy sigh scratches from within the speaker of my phone. "I would never dream of disturbing Amelia's happiness, nor the wonderful life she made for herself."

"Charlie, I think you are, and always have been her happiness."

"I've waited a long time to hear that, Emma. Patience *is* a great asset, and it eventually gives back to those who unnervingly wait.

I was starting to give up hope, though. It has been quite a long road."

While I pace back and forth, feeling Jackson's gaze burn against the side of my face, I try not to cry for the emptiness that Charlie has endured all these years, but even more so because of the irony. All they wanted was to be together, and if they find each other now, at the end of their lives, they will have such a short time to experience the life they deserved to have. "Charlie, I'm very much looking forward to meeting you tomorrow. Thank you for doing this for my grandmother. I only wish I had found you sooner."

"The pleasure has always been mine, sweetheart, and I look forward to meeting you, as well."

"Bye," I whisper through an almost voiceless breath.

"Goodbye, dear."

I hang up the phone and fall into the seat beside Jackson. "I don't even know what to say right now," I tell him.

"You should be proud of yourself. You did it," he said.

"Well, with your help. I'm not sure I would have had the courage to pick up the phone and call him like you did."

"You would have for your grandmother."

"Do I tell her?" I know the answer, but I felt the need to ask out loud.

Jackson shakes his head with a smile. "No, just be there when he walks through that door tomorrow. Never in your lifetime will you experience another moment like that."

"I have to finish the diary tonight," I tell him. "I have to know everything there is to know first."

"Mind if I join you? I feel like I'm invested in this romance as much as you are," he says while running his fingers through his hair. He even looks stressed out like I am. It's cute and amazing at the same.

"I want you to be with me when I read it, yes."

Jackson leans in and cups his hand around the side of my face as he kisses me hard, forcing my heart to pound just a little harder than it already is.

The door to the waiting room opens, and a gasp follows. Startled, I pull away from Jackson and drag the back of my hand under my lips as I face Mom and Annie. *Oh no.*

"Oh my, I'm sorry. I mean, I'm not sorry that you're kissing, but I'm sorry I walked in on you," Mom says.

Jackson stands up, scratching at his brow with the back of his thumb. "Ladies, it was a pleasure to see you today. I'll catch you later, Emma."

"I think I'm going to get going too, actually," I tell them.

"You sit here all day until we show up and then you have to leave?" Mom asks.

"Wouldn't you if you were me?" I ask with a raised brow.

"If you even think for a second that your grandmother didn't do the very same thing to us, you're wrong," Mom says.

"She forced you to marry Dad?"

"No, actually, she tried to keep us apart. She told me it would never work out."

What she's trying to say is, Grams knows everything and has a sixth sense. "Well, if you had listened, I wouldn't be here."

"Emma, everything in life happens for a reason, and while we think we have control over it, the truth is, we don't. Our life lessons shape us, our future, our kids' futures, and so on," Mom offers as her form of a lecture.

I know. I've heard it all before. "Okay, well on that note, I'm going to go get some fresh air. I think I at least have control over that," I tell her with a snarky smile.

"Oh, by the way, did you ever find that book Grams was asking for?"

I don't know what my face looks like right now, but I'm not so great at lying, especially when I'm being stared at by two pairs of eyes. "Uh, yes, I found it."

"Well, what was it?"

"Just some old photos, nothing really," I tell her as I place my laptop into my bag beside the diary.

"You're lying. What was in the book?"

"It's something Grams wants to keep private, I guess. I don't know."

I walk past the two of them, but Mom grabs my arm. "Emma Hill, at a time like this, we're not keeping secrets."

"Mom, please ask Grams yourself then. Don't put me in the middle of you two. Not at a time like this."

She releases my arm. "Fine, I'll ask her myself."

"That sounds good. I'll see you in a bit," I tell her, rushing out of the room before she continues pressing me for more information.

"Thank you for dinner," I tell Jackson as I blot my lips with a napkin.

"I can order pizza like no one's business," he says.

"But, can you cook?" I ask, teasing him.

"Not to save my life," he says.

"Well, if this whole plan of my grandmother's works out, we'll be eating out a lot because I can't cook either."

"There are plenty of good cookbooks out there. We may need to learn how to cook together," he says.

"Maybe."

"You know what we don't need to learn how to do?" he whispers.

"What?" The look in his eyes makes me bite down on my bottom lip. He leans forward and pulls me from my stool at his kitchen's bar table. His arms wrap tightly around me, and he leans down slowly as he seems to enjoy each time he's stealing a kiss. It gives me a moment to take in the view. He's slow with his movements when he touches his lips to mine. It's almost as if he wants to memorize the texture, the taste, and the way I return the gesture. It's like nothing else I've experienced, and it's just a kiss, but so much can be conveyed by the sensations, and it's my favorite part of being with him.

As he pulls away and sweeps his knuckles down the side of my cheek, I notice a pink hue spreading across his face. "You make me feel things I haven't felt before—things I'm sure I've been missing out on."

"You know, some people would call us crazy and insane, talking like this after only knowing each other a few days."

"Some would call us lucky," he argues.

"I'm one of those people. We are lucky. I hope this lasts, Jackson. I'm not afraid of going all in, even knowing I could end up with a broken heart, but I know I don't want it to end that way."

"Don't break my heart, Emma, and I won't break yours. How about that?"

"Sounds easy enough," I tell him.

"I don't understand why some people make it out to be so hard."

"I suppose it's like wearing a shoe that's two sizes too small," I add in.

He chuckles. "Why do I have a feeling you've had experience in that department, Miss Shoe Addict?"

"Been there, not fun."

"Em, I'm not sure I can focus on anything else until we finish reading the diary."

"I've been thinking the same thing." I rush over to where I left my bag near his couch and pull out the worn book. "I don't know if I'm ready for this though."

"Hang on then." He jogs around the bar and into the kitchen where he pulls out two beers from the fridge. "This will help you relax."

"Yes," I agree with laughter. "Who knows what we might need

after finishing this. It's supposedly going to make me want to get married, so it has to be something pretty crazy."

Jackson drops down beside me on the couch and lifts his feet up to rest them on the table, then hands me one of the beer bottles. "Okay, ready."

CHAPTER TWENTY-THREE

AMELIA

MAY 1943 - DAY 523

"*A*re you ready?" Charlie whispered in my ear, long after I had woken up. I was used to waking up to whistles and shouts at around three in the morning. Sleeping until nearly four-thirty that day was a gift.

"Yes," I told him.

"We have an hour until sunrise," he said.

"That's a good thing, right?"

"For us," he continued, but I wasn't sure what he was planning.

He peered over to Lucie, who was still fast asleep in her makeshift crib we made from blankets. "She, on the other hand, might need a bit more sleep before we wake her," he observed.

"Oh," I said.

Still wondering what Charlie was trying to say, he rolled to his side and soothingly stroked his finger around my ear and beneath my chin, sending a wave of chills down my warm spine. "Being with you before leaving for the war was a mistake," he said.

I pulled my head back with surprise. I wondered how he could say a thing like that. Despite living in terror, it was one of the most amazing times of my life. "Why?"

He smiled weakly, lovingly. "Amelia, I had to relive those moments for almost an entire year, dreaming of what I could have had, what I may never have again—what I desperately wanted and needed. If I hadn't known, I wouldn't have spent so many nights with a heavy heart."

"I know the feeling well," I told him.

His fingers traced down the length of my neck toward the collar of my dress. "Do you still want to be with me even though my body is maimed now?"

The question surprised me. "What do you mean? You look the same to me as when you left, Charlie." I meant that. The superficial scars and one arm less didn't change a thing about him or who he was.

"But my face has been torn to shreds, and my arm is missing. I'm not a full person anymore," he explained. Each of his words chipped another piece of my steel heart away.

"Charlie, if I were left with only the memories of your life, I'd still want to be with you. You could look like a monster for all I care, and I'd still only see the beautiful man you are inside. I see what my heart sees—an amazing man."

It wasn't long before we quietly intertwined our bodies into a partially clothed mess of breathless whispers that would forever leave its imprint inside of me. Being with Charlie in that way wasn't about the sensations as much as it was about the bond between us. It was a seamless line in our lives that offered us power and control in our own little world. The love we shared was warm and soul-shattering, offering awareness from within my body that I accepted Charlie, as not the enemy, but my ally, and my love. He was my safety, my shelter, and my home.

I looked intently into his eyes each time he rocked against me, seeing a type of forever I wanted more than anything. With passion firing through me, I pressed my fingertips firmly into his shoulders as I felt a release flow through my body that made me want to call out his name, so I locked my lips shut in fear of making a sound, and I gritted my teeth, feeling a quiver run through me as his body trembled against mine. I assumed it was from holding his weight above my body with one arm, but he soon unraveled and collapsed on top of me while breathing at the same pace I was. "Amelia, you are everything worth fighting for," he said as he kissed me with a power that showed fury. One long moment of an unbreakable bond between our mouths broke into a dozen more kisses we shared between quick inhales and exhales of short breaths.

As our bodies fought for steady pulses, our dewy steam swirled together like watercolor on a canvas. Nothing could take away what we had. It would always be with us.

"You saved my life, and Lucie's," I told him.

"And we're going to get out of here, make it across that border, and find a small place to live in peace where we can start our lives together without the shadow of doom hovering over us. Is that what you want?" he asked.

"That's exactly what I want, Charlie. My dream, though—"

"What is your dream, sweetheart?"

"I want to go to the United States. Maybe New York or Massachusetts. It's safe there, with endless opportunities that you can't even imagine. It has always been my dream."

Charlie smiled as he wrapped a fallen strand of hair behind my ear. "That sounds like heaven," he said. "That's our plan, Amelia. We're going to have it all."

"What are we waiting for?" I said with a bit of excitement filling my voice. I was hopeful. It felt like a new beginning, even though we hadn't made it out of the country yet, but everything was falling into place. Freedom was so close, I could almost taste it.

Charlie stood up quickly and re-dressed. I did the same, then folded up the blankets Svaya and Louis were kind enough to share with us. I lifted Lucie up carefully so she could continue sleeping, and we left the room as we found it.

On the way out, I saw a stack of notepaper next to a pen. So, I wrote a short thank you to Svaya and Louis for their kindness, and wished them well. I didn't blame them for their reaction the previous night. I was just grateful for the time they allowed us to stay.

We left the house, making sure to secure the door behind us. The glow of the rising sun was off to the right, and we headed left through the woods. The ground was covered in matted leaves, and broken sticks left over from the winter damage, which made our presence known if anyone were to be in hearing distance. Though, it was still safer to be in the woods than on the road.

We kept walking, knowing the country line was two miles from Louis and Svaya's house, but we weren't walking on a straight path like the road, so it seemed to take longer than it should have by the time we reached the bottom of a very steep hill. It took everything I had to make it up the next upward trek, even though Charlie was carrying Lucie.

When we reached the top, there was nothing to see but barbed wire. There was no place to cross. There was no way out. Before I could see the entire scope of land, Charlie pulled me to the ground, hiding us within the tall grass. "There's a watch tower over the main customs area. If they see us, we won't stand a chance."

"What are we going to do?" I pleaded for an answer I knew he didn't have, or at least didn't think he had.

"We're going through those gates," he said. His voice was calm and sure as day. "Your name is Emille. We were on our way to visit your family in Austria, but our car broke down some ways back, and your family agreed to meet us just inside the nearby town to pick us up."

"Charlie, do you really think that's going to work?" I asked him.

"We just need to be curt with them and appear calm. If we don't look like we have something to worry about, they won't doubt our story."

"They won't doubt you," I argued. "You are a soldier in uniform. I am no one."

"You, Amelia, are the world, and shame on them if they don't know it yet."

I nodded my head, still not quite believing his words. After all, I looked emaciated, but I tried my best to smile a little. "Maybe if you explained that to them, they would just let us walk on through."

"I don't know why I didn't think of that myself," Charlie said, smiling as he pulled himself up to his feet with Lucie still snugly held within his bent arm. "Come, it'll only take a few minutes to go down the hill and around the corner." He placed a kiss on Lucie's head and looked down at her with a loving look. "I'll be her papa. I want to be that person for her."

My heart ached with adoration as I listened to his beautiful confession. "You are incredible, Charlie Crane."

We carefully made our way back down the steep grassy mound and headed toward the road, trying to avoid looking suspicious. I needed to convince myself that I was Emille—Charlie's wife, and that our car broke down a couple of miles back. Lying was hard for me, but our lives depended on it. I had essentially been lying for more than a year, as I had been breaking the rules almost daily to help the other women in my barrack. I was also taking food from Charlie, which I was not supposed to have. Of course, in addition, I had snuck off and escaped too. I broke every rule in the book. What was one more lie?

My heart thudded heavily as the bordering iron gates blurred in the distance. Knowing we'd have to go through a checkpoint twice was already a hard fact to swallow, though entering Switzerland would be much easier, I had assumed—hoped.

"Charlie, how will we make it across Austria? Are we walking into another war zone?" In truth, I didn't know where the war started and where it stopped. Information was not given to us inside of the camp. It was as if the world had stopped outside those walls, but if the war was over, would we have been left to rot there?

"There's a train station just over the border. We're going to get on that train. I have plenty of schillings saved up to get us to Zurich."

He looked over at me as we continued to walk, likely seeing the nervous expression on my face. "Here," he said. "Take Lucie for a moment."

I took Lucie from his arm, and he reached into his pocket, pulling out a handful of schillings. "I want you to have enough just in case."

"Just in case of what, Charlie?"

"In case you make it and I don't," he said pointedly. "No more questions, okay?"

We continued walking down the gravel path. While spotting the patrols in the watch tower, we noticed they were studying our every move as we came closer.

"Soldier, is everything okay?" one of the guards asked.

"Yes, yes, we had some car trouble a couple of miles back, and my wife and I are on leave to go visit her family across the border. They plan to pick us up just inside the town." Charlie pointed off into the distance, past the gates.

I swallowed hard and squeezed Lucie tightly within my arms. The guard looked over at me and inspected my clothing with a curious look in his eyes. "Your wife looks ill," the soldier replied.

"Oh, you know how it is in the spring time. I've had a terrible cold for a week, but it's passing now. I just hope our daughter doesn't catch it. A baby with a cold is not an enjoyable time," I countered. I was proud of myself for the act I put on, but whether it was enough of a performance, I wasn't sure. We were still on the wrong side of the gate.

"I see," the guard said. "What is your name, soldier?"

"Charlie Crane," he replied. Charlie Crane is supposed to be receiving medical attention for his arm at that moment, and yet he had just mentioned he was on leave.

"Where are you stationed?" He can't possibly tell him the truth, or they'll know for sure.

"I'm in transition at the moment," Charlie said. "Due to my injury." Charlie pointed to his shoulder.

"I suppose that's a good time for leave," the guard said. "Give me a moment to call in your name. What is your wife's name?" he asked.

"Emille Crane," Charlie replied. I knew I wasn't fooling anyone into believing I was German, but we had to try. As the guard walked to the office beneath the tower, I began to shake. I could bet on the fact that there was no one by the name of Emille Crane. He would also find out Charlie was lying about where he was stationed. I could feel our freedom disappearing by the second. I felt death approaching. Maybe Lucie would have survived if I had just left her back at the camp. At that moment, I knew it would be my fault if she died.

The guard returned, and my throat narrowed, making it hard to swallow. My palms were wet with sweat as I pressed them against Lucie's back, rocking her from side to side, hoping to keep us both calm. "You can go on through," the guard said.

I wasn't sure if my body was confused with how to react, or if all my fears just went away, but it was as if my legs walked on their own accord, nearing the gate that was slowly being pulled open by a second guard.

Charlie placed his hand softly on my back as we walked side by side toward the Austrian border. It was probably in my head, but I could smell fresher air wafting through the gate from the new country we were entering. Whether it was safer or not, I didn't know, but it appeared better from where we were standing just a moment earlier.

"Jews don't belong in Austria either," the guard said, his voice deep with contempt.

I could hear my pulse beating inside of my ears, unsure if I should turn around and address the guard's statement or if I should continue walking and ignore the insult he was offering.

"Don't turn around, Amelia, keep walking, and then run," Charlie said. His words were so quiet, they were softer than a whisper, but I heard him clearly. I did as he said, and with only a handful of seconds passing between the guard's comments and the sound of a gunshot—two gunshots, I turned around, finding Charlie holding his already injured shoulder, guarding me as I continued forward. There was blood pouring out of his arm and onto the ground below him.

"Let her go." Charlie's words were demanding. "Or I'll kill you."

"You'll kill me?" the guard questioned Charlie while laughing out loud at him.

I turned back around and looked at Charlie. He looked scared, but I saw an inner strength in him that I hadn't seen before.

"Run, Amelia. Run as fast as you can," Charlie shouted once more. I did as he said, but my body was in so much pain, I didn't know if I'd make it.

"Amelia, do it for me. Go as far as you can go. Go on, Amelia. I'll find you. I promise. I love you."

He was hurt. I should have gone back for him, but when I turned around, I watched as the guard dragged him off toward the tower. I had to protect Lucie too, and if I went back, they would have killed both of us.

Charlie saved me, and I left him there to fight for his life.

I looked back several times, but there wasn't a trace of him in sight.

Charlie took a bullet for me. Lucie and I were alive because of him, and yet I had no idea if he was dead or alive. I wanted to drop to the ground and cry, but there was no time. I held back the tears and kept running. I think it was the pure adrenaline running through my body that kept me going until I finally saw the train station Charlie had mentioned. Shouting in the distance from where we had just come from continued, which told me that there were soldiers after us. Nothing was going to stop me from getting onto that train, though. Charlie just gave up his freedom, and very likely his life, and I could not let that selfless act be in vain.

Lucie was crying in my arms as if she knew what had happened. The poor thing watched all of it as she rested her head on my shoulder.

Lucie and I snuck onto one of the trains that was boarding. I found a coat closet in an empty car and buried us behind some stored bags.

If he survived, Charlie would find us. I had to keep telling myself that we would somehow be reunited. He would find us. It couldn't end like that. It just couldn't. "Lucie," I whispered. "I promise you, Charlie will find us. He said he wanted to be your papa, and he is—he will be. I'm going to make sure you and I have a good life so that when he does find us, we can share it with him, sweet girl. We can start over. We can go to America. I know I didn't put you on this earth, but I will do anything in the world for you, and I'll keep you safe. I will show you undying love, and I will keep you close to me like your mama did for you before she was taken, and like my mama did for me." Lucie looked at me with her doll-like, blue eyes that glimmered from the crack of light pouring in from the closet door. "I need to change your name, sweet girl." I thought for a moment, pondering a good, strong name. Mama's middle name was Annie, and I felt it would be the perfect way to carry on her undying strength. "You will always be Lucie to me, but I'm going to call you Annie from now on because I don't want those horrible men to ever find you. I will be your

Mama, and you will be my daughter. You will never have to know of the life of murder and hatred that we left behind. This is my promise to you, sweet girl."

Lucie couldn't respond, but she smiled as if she understood. Her hand reached for my hair as if she was reaching for the stars, and I knew that with all the horror we had been through—all the misery and heartache—that I had at least saved one life; the precious little girl and I would never take that for granted.

Life wasn't fair, and to know I didn't tell Charlie how I truly felt about him would forever torment me. I didn't tell him how much I loved him because terror stood in the way, and in the end, he was taken from me anyway. It was all for nothing.

I loved him. I love him, and love like that only comes around once in a lifetime. I'm sure of it. Yes, there are second chances to be had, but only one first love—only one who would sacrifice his own life for another. If I could only do it all over again, I would so that I could tell him the last words that he deserved to hear. I hope he knows that I loved him. I'll never forgive myself for not expressing that with words.

CHAPTER TWENTY-FOUR

AMELIA

I still love you, Charlie. I waited years for you to find me, but I've sadly moved on with an everlasting pain in my heart. I needed a new life as I continue trying to let go of the pain that may still eat me alive. The universe didn't want us to be together, so it seems, and when you fight the forbidden, there will always be loss. Throughout my despair, I'm grateful for the gifts God gave me—two beautiful daughters. One of them looks exactly like you. She's yours, Charlie. I see you in her every time I look at those gorgeous blue eyes. I will raise our two girls with every ounce of love that you showed me. Most importantly, I will never let either of them know the real pain you and I experienced. I will shelter them from harm and give them the best life I can. I know if you are watching us, that you will be proud.

No one will ever read the words I have written. My memories will live in a box under my bed like the monsters that threaten to come out in the dark. Only I know where the memories are, and if I tell them to go away, then they can't hurt me anymore.

You are the only memory I will hold on to, Charlie. For as long as I live, I will forever be waiting to see you again, here on earth or in heaven. You are and always will be the love of my life.

CHAPTER TWENTY-FIVE

CHARLIE

"Thank you, sir. Your seat is right over here," says the gentleman whom I assume to be the conductor. He is kind enough to help me with my bag, placing it in the overhead compartment above my seat.

I ease into the blue cushion next to a young man who appears to be traveling alone. He is wearing an expensive-looking pair of headphones, has a phone is resting on his lap, and he looks slightly bored. I'm sure he's oblivious to the fact that he's experiencing luxury at its finest compared to what I knew when I was young. I doubt he'd even be able to comprehend what a train ride during World War II would have been like for the prisoners of that war.

"I love the train," I tell the boy, guessing he probably can't hear me anyway. His gaze floats to the left, studying me for a moment. I'm quite surprised when he twists his head to take a longer look at me, though I'm not surprised with the expression on his face—one that tells me I've annoyed him before he quickly looks down at his phone. I suppose I'm not that interesting to look at, but I don't give up that easily.

"You know, I used to ride the train because it was the best place to people watch," I say, seeing the boy shift his weight around with discomfort. He seems a little more irritated now. "I was people watching so I could find a particular woman. I figured if I rode the train enough times, I would eventually see her. Did you know that seven hundred and fifty-thousand people travel through Grand Central Station each day? Can you imagine that?"

Rather than respond, the boy hits the volume button on his phone, probably increasing the loudness of his music, then turns his head toward the window.

"The ironic part about my train rides was that I ended up seeing the woman I was looking for at the small airport in Rhode Island—in the smallest state of this country. What are those odds?"

When I get no response, I decide to leave the poor lad alone for a few minutes. I realize I'm likely making him uncomfortable, but what he doesn't realize, is that by the end of the ride, he'll be asking me for more stories.

Amelia. Her name still brings a smile to my face, but also a deep feeling of longing, even though it's just thoughts running silently through my mind. I've felt an overwhelming sense of sadness ever since I heard from her granddaughter yesterday. Amelia is ninety-two years old, and although it's an accomplishment to reach such an age, it's hard to bear the thought of her leaving this earth without her lips touching mine one more time. I'm almost embarrassed to be having these thoughts, but it's beyond my control. Not a day has gone by that I haven't thought of her. Not a night has gone by that I haven't dreamed about her. I know I did the right thing by not interfering with her life, but my heart aches to think that we will never have the chance to spend our lives together. The years flew by, but the reality of never being able to gaze into her eyes or touch her sweet face again has almost been too much to bear over the years. I never reached out to her because I didn't want to be selfish. However, now I don't have to feel bad because I was asked to come.

"When I saw Amelia, the woman I'm talking about, in the airport that day, she had her arms full—two little girls, one with dark brown curls and the other with long blonde hair. They were both talking to her at the same moment, begging her to buy a bag of candy in the store they were sitting across from. I sat in the distance within the gate's waiting area, just watching her. Once she gave in to her daughters, she leaned back into her seat, pulled in a deep breath and smiled. I saw happiness on her beautiful face."

The boy looks over at me and removes his headphones from his ears. "You like to talk, huh?" he asks. His voice must have just started changing because it sounded very deep for the age he looked. I wondered why he was traveling alone. Was he was visiting family, or maybe running away?

"When I stop talking, I start to think, and that's never a good thing. Talking cleanses the soul."

"That makes sense," he says, which surprises me.

"So, do you want to know if I went up and talked to her?" I ask him.

The boy shrugs. "Sure, I guess." He's acting like he doesn't care, but I think he's curious where this story is going.

"I didn't approach her right away. After spending such a long time searching for her, I needed to consider what to do. Within a few minutes of watching her, a well-dressed man, who I assumed to be her husband, sat down beside her." The man appeared charming, and she smiled happily as they conversed. "I remember watching as he told her something that made her laugh, and then they each went about reading their respective magazines. She elbowed him once to show him a picture in the one she was reading, and he chuckled in return." She was happy. It was apparent. "Then, when their daughters came back from the store, they both hugged them and gave each girl a kiss on her cheek before the darlings sat down on the ground to eat their candy." The family looked like a picture of perfection. I envied her husband since he had everything I always wanted. "Anyway, after all the time I had spent looking for her, I felt a sense of relief to know she was happy and well. It was the closure I thought I needed before moving on with my life. I figured I wouldn't have to wonder anymore."

"You didn't even say hi?" the boy asks.

"No, I did not, and do you know why?"

He shakes his head with confusion. "Why?"

"If I had walked up to her, every memory she had, both bad and good, would have come rushing back, and I didn't want that for her. She had been through some terrible things, and it appeared she was living a good life. While I had always dreamed of being a part of it, I was satisfied enough, knowing her dream had come true."

"I would have gone over to her," the boy says. "What if she was only somewhat happy, you know?"

"Somewhat happy?" I ask him.

"Yeah, like my mom acted for most of my life until last year."

Divorce. The poor kid. I'm sure that must be hard for him. "Divorce?" I ask to confirm my assumption.

"Yeah, I told my mom that if she wanted to be happy, she needed to leave my dad and get her own life." I'm stunned by his words. He is so mature and rational for such a young man.

"You're a smart kid; you know that?"

"I just know I would not want to grow up to be a miserable person," he says. "That's why I would have gone after the woman."

"I haven't been miserable," I correct him.

"You let some other guy be with your woman? I don't think that would make me very happy," he says.

"How old are you, son?"

"Fifteen," he answers while straightening his shoulders to appear a bit taller.

"Ah, so you're just starting to date then, huh?" I ask him.

He shrugs again. "Eh, the girls at my school kind of su— they're stuck up."

"I can understand. Most women were like that back in the forties too, but not my Amelia. She was such a sweetheart."

"Where did you two meet?" He asks the question that makes my throat tighten each time I'm asked, even after seventy-four years. I don't believe in hiding my story, but it hasn't gotten much easier to discuss over the years.

"During World War II in a concentration camp."

Being fifteen, I assume he's already learned about the Holocaust in his history classes, which is likely the reason his jaw drops. "You survived the Holocaust?" he asks while looking at me as if I were a living ghost.

I glance out the window into the blur of trees we're passing, stealing a moment to avoid eye contact while I confess the truth. "I was one of the bad guys," I tell him.

"You were a—Natz—a—ah." The word is said as if it's a cuss— an insult. It should be; the truth hurts whether it was a path I chose or not.

"We were referred to as Nazis, yes, but I called myself a soldier. I was enlisted by my parents and never given a choice. Sometimes, life takes you for a ride, and when you don't know where your stop is, you just keep moving until the ride ends?" He doesn't understand what I'm talking about, and that's fine.

"Wow," he replies.

The look on his face and his gasping word are a typical response from people of all ages. "I was sentenced to ten years in prison, but I had never hurt a fly. I was punished because I did the right thing."

"Whoa," the boy says. "Was Amelia a—um—soldier too?"

"No, son, she was the victim."

"A Jew?" he clarifies as his eyes widen with shock.

"A person," I clarify. "A beautiful, wonderful, loving human being who I adored more than my own life."

"That's crazy," he says. "And you never talked to her again?"

"No, I haven't yet."

There's silence for a few moments before the boy continues talking. "Sir, with all due respect, you seem like you've lived a long life. What exactly are you waiting for?"

I lean my head back into my seat and shut my eyes, knowing a nap will make this ride go by much faster. "I'm waiting for the end of this ride," I tell him, "and it's almost over."

"You're going to see Amelia?" he asks, elated with curiosity.

"I am, indeed. Seventy-four years late, but I'll finally be able to talk to my love again."

"That's awesome, sir."

"Yes, it is quite awesome, if I do say so myself." The boy smiles as he lifts his headphones from his lap. "Son, do me a favor," I say before his headphones are secured over his ears. "Don't fall in love until you're ready to hold on to her for the rest of your life." There's my unsolicited advice for the day.

My nap aligned perfectly with the end of the ride as we pulled into South Station in Boston.

"Hey, son, would you mind helping me with my bag? I've got a bad arm." The boy looks down at my prosthetic arm, and his mouth falls open, ready to ask another round of questions, I assume.

"Is that because of the war?" He asks in a way that a boy would sound when comparing scars for measures of toughness.

"It's not an achievement, but yes, it is."

"Did it hurt?"

"It did hurt, but I've felt worse pain." Many people don't know what the heart is capable of doing to a body. In my experience, physical pain has never been able to compete with the emotional turmoil my heart went through. He grabs my bag and hands it over to my good hand.

"It was nice to meet you, sir."

"Charlie," I tell him as I place my bag down and reach out my hand to shake his.

"Danny," he says. "I'm glad you sat next to me today."

"The pleasure was all mine." I tip my head and retrieve my bag from the ground.

We exit the train, and I find my way through the terminal to catch a cab, but just as I'm reaching the exit, a young woman places her hand on my arm. "Excuse me, but are you Charlie Crane?" The voice is familiar. Not many people know me by name in Boston, so I assume this is the young lady I spoke to on the phone yesterday.

I turn toward her, finding a spitting image of Amelia—the auburn hair, chestnut eyes, and the worry written in her nervous smile. "And you are?"

"Emma Hill," she says.

I press my lips together because my chest aches, and I'm afraid of what I'll say if I don't take a second to breathe. "She really asked for me?"

Emma wraps her arms around her shoulders as if she were cold inside the warm train station. Her bottom lip quivers for a second, but then she speaks. "She's been asking for you throughout the past week now...but she's been thinking about you since the moment she last saw you."

I feel a bit confused by what she's saying. I suppose Amelia could have mentioned me, though I can't imagine it being an easy topic for her to bring up due to our unusual circumstance. "Did she tell you our story?" I ask.

The man Emma is with places his arm around her shoulders, probably trying to calm the rest of her body that is visibly trembling with discomfort. "Her diary. It has your whole story inside. She asked me to read it, so I did."

I place my hand on my chest, feeling the beat of my heart—and finding it thumping so hard, it scares me a little. "Well, I'll be," I say. "How long does she have?"

"There is no definitive time, but probably not years. We're working on a long-term plan so she will receive the best care possible," the man Emma is with speaks up, and I'm assuming he must be her boyfriend or husband.

"Are you Emma's husband?" I ask, curiously.

"If my grandmother has her way, he will be," Emma laughs, and a hitched breath catches within the sweet sound.

"I'm Amelia's doctor," the young man says. "Jackson Beck. It's such a pleasure to meet you, sir. I've heard a lot about you from Emma."

"Wait a minute," I say, waving my hand in the air, trying to clarify some scattered pieces to this situation. "What does your grandmother have to do with the two of you getting married?"

Emma looks over at Jackson with an adorable smile—a look I recognize. That's Amelia's smile—the one she had every time I told her I loved her.

"Grams told me that her dying wish was for us to get married," Emma tells me.

"I see she hasn't lost her nerve," I reply.

Emma laughs again and tucks her hair behind her shoulder. "She's one tough cookie."

"Take me to her, please," I plead.

"That's why we're here," Jackson says.

"How did you know when my train was coming in?" I ask them as we walk toward the parking garage signs.

"There were only a couple of trains arriving this morning from

New York, so we sat here and watched all the people passing by until we saw you."

"My goodness, you sound like me, kid."

Emma claps her hands over her mouth and tears burst from her eyes as she flings her arms around my neck. "I'm sorry," she cries. "I'm just so happy you're here."

I'm taken aback by her welcome, but at the same, it's nice after not having any family around. I came to the United States alone, and my friends here became my family, but it's different. It has never been like my life growing up before the war.

Jackson takes Emma's hand and pulls it to his lips to kiss her knuckles. What a gentleman. He looks completely smitten by her. I wonder how long they have been together.

We make it out to the car. "Very nice automobile you have here, son," I tell Jackson. "It looks like you've done well for yourself."

"I've worked hard, sir."

"Good for you," I tell him. "Emma, I know I just met both of you, but I think your grandmother might be onto something here. How long have you two known each other? A year or so?"

"A week," Emma says, appearing embarrassed as she places her hands over her cheeks to hide the pink warmth glowing across her face.

"Well, love isn't measured by time, sweetheart. There's nothing to be ashamed of because if it's meant to be, it's meant to be, and there's not much you can do to change that. Life is too short and precious not to take a chance on love."

"Charlie, do you need to stop anywhere before we arrive at the hospital?" Jackson asks me.

"Actually, do you mind if we stop at a pastry shop first? I'm quite hungry," I tell him.

"Absolutely," Jackson says.

He kindly pulls into a small parking lot in front of an old-fashioned bakery. "I'll just be a moment."

The shop is somewhat empty, and I'm able to check out within a matter of minutes. "Did you find what you needed?" Jackson asks as I slip back into his car.

"I did. Thank you very much," I offer.

It doesn't take long before we pull into another parking lot—it looks like the doctor's parking area. Jackson opens my door first and runs around to open Emma's door too, though she's already opened it by the time he gets there. "I told you that you don't have to keep doing that," she says quietly, along with a soft love tap to his arm.

"I want to," he says.

She rolls her eyes at him and laughs. "You're a goof, but a chivalrous one."

She is her grandmother.

Emma appears more nervous than I am as we take the elevator up to the eighth floor. I feel like the world is moving toward me in slow motion as we walk down the hall. I've been waiting so long for this day that I'm scared I may wake up from this dream again, and as usual, it won't be real. We turn the corner, and in an instant, it feels as if time stood still. It doesn't matter how many years have passed. It doesn't matter that she has white hair and that there are lines on her face. She is still the most beautiful woman I have ever seen.

"Amelia, my darling. You look as beautiful today as the last time I saw you," I say as I walk toward her. The surprised glimmer in her eyes tells me that Emma wanted to keep my arrival a secret, which makes me happy. I've wondered what the look on Amelia's face might be if we were to run into each other unexpectedly. This was the look I imagined.

"Charlie?" she says, recognizing me immediately. Her eyes are open wide, and tears trickle down her cheeks.

I take her hands in mine and immediately feel the undying connection between us. I remember the sensation running through my body as if it were only yesterday that I laid eyes on her for the first time.

I haven't cried since that day when they took me away from her, but the tears are flowing freely from my eyes now. I'm not ashamed to cry because I've been holding it in, waiting for this day for seventy-four years.

CHAPTER TWENTY-SIX

EMMA

I didn't tell Grams I found Charlie or that he would be here this morning, just in case it didn't happen. I couldn't bear to disappoint her. However, I also wanted to see the look on her face as he walked through the door. Mom and Annie aren't here yet, which is a good thing because I think they might interfere with Grams and Charlie's reunion, but I have to be here for this because Grams entrusted me with her secret.

"Emma," Jackson whispers into my ear. "Maybe we should give them a minute."

"I can't leave," I whisper back. Both of us are standing at the door, and I know Jackson wants to hear what happens just as much as I do.

"All right," he says.

"Amelia," Charlie speaks her name again as if he just wants to hear it out loud. He's caressing her cheek and wiping her tears away. He leans forward and gives her a long hug. Grams closes her eyes, and her lips quiver as her chest rises and falls.

I'm having a hard time breathing just watching them. The honor of watching a love story that has spanned seven decades is nothing I'll ever forget. After a moment, Charlie turns and takes ahold of a chair by the bed, pulling it up beside Grams and takes her hand within his again.

Charlie is gazing into Grams's eyes, and it looks like he is struggling to find the right words to say. "I brought you something," he tells her.

"You brought me something?" Grams asks, trying to laugh against her tears.

"I was worried you might be hungry," Charlie says as he hands her the pastry bag he had been carrying.

Grams peers inside and cups her hand over mouth. "Charlie Crane," she says, weakly.

"A sweet roll for my sweetheart—your favorite," he says.

Grams's eyes well up again as she continues looking at the fresh pastry in the bag. She swallows hard and finally looks back up at him. "I thought you died, Charlie. I waited in Switzerland for a year, but when you didn't come back to me, I assumed you had been killed, so I made the decision to move here. I thought if by God's grace you were still alive and you were ever going to find me, it would be here—where our dreams were supposed to come true."

Charlie rests his hand on Grams's and encloses her fingers in his. "I was sent to prison for ten years when they took me away from you that day. I was so angry that they ripped us apart, but I saw you get far enough away that I had some relief knowing you would be able to escape. When I was released, I looked everywhere for you. I wasn't sure if you were even alive, but I didn't stop, Amelia, not until I found you."

"Oh Charlie, my sweet Charlie. It took seventy-four years, but you found me, my love," she says.

Charlie looks down at their hands for a moment before gazing back up at her. "Amelia, I have to be honest with you about something."

"What is it?" Grams asks with wonder, and her voice cracks with a sound of weakness.

"I—I found you a long time ago," Charlie says. He takes a deep breath and looks back up at her. "It didn't take seventy-five years, Amelia. I wanted to have you back in my life so badly, but I saw you at an airport one day with your family, and I accepted the fact that you were happily married with two daughters. I wasn't going to interfere with the life you made for yourself. I just couldn't be that selfish."

I gasp, making my presence known at the doorway, and Charlie turns around as Grams stares at him with her mouth wide open. "Give us a moment, will you, sweetheart?" Charlie says to me.

Jackson pulls me from the doorway but just around to the wall so we can still hear their conversation.

"You're a doctor, you know, you shouldn't be spying on patients," I tell him.

"Shush, I can do what I want. This is not a violation of patient privacy. It's about a love story."

"That's my grandfather in there," I tell Jackson. "I think he's Mom's dad, and she doesn't even know. I know the truth, and she doesn't. That's not fair to her."

"Em, your grandmother may not want your mom and Annie to know, and you have to respect that. That information could destroy them."

"Grams wouldn't ask me to keep a secret like that," I tell him.

Jackson leans forward, bringing himself down to eye level with me. "She kept a secret for seventy-four years. I wouldn't be so sure."

I rest my head against the wall, exhaling despair. I can't keep that kind of secret from Mom. I hope Grams tells them the truth.

"Charlie, how could you? And what do you mean, you saw me at the airport?" I hear Grams speaking louder than before.

"I was at the airport in Rhode Island one day many years ago, and I saw you from a distance. I couldn't believe it was really you, but it was. I was so happy, so overjoyed. I headed toward you, but as I got closer, I saw you were sitting there with your family. You were smiling and laughing. You were happy, Amelia. I saw it with my own two eyes. That's all I wanted for you," he explains.

"Charlie Crane," Grams scolds him. "That wasn't for you to decide by yourself. You should have given me a choice. I deserved a say." Grams's voice was growing louder by the second, and I couldn't tell if it was out of anger or pain, but she didn't sound happy. I didn't see their reunion going this way.

"You're right, but at the time, I thought I was doing the right thing. Please forgive me?" Charlie begged.

A few more loud exhales bounce off the wall of her room before either speak again. "There's something you need to know, Charlie, something you would have known had you come up to me in the airport that day," Grams says.

I move an inch closer to the door, needing to make sure I don't miss any of this. "What is it?" he asks her.

"We have a daughter," she says, her words shaky, but firm.

There's deafening silence in the pause between them. "As well as a granddaughter." Again, there is silence.

"I have a daughter?" he musters the word as if his tongue is lodged in his throat.

"Yes, her name is Clara." *I was right...Mom. Mom has no clue.*

"All this time, I've had a daughter, and she grew up without me. Dear God," Charlie says with muffled words.

"But who was that man I saw you with?" he asks.

"My late husband," she said. "Max and I became friends when I moved into my first apartment in New York. He lived in the same building, and he was always bringing food for us, and toys for the girls. He just loved spending time with us, and he was a good man. As our friendship grew, he told me he'd help me with everything, and I wouldn't have to take care of my family alone. He asked me to marry him, and I said yes."

"He married you even though you had a daughter with another man? Did you love him?" Charlie asked.

"Of course, I did. He helped me take care of my family. What's not to love?" I roll my eyes at a comment only Grams could come out with.

"That's not what I'm asking you, Amelia," Charlie says.

Grams's voice lowers to a whisper. "Let me finish the story, Charlie. Max was homosexual. You know it wasn't common back then for somebody to admit to that, and nobody knew the truth except me. We had a good life together. I was married to a man I could laugh and cry with, and we took care of each other. It was easy. It was nice."

As I peek around the corner, Charlie looks dazed. I'm sure it's a lot for him to take in all at once. First, he reconnects with the love of his life after decades of being apart. Then he finds out that she's been waiting for him all these years, while he was staying away so she could be happy. What kind of cruel irony is that? "What about you, Charlie? Did you ever marry?" Grams asks.

"No," he says, simply. "No one ever held a flame to you. I dated a few women, but honestly, I gave up trying after a while. I was meant to be with you, and if I couldn't have you, I was surely meant to do something different with my life. I always felt like losing you was my punishment for the wrong I did in this world."

There is a sudden silence between them. It's killing me, and I can't stand out here wondering what's going on. I turn the corner, going back into the room even as Jackson is trying to keep me where I was.

Instantly wishing I had just listened to him, I quickly return to the hallway and press my back up against the wall.

"I told you to leave them alone," Jackson says. "What's the matter?"

"They're kissing," I tell him.

"That's a man who knows what he wants," Jackson says, his eyes filled with mirth. "I could see it as soon as I met him."

I elbow Jackson gently in his side, "Stop that," I say.

"Hey, give him a break. He waited more than seventy years to kiss her."

With a deep breath and my eyes closed, I knock on Grams's door because I'm worried about the effect on her heart if she gets too excited.

I open my eyes after a long second, finding two sets of eyes gazing at me with pride. "Emma, my dear, you are my granddaughter," Charlie says as he approaches me with his arm stretched out wide.

He holds me tightly, and I return the embrace. I don't know this man other than what I've read, but if he was good enough for my grandmother to love, then I want nothing more than to get to know him.

"Apparently so. I just found this out myself last night," I tell him.

"Your grandmother is good at keeping secrets," he says with a proud smile.

"Hey, doc?" Charlie calls out.

Jackson walks right in when called, in case they had any doubt he was standing in the hall with me. "Yes, sir?"

"What can we do about getting this woman back on her feet?"

Jackson seems caught off guard as he runs his fingers through his hair. "Well, there are two options. Both are risky, but one is more dangerous than the other. We can do nothing and hope that the progression of Amelia's condition is slow. The other option is surgery, which would consist of replacing the aortic valve. It's a risky procedure in a younger person, but even more so for Amelia because of her age."

"If I don't have the surgery, I'll be dead within a year, right?" Grams asks.

"No, not necessarily. It could be longer, but probably not by much. I just can't predict or make any promises."

"Do the surgery," Grams blurts out without even giving it a moment's thought.

"Amelia, are you sure about this? Don't you want to discuss it with your daughters first."

"Daughters? Wait..." Charlie says, shaking his head and looking confused.

"I saw two little girls with you in the airport that day. Who was that other little girl? Do you have another daughter? Who is *her* father?" Charlie asks.

Grams's lips press firmly together as she takes the time to look at each of us. "You said you would be her papa, so she's just as much your daughter as she is mine," Grams says to Charlie.

"Lucie?" Charlie asks.

Grams smiles and bites down on her bottom lip. "Yes, I changed Lucie's name to Annie so I could keep her safe, and then I kept her as my own."

"Oh my goodness, you raised these two precious girls without me?" Charlie asks with a profound look of sadness on his face.

Grams looks upset for a moment, maybe thinking Charlie is angry, but his expression changes quickly, and he lifts his face to look directly into her eyes.

"You still amaze me, Amelia. What a wonderful thing you did for your girls," Charlie says with pride written on his face.

Relief spills through Grams's eyes as she continues, "Annie doesn't technically belong to either of us," Grams says, and I immediately understand why it's so important for the truth to remain hidden from Mom and Annie. It would hurt them so much. Looking at it from the outside, I find an immediate under-standing of what love is.

Love is keeping someone safe, taking a bullet for them, and letting them live in happiness. I get it now.

"You're right, Amelia, she may not belong to us by blood, but she belongs to us by love. We loved her then, and I love her now just like you do."

"You haven't changed a bit, Charlie Crane."

Charlie leans forward and shamelessly kisses Grams again, without a care in the world, even though we're standing here watching.

"So, about the surgery," Grams says as she wipes away her tears again. "How quickly can I start the rest of my life?"

"Amelia, are you sure about this?" Jackson asks.

"Jackson, come here," Grams says, waving him over.

He walks over to her, and she takes his hand in hers.

"I've already handed you a part of my heart," she says, pointing at me. "Now fix the other part. You're the best cardiologist in this hospital, aren't you?"

"Well, I—"

"Quit being so humble," Grams says. "Fix my damn heart, Dr. Beck. I need more time."

"As long as you are aware of the risks involved. I understand where you're coming from—I'll perform the surgery, and you know I'll do my very best," Jackson says. "I'll have the pre-op tests done this afternoon, and we'll schedule you for surgery tomorrow morning."

"On a Saturday?" she asks.

"For you, I'll make it happen," he tells her. "I know better than to stand in your way on this."

"Okay, just remember, you promised to marry Emma before I die, so keep that in mind tomorrow. You don't want to go breaking promises to an old lady now, do you?"

"No, ma'am," Jackson responds. I can see how nervous he is, and yet, I believe I may be more nervous, but hopeful at the same time. This could give Grams a second chance at life, and while she may be ninety-two, her will to live is stronger than her weakened heart.

"I have some scheduling to do," Jackson says. "I'll be back in a bit to check on you." Jackson turns to shake Charlie's hand. "Again, it was a pleasure to meet you, Mr. Crane."

"Well, he's a keeper," Charlie says to Grams as Jackson leaves the room.

"Exactly what I told Miss Emma over here," Grams says with a raised brow.

"Listen to your grandma; she knows what she's talking about," Charlie says. I guess he's got the right to say what he wants. After all, he is my grandpa, and they sure do look good together.

"When do I get to meet my daughters?" Charlie asks Grams.

Grams fidgets with a thread on the bed sheet, appearing lost in thought for a moment.

"Charlie, the girls believe that their father passed away ten years ago. They loved him dearly and mourned the loss of him for a long time after his passing."

"You didn't want to hurt them," Charlie says, understanding more than I would ever be able to. "You were right to keep this secret, and it would be unfair to disrupt their lives now."

"I'm afraid they would never forgive me," Grams says to Charlie. Charlie and Grams both look over at me. "Emma, this is a big secret. It's a lot to ask of you to keep it for me. Is it going to be too much for you? Because I would understand if it is."

"I love Mom and Annie, so, no," I answer simply. It hurts to know they'll never know the truth, but I understand that going through half your life and then learning that the one person who always cared for you withheld the truth about who you are, might be too painful to comprehend, no matter the reason. I have to live with this fact, but no one in our family deserves any more pain after the suffering that's already been done.

"Thank you," Grams says. "You *are* just like me, you know that?"

I smile, unable to respond with words that will do justice. I don't think I have done enough to deserve a comparison to her strength and greatness, but the fact that she thinks I do, means everything to me.

"Mom and Annie are supposed to be here in a few minutes," I tell them.

"I'm your grandmother's close friend from before the war. We grew up together, and I happened to see her name on the wall as I was visiting another sick patient," Charlie says.

"Close friend?" Grams asks him. "That part is the truth. The part where we fell in love and had a daughter together is something we'll just keep between us," Grams says as she beams with utter happiness.

"You're sure about this surgery tomorrow?" I ask Grams one last time.

"Yes, and I need you to back me up with your mother and aunt, all right?"

"I promise," I agree.

As expected, Mom and Annie walk in with coffees in hand.

"Good morning, Mom," Annie says, before noticing a man sitting in the visitor seat. "Oh, who's this?"

Charlie is gazing at Annie and Mom. He clears his throat after a long second. "I'm—I'm Charlie," he says, standing from his chair to offer his hand to each of them.

"Charlie," Mom says as if she's running the name through her head, trying to place it. "It's nice to meet you, Charlie." She reaches over for his hand, looking at him quizzically as if she's trying to dissect his thoughts. Next, Mom glances at me questioningly, but I shrug.

"Are you a friend of my mom's?" Annie asks.

"Indeed. Amelia and I are old, old dear friends. I saw your mother's name on the wall as I was visiting another patient, and it seemed too good to be true."

"Sure does," Annie says with a bit of apprehension. "Mom has mentioned a 'Charlie' several times in the past week. Is this the same Charlie, Mom?" She's studying Charlie intently but doesn't haven't much else to say. Annie has no idea she has met him before.

"Yes," Grams says without elaborating. "What a coincidence, huh? This is Charlie, and he's right; we go way back. He's a dear old friend, and I'm glad he found me today."

Annie takes a moment to look between Grams and Charlie again, and I can tell she's more curious than she's letting on. "Oh, that explains it. She must have seen him walking around the hospital," Annie says. "Well, it's so nice to meet you, Charlie. Any friend of Mom's is a friend of ours, of course."

Charlie is quieter than he's been since we picked him up, and I feel a need to leave the room before I give anything away with my facial expressions since Mom knows me too well, but I promised to help Grams with this battle about the surgery tomorrow.

"Girls, take a seat," Grams tells them.

They look at her warily for a moment before sitting down. "What's going on, Mom?" Mom and Annie peer over at Charlie next, maybe wondering why someone who's practically a stranger is standing there when they are about to have what sounds like a serious conversation. I would feel that way if I didn't know better.

"I'm going to have the surgery tomorrow. I have to give my heart one more chance, and there's nothing either of you can do to talk me out of it." Grams gets right to the point.

"Mom, Jackson said it was dangerous, and it could kill you," Annie says, immediately upset—obviously against the idea, and Mom is right behind her. There's no winning with this. It's a gamble either way.

"Clara and Annie, I'm going to die anyway. If it's my time, then it's my time. Let me die when I choose to die, okay?"

Annie and Mom give each other a knowing look, silently agreeing that there is no arguing with Grams about her health. She has always overseen her own life, and it will continue to be like that until the day she dies.

We're all gathered in Grams's room this morning at six o'clock since Jackson scheduled the surgery for seven. He said it could take several hours, and he wanted to start as early as possible. I'm stealing half of Grams's bed, resting with her, needing to be as close as possible. Annie and Mom are sharing the space on her other side, and Charlie is beside me with his hand on my shoulder. "You're going to make it," Charlie says. "You're a survivor, Amelia. You know that."

"I know," Grams says. She doesn't seem like herself today, kind of like the day when she was telling me she was going to die, and it scares me.

"Do you think I'm doing the wrong thing?" she asks.

"No," I tell her. "If you have a chance at more, I say take it."

I must be able to live with the outcome if today doesn't go well, but Grams has always focused on living in the moment and taking risks so she never had to wonder what could have been, except with Charlie. In any case, if this is what she believes is right, then I have to be okay with it.

Jackson knocks on the door and walks into the crowded room. He's in his scrubs with a surgical cap already in place. "Good morning, Amelia," he says.

"How is my future grandson-in-law?" she asks, teasing him with a pointed finger.

Jackson laughs. "I'm doing well. I'm ready to save a heart today. How are you doing?"

"I'm scared," she says honestly.

Jackson moves in slowly as we all part ways from Grams's side to give him space. "You're going to be set up in just a few minutes, but I wanted to make sure you don't have any last-minute questions or concerns."

"I don't think so," Grams says. "I'm ready to get this over with."

"Understandable." He places his hand on Grams's shoulder and smiles at her, looking calm and relaxed, which is exactly what she needs. I appreciate it, especially since we all know how risky this surgery is.

"I'll give you all another minute before the nurses come in to get you," Jackson says.

He looks at me and subtly asks if I'm okay with a gesture of his raised brows. I nod and shrug, unsure how to respond. "I'll take good care of her," he mouths before leaving.

It's hard to imagine saying goodbye, but how can I not prepare for the worst? I lean over Grams and wrap my hands around her face, staring into her hazy eyes as she gives me the same look in return. No matter the outcome, I need to remember this moment for the rest of my life. I need to remember everything about her because I'm so much a part of her. She can't leave me...she can't. I break my gaze for a moment, looking up at the ceiling to stop the pooling tears from falling down my cheeks. I exhale slowly, pleadingly for this pain in my chest to go away. Right now, I feel like I need a heart doctor too.

"I love you so much, Grams, and you are going to make it through this, okay?" My chest is tight, and my throat is dry. My heart hurts, and I'm not going to be able to keep it together much longer.

"I know you love me. You will always be my sweetheart, Emma. Always."

"And my girls...you are my special, special girls. You have made my life worth living. Every moment. Every single moment has been worth it for you. I don't know what I'd do without you. I really don't," Grams tells them.

"Don't talk like that, Mom," Annie says. "We love you. You're going to make it. You have to."

Mom and Annie release an ocean of tears as they hold each other, walking out of the room. "Charlie, are you coming with us?" Mom asks him through a hiccup. They haven't asked him many questions, which I find odd, but at the same time, I'm grateful.

"I'll be right there," he says to them.

Mom and Annie offer each other a look, and I can't decipher the exchange. Maybe they know something, or maybe I am truly the only one who knows. Maybe none of us are meant to ever speak of it with one another. It's so confusing, yet I understand it all so clearly.

Charlie is the only one left beside me, and he sits down on Grams's bed and leans back into the pillow with her.

"Amelia, we've made it this far. I know this is what's right. I still love you, darling, just as much as I did all those years ago."

Grams reaches up and touches Charlie's cheek with the tips of her fingers, gazing at him as if she were a young girl in love for the first time. "You know what my biggest regret was, Charlie?" Grams asks.

With a small smile on Charlie's face, he presses his fingers gently through Grams's hair. "What's that?"

Grams shakes her head from side to side with small movements. "I never got to tell you how I truly felt that day when you saved me, Charlie."

With his hand now cupped around her chin, forcing her to focus on his face, he smiles. "It doesn't matter," he says. Charlie's eyes well up, but it looks like the tears are made from contentment and joy. He lays his head on Grams's chest and holds her tightly. "I could die knowing you never said those words because I knew how you felt, and that was enough for me."

Grams pulls in a deep breath and holds it for a moment. "Charlie, it's not enough, and if this is it for me, I need for you to know—"

"No," Charlie says as he places his finger over Grams's lips. "You don't owe me that. Love isn't words, Amelia. Love is so much more than letters and sounds, and we know that."

"Yes, that's true, and I was sure if said those deadly words to you, then you would be the next person taken from me. Before I met you, I lost everyone I loved. I couldn't bear to take a chance on that with you, as well. However, now that I might be the next to go, you should hear those last words."

"Don't say your last words, Amelia. Don't."

"Charlie, I have waited all these years to tell you what I couldn't say back then."

"Don't say it," he croaks, sounding as if he may shatter. His face crumples with pain and anger as he continues to plead. "Please, don't. Save them for later."

"I love you, Charlie. I have loved you since the beginning of our time together, and if this is it for me, then these words—'*I love you*' are my last words, and they will always belong to you."

EPILOGUE

he chairs are all aligned in a row, one after another, filled with friends and family. I've learned a lot over the course of my life, and I know there are many beginnings but only one end. Life has its path set out for us, and whether we try to change it or just understand it, we'll never have everything figured out. That's just the way it is.

Everyone is gathered in their best attire, waiting silently for the ceremony to begin. Tears that have been waiting a long time fall from my eyes as Jackson walks with me down between the rows of chairs. My heart pounds heavily, reminding me of the journeys I've been through as Jackson helps me down to the seat in the front row. I pull a tissue out of my purse and hold it against my chest, knowing it won't be long before it has soaked up all my falling tears.

Debussy's Reverie chimes from the small three-piece orchestra in front of me, and I turn to watch the others walking in my direction.

As the rows are filled and silence washes over the enclosed area like a breeze on a beautiful summer's day, my attention is drawn toward the most beautiful vision.

Charlie's arm is looped through Emma's as he escorts her down the aisle toward the love of her life. Knowing he has had the privilege of walking his granddaughter down the aisle is more than I could ask for, other than the little more time I've been gifted. It will be the best memory of my whole life.

Jackson has a tear rolling down his cheek as he smiles wider than I've seen him smile in the last year. He sees his forever walking toward him, and he told me yesterday that if it weren't for me, he wouldn't be the luckiest man in the world today.

They promised me they would marry before I died, but Jackson gave me the gift of more time, so not only do I have the pleasure of watching my only granddaughter entering into a life of happiness and joy, but I have my Charlie by my side—the way it was always meant to be.

Annie and Clara accepted me—their old mother—dating a man at ninety-two and didn't put up much of a stink. Charlie has added laughter and love to our lives, and it has felt purely instinctual the way both girls warmed up to him without knowing the true connection between us all. To me, it's just another way of witnessing the depths to which love travels.

With my life's truths floating from secret to secret, Charlie and I found it appropriate to privately sneak away to Ellis Island a few months ago and marry one another in front of the Statue of Liberty. It was a day to celebrate, but just for the two of us. It's still a secret, but it's our secret now instead of just my own, although I think Emma suspects something. I know it was our destiny to live until we found freedom and each other.

I've seen it all. I've been through more than I want to remember some days, but my stories and memories made me who I am. I can speak freely about the difference between love and hate, peace and war, and I don't feel the need to keep it tucked away in my diary under my bed any longer—most of it, anyway.

Charlie and I may not have all the time in the world, but we have the rest of our lives together, and we intend to make the most of it.

I never gave up.

He never gave up.

We're survivors from opposite sides, brought together through the enemy who only believed in hate.

Charlie promised he'd come back for me. He kept his promise —his last words. and I will keep mine.

In the end, we won our war.

AFTERWORD

I love you.

Three simple words, never spoken by my flesh and blood.

Thirty-three years came and went, and I never heard those words from my grandmother. I went through life wondering if she loved me at all, wondering if I wasn't adequate or worthy enough, wondering if I was a disappointment. Her feelings came to me in waves of confusion—explanations of why she was the way she was —who she was and who she had been.

My grandmother was a survivor in every sense of the word. She lived through three years of torment during the Holocaust at Theresienstadt, a concentration camp in what was then Czechoslovakia. The conditions in the camp were horrendous, even worse than what I wrote about in this story.

Writing this book was a journey for me—it was a way for me to heal and understand who my grandmother was. After thirty-three years of pushing away and blocking out the historically terrifying stories she willing shared with me, she passed away. Now, all I want to do is ask her questions, learn more about her life, and find out about the monsters under her bed. It's too late for that, but the information is still there even though it has been denied and erased by so many people. That saddens me.

I was in pain after she died, but I could not show it. She told me crying was not a way to express emotion, but instead, it was a form of weakness. We weren't supposed to cry at funerals. Instead, we should always remember the good times.

No one cried at my grandmother's funeral. It was out of respect for her.

We all told her we loved her, knowing we would never hear the words in return. It took the writing of this book to help me understand why she couldn't say it.

My grandmother lost her brother, her father, aunts, uncles, and cousins in the Holocaust. Everyone was gone except for her mother. She carried on through life—existing, learning, teaching, researching, and writing. Unlike Amelia, she didn't want to forget. She wanted to remember. She carried it all with her—the habits she learned in the camp, and the way of life no one should willingly choose. It made me angry and upset, and I couldn't understand why she was cold when I was so warm. Now, I finally understand. What she experienced at that camp had such a profound effect on her that it became part of who she was.

She may be gone, but I hope she's watching over me and knows how much of my heart I put into this book to honor her. I hope that if she were still here, she would feel a sense of peace and pride to know that I understand why she was the way she was, and that I accept, appreciate, and respect her and the unique ways she chose to live life.

If she didn't fight to survive, I wouldn't be here. I'm grateful for her strength and courage, and I hope I've inherited just an ounce of her passionate spirit.

UNSPOKEN WORDS

If you enjoyed Last Words, Unspoken Words will give offer you a completely different, yet heartbreaking, perspective from Charlie Crane.

"Women and children to the right. Men, to the left," I once said.

From 1942 to 1944 I was what some called a Jew killer. Though, I have never hurt a soul, I was responsible for separating Jewish families, ensuring they would never see each other again. Those who were sick, were sent to their death ... by me because I was forced to follow the enemy. The war stole my right of beliefs, my goals for a future, my left arm, and the love of my life.

I saved Amelia ...

... then I lost her.

And after more than seventy years, I'm told she's alive and asking for me.

Will love be enough to overcome the silence of more than seven decades?

PROLOGUE

he house in front of me was a vivid shade of blue—bluer than the sky, but not as dark as the ocean. The color reminded me of a bluebird. The framed windows were a shade of forest green, and there were two small windows on each side of the matching door. The roof was old and tattered but supported the one lonesome dormer-window in the attic. The flower beds beneath the front windows were empty, but I imagine they were full of vibrant blossoms in the spring and summer. Trinkets clung to the windows from the inside, where a fire illuminated a lonely table covered with a freshly prepared dinner.

I wasn't standing in front of that house to admire the unique colors and decor.

I had a task.

Sven shoved his elbow into my side as he walked past me, continuing down a line of Jews who were waiting for their next order. "Charlie, kill that woman. She is out of line," Sven asserted his command with an authoritative intonation.

I tried to step forward along the uneven cobblestones from where I was standing. The sight in front of me had me frozen. Through wisps of fog, I set my focus on the middle-aged woman. With dark hair, tied in an unkempt knot at the base of her skull, and loose strands hanging in front of her eyes, she appeared forlorn while shouting for her children. She was wearing an apron, probably from the food she had just finished preparing for her family when a group of soldiers broke into her quaint blue house. "Let my children go!" The woman was trying to protect her family—her daughter and son. Sven told me to kill her because she was crying for her children, and we aren't supposed to tolerate such a disgusting display of emotion from a Jew.

Sven stopped walking when he noticed I wasn't following him. He stood, staring at me, waiting on me to fulfill his command. I still couldn't move. Rather than follow orders, I glanced back and forth between the woman's daughter, who was being pulled away by a comrade I didn't know, and then again at the distraught mother. She was reaching her arms out for her daughter, who was already so far away. At that moment, I knew the two would never reunite. The thought made me feel sick.

"Kill her," Sven shouted. "Do it now, Charlie."

I knew of the punishment I would receive for not following orders from a superior, but I couldn't move my arms, let alone, handle a weapon.

Sven's hand pressed against the lapel of my coat as he pushed me away. "Coward," he muttered, passing by me.

Sven retrieved his rifle from the left side of his belt and aimed it at the mother's head, while the other comrade had the woman bent over in shame.

I couldn't do much else but watch her daughter grieve what would be an extraordinary loss in a matter of seconds. "I love you, Mama. Please don't hurt her!" the girl shouted in a plea.

"Amelia," the woman countered. "Fight and be strong. For me."

Amelia was the girl's name.

Amelia deserved a mother to face the horrors she was about to encounter.

"Mama, no," Amelia grunted. "Please, don't leave me!" Amelia pleaded as if her mother had a say in the matter. Though we all knew, only one person had the final decision, and Sven no longer had a heart in his chest.

Amelia's words buzzed over the blasting weapon. Her mother was taken down with one bullet. To the ground, she fell. Blood pooled instantly. The smell of gunpowder was potent, even through the thick air.

The world went silent for me even though screams were coming from all *sides. The Jews were scared, especially while watching one of their own sacrificed as an example of what disrespect earns.*

I watched that woman's daughter, Amelia; the pale complexion wash through her face as she stared doe-eyed at her mother's corpse. Amelia's head shook slightly with disbelief as she was pushed within a herded line, farther and farther away from her mother's body. Amelia couldn't have been older than sixteen or seventeen, and in an instant, her world had become darker than she likely ever could have imagined it would.

My chest felt as though it was caving in. No matter how many Jews I watched meet their ending as Amelia's mother had, the pain never lessened, and the heartache only grew stronger with the sight of every new-fallen body.

I was not meant to be a killer.

I refused to hate, no matter what I was supposed to believe.

Hello. I'm Charlie Crane.

Like many people who lived through World War II, I have spent years reminiscing about those years—the memories, decisions, losses, and gains. While I know plenty of older folk like myself who put the past behind them, I prefer to keep my past current to avoid letting anything I left behind, die.

My life has had many ups and downs, trials and tribulations, and enough death and destruction that has made me wonder if my birth was a mistake. Surely, I was not meant to live the way I have. Though beyond my dismay, I will carry the shadows from eradication within my heart.

I was born in the small town of Lindau within Bavaria, Germany—a place where houses and buildings replicate much of the fairytales modern parents tell their children about today. Colored facades, in every hue, with gabled roofs, white-framed windows, cross-hatch decor lining the walls, stone-work adorned with deliciously pungent flowers; the world as I saw it was picturesque, and I was none the wiser that a place outside of Bavaria could look any different.

My mama and papa were Hans and Anja, a bread baker and a seamstress—both innocent and quiet.

My family didn't have a lot, but we made do to get by; always dreaming of a day when life might become more comfortable for us all. We weren't shy about our wishes and hopes, but as I became an older boy, I often wondered if we were too open about our desires. I began to think that by having enough and recognizing what we had, my family would someday have more than enough. Although, who was I to tell someone how to dream? Especially when that someone was Mama or Papa.

"He will change the world," I remember Mama saying, speaking of our country's new chancellor. "You watch, Charlie, he will make things better for us all. We will have an answer to our prayers."

There was no answer to our prayers. *Hitler* did not make life better for anyone. Instead, *he* stole everything from everyone.

"I don't like that man, Mama," I replied, speaking out of turn.

"Charlie, do not talk that way. That is pure blasphemy. Our country needs change, and Adolf Hitler will do just that. You watch, he will." With a smart tap on my cheek, Mama pointed her finger, making her point clear, which only left me with more thoughts.

I was too young to understand the complexity and meaning of a country adopting a dictator as a leader. However, it might not have mattered how old I was, because Hitler's promises blinded many of us.

History was developing every single day. Life changed quickly for all young and old, men and women. No one was safe with their thoughts and opinions because we were no longer allowed to think on our own.

Hitler's troops tried to mold us—me, but I was a strong boy and a stronger man.

I bent, but I did not break.

Adolf Hitler made laws against loving a different kind.

Then, I broke the law.

It was the best decision I have ever made. **[Continue Reading]**

THE OTHER BLUE SKY

I WAS ONE OF THE LUCKY MISSING CHILDREN OF THE HOLOCAUST

READY FOR ANNIE'S SECRET, HEARTBREAKING STORY?

*V*ery few people can say they were born inside a concentration camp during the Holocaust. Disease, starvation, and much worse, prevented most prisoners from surviving.

For infants, it was nearly impossible.

I became an anomaly. I shouldn't be alive.

As a child, I didn't know my life was different from that of others. I had nothing to compare it to, and I had no insight about the day I was born ... until the moment I overheard the truth.

In a split second, I became a stranger to my reflection, my name, and my reason for being. I was not Annie anymore, and the people raising me were not my parents. Even the blue sky I cherished became an unfamiliar sight.

I felt utterly alone in a foreign world, but that changed when I met another person who was lost, like me. Fisher offered his hand to hold and began to prove his theory: "When two missing people find one another, they can consider themselves found."

Fisher enlightened me, and through him, I gained a deeper understanding of life. Now, I know there are two sides of the beautiful, blue sky. I'm on one side, and my lost loved ones are on the other, but at the end of it all, we'll be together again under the one and only sky. [Continue Reading]

PREVIEW OF THE OTHER BLUE SKY

PREFACE

I didn't know one could be missing when a visible reflection states otherwise. I also didn't realize how many of us, former prisoners, are still considered missing people, especially since we were once missing children. There's a bond between the strangers we are, and though many of us haven't met, we think of ourselves as a family, in a sense because our stories are the same.

There is a book cover with a simple image, one that could tell any story. There's a spine—strong and built to hold everything inside, and though there isn't much of a description written on the back, inside ... on the yellowed pages ... is where our stories line up perfectly. For the thousands of us who have not been accounted for, there are no words to trail in our footsteps.

During the time of the Holocaust, people were taken, murdered, and tortured. All different types of people—mothers, fathers, sisters, and brothers. Books were burned, money stolen, and heirlooms were left to rot. Those who survived curated the information we have in our history books, passing forward the stories we read about and could never imagine, but many stories remain untold, hidden within memories too painful to revisit.

My mother lived through this horrible time, and she is one of the survivors who has chosen to remain silent about her time in the prisoner camp. I didn't earn a right to comment on her choice because unlike me, she has memories that linger inside her mind, memories that likely haunt her every night.

As for me, I have spent my entire life trying to figure out who I really am. I've been a humble person, appreciative and grateful for the life I have, but there is one thing I need—the truth. I desperately need to know who I am and where I came from, but it must come from the person who is responsible for making me one of the *lucky* missing prisoners of the Holocaust.

ONE - CURRENT DAY

I've decided without knowing the effects it may cause. However, life moves too quickly, and the idea of forever is variable. Nobody really knows how much time they have. I should certainly know the importance of living in the moment. I understand what a moment's decision can influence. All these years, I've been sure about keeping certain thoughts to myself, but I can't hold them inside any longer.

I pull out the heavy, black iron chair from the garden table and slowly ease down into the seat, resting in front of a steaming cup of tea and two sets of eyes, both full of wonderment.

"Annie, you're scaring me," Mom says, her voice frail and meek, as it has been since she had the stroke last year. "You look ill or upset. What's bothering you, dear?"

I inhale slowly, taking in the late spring air infused with a mixture of lilacs and hydrangea. The mist from last night's rain still lingers, leaving the morning damp but warm enough for comfort. The trees around us fold us in their embrace, offering us a feeling of protection from the outside world. It's lovely here, and I'm often jealous of the assisted living community that Mom finally agreed to move into. It would be a little bit like heaven, if I were to imagine such a place.

I've lost my train of thought as I subconsciously avoid the task at hand. I'm about to place a heavy burden onto their shoulders. As my attention snaps back to the anxious looks on Mom and Charlie's faces, a knot of uncertainty tightens in my stomach, but I need to get it out. They need to hear this. I clear my throat and take a quick sip of the steaming tea, hoping the sweet, chamomile-infused water will alleviate some of the tension in my chest. "I don't want scare you, either of you. I've—" the words aren't forming as I had hoped they might. "I have something I want to give to you."

Mom clutches her hand over her heart with what appears to be relief. Maybe she thought I would say I'm sick, or something else along that line, though I'm not sure this gift will be any easier for her to receive.

I place a brown, paper-wrapped package down onto the woven metal slats, settling it gently between the plate of pastries, the vase of fresh lilacs and their two teacups. Mom gazes at it for a moment as if she's trying to see what's inside without removing the paper wrapping. She runs her puckered fingertips across the top, and the sound of her soft skin gliding against the coarse paper causes my shoulders to tighten. "What is this, Annie?" Mom asks. Her question is filled with curiosity, but no concern. I hope she feels the same way once she looks inside.

I stare into Mom's eyes, noticing the faded grayish-blue hues filling her once vibrant, sapphire-coated irises. Old age has taken its toll on her body throughout the last year, and the evidence is overwhelmingly obvious.

"Annie, may I have a word with you for a moment?" Charlie interrupts. He lifts his forefinger from the table top, and the slight gesture from his hand matches the rise in his left brow. I've learned that this particular look of his is full of contemplation and worry. He protects Mom from the air she breathes, and I've found his love for her to be quite endearing, especially considering how late in life they found one another.

A small smile flutters through my lips as I attempt to appear happy and unafraid of what thoughts he has, but speaking to Charlie, as he wishes, is the very least I can do for him after everything he has done for me.

"Of course." I lift my purse from the stone slabs beneath the table and place it down on the chair in my place. "We'll just be a moment, Mom."

"Take your time," she sings, waving us off as if we were pesky bugs.

Charlie grumbles a bit as he stands from his chair, so I offer a hand, which he denies as usual. "Don't treat me like I'm an old man, young lady," he always says. His replay of words eases my tension and allows a soft laugh to break up the clusters of fog in my head.

Charlie places his hand on my back and guides me down the dirt path toward their condominium. No more than a hundred feet from where Mom is seated, we stop in front of a group of trees and take a seat on a stone bench left behind as a tribute to the owner of this community.

I feel restless, waiting to hear what Charlie would like to say, and I find myself brushing away a small pile of sandy dirt from the space between us.

"Annie, I only have one question to ask you before your mother opens that package."

"Of course. What's the question?" I ask, sounding short of breath, which I am.

He places his hand down on top of mine before speaking. "Are you sure you want to do this?"

"Do what?" I ask, wondering what he knows, or how he knows the solemnity of what it is I have to share.

Charlie turns and leans in, staring at me with his freckled brown and green eyes. "Are you sure you want to reopen the past?"

"How—"

"I know the look on your face. I've seen the way you've studied me. You, Annie, are a wonderful woman who has gifted your mother exactly what she tried to gift you."

I'm not sure if Charlie knows precisely what I am giving Mom, but it seems as though he has more insight than I might have assumed. "With your blessing, Charlie, I'm sure I want to say what's in my heart," I tell him.

Charlie's lips tighten and curve into a slight bend. "Very well, sweet girl. My only request is that you unravel your story slowly. She's weak, but I agree, she should know. Secrets don't truly help anyone, do they?"

I lose my words as he throws an unexpected curveball. *Secrets.* My life has been built upon secrets. "No, secrets don't help at all. Thank you for understanding," I tell him in a mere whisper, a tightening in my throat leaving me momentarily unable to speak. When a breeze settles over us, I relax enough to say one last thing to Charlie. "Thank you … for more than I will ever have words for."

Without thought or a need for further explanation, Charlie places his hand on my cheek and smiles, grimly. A tear percolates in the corner of my eye, then slowly spills down the side of my cheek, leaving a cool chill in its trail. *It's been such a long time with these secrets.* "Sweet girl, you don't have to thank me for doing what I wanted to do. It was the best decision I have made throughout my entire life." He knows. There isn't a doubt in my mind about what he knows.

In silence, we stand from the stone bench and make our way back to Mom. She's gazing off into the distance where the trees are grouped together. With the leaves starting to fall, the woods we couldn't see through just a month ago are now showing their cavernous depth. I wonder what she's thinking. I always wonder what she's thinking when I notice that look in her eyes. It's as if she's not present in her body, but lives in another world that exists only in her mind.

There is another world …

We take our seats at the table, and I move my purse back down by my feet. "I may be old, but I'm not stupid," Mom says.

"What do you mean?" I ask, placing my elbows down as I lean toward her.

"I already know what's in the package, Annie. When you've lived as long as I have, there is little surprise left in the world."

Charlie's recent reappearance in her life surprised her. I know that much.

"Oh really?" I ask. "Well, then, I suppose you don't need to open it."

Her focus switches to my face, and she stares intently into my eyes. The grounds here are so peaceful and quiet that I can hear my breaths, even in the open space. I also hear the orchestra of crickets and birds emanating from within the barricading woods.

Mom finally lifts the package and plucks the adhesive tape from the paper's edges, freeing what's inside.

"Just as I thought," she says without surprise.

"You knew?"

"That you had a journal? Yes, of course, I watched you write in it many nights when you were a child. I watched you write in it until you were eighteen and moved out. I assumed you kept up with it, but as journals should be private, I never asked what was inside."

"I did keep it private," I assure her.

She lifts the lavender, velvet-covered notebook and holds it against her chest. "Then why are you handing it to me as a gift right now? These are your personal thoughts, Annie. Plus, I'm not dying right now, if that is what's going through your head."

My chest tightens at the mention of Mom dying, especially

after the strokes she suffered. "This isn't about you dying, Mom. This is about freeing something from my soul—my heart."

"Annie, I'm not sure I want to know the secrets of your adolescence. I do feel that a healthy dose of mystery in your child is necessary for the longevity of a parent's heart. You were such a good girl. I didn't, and still don't, feel the need to consider the thoughts that are contained within this binding."

"My birth name is not Annie, Mom," I say, sharply.

Charlie takes Mom's hand and compresses it between his. "Annie—"

"You don't have to explain anything."

"I didn't want you to experience the pain of knowing what that would bring," she says. "How long have you known?"

A tight-lipped smile presses into my cheeks with a sense of guilt—the guilt I knew was coming. "Most of my life—from the time I was old enough to understand, I suppose."

"But—" Mom tries to speak, though what is there to say?

"It's all inside—everything. I need you to know," I tell her. "I don't want there to be any more secrets. I can't live with them anymore."

"I am so sorry, Annie," she says with disdain. I knew this was going to be painful for her, which is why I have put it off for so long, but I can't wait any longer.

"Mom, you have nothing to be sorry about. That's the reason I want you to read what's inside the book."

Mom places the journal back down on top of the brown paper. "I want to hear it all—I'm sure Charlie does too—but we need to hear it through your voice."

"My search for answers started on my twelfth birthday," I told Mom.

"What? What happened that particular day?" she asks.

It was the beginning of a new world filled with questions and no answers.

It was my twelfth birthday. Each birthday prior to that day, I would receive a teddy bear or charm bracelet, but I told Mom I didn't need anything extraordinary since I was becoming older. I knew money was a burdening factor in our lives since we didn't have much of it. The last thing I wanted to do was ask for something I didn't need. Still, Mom wouldn't let a birthday pass without some type of gift.

To my surprise, I received a beautiful, purple velvet book, filled with blank pages just waiting for me to write down my thoughts in. I was even more pleased with the texture of the cover than the thought-provoking pages inside. "I'm not sure what to write in here," I told Mom. "The pages are all so clean and crisp. It would be a shame to ruin them with ink. Don't you think?" For some reason, I couldn't fathom tarnishing the insides of the book, although at that time, there weren't words in my head that felt adequate to leave a mark anyway.

"Annie," Mom said sweetly. Her smile lit up the room, and she took the book from my hands, opening it against the crinkling scream from the inner binding. The pages fanned from one side to the other. "It is healthy to write down the way we feel because it cures us of our fears, aches, and pains."

I didn't understand what she meant because I hadn't experienced those types of emotions yet. "I don't have those kinds of feelings, though, so how can I write about them?"

She closed the book and handed it back to me before continuing with her reason. "It doesn't have to be today, Annie. It can be whenever you feel the need to write down how you feel." I remember her eyes lit up like the sky as she stared up toward our discolored ceiling like it was a beautiful piece of art instead of a hideous slab of plaster. "Journals are like treasure chests ... places that can keep all our feelings secure and safe from everyone else. I strongly believe every girl should have one."

"What about me, Mom?" Clara piped in, as she always had when the topic was about me rather than her.

"Next year, when you turn twelve, I will buy you a journal to write in, as well." She cupped her long, narrow fingers around Clara's chin and pinched gently. "It is time for bed, girls. Go get washed up, and I'll be there to tuck you in shortly."

Clara, being dramatic, scuffled her feet against the wooden floor and ran to the bathroom. It was our nightly routine. She would slam the flimsy wooden door in my face and laugh because she got there first, and I would have to wait. It bothered me for a while, but eventually, I preferred to take those few extra moments and sit by our bedroom window, staring out at the millions of glittering lights throughout the New York City skyline. I tried to count the lights, but my eyes would eventually tire, and the glowing flickers would blur into one. By that time, the bathroom would be free, and Clara would be on to her next nightly routine of singing at the top of her lungs while changing into her nightgown.

I placed my new journal down on top of my bureau and claimed my time slot in the bathroom. I was quick as usual, knowing the one small bathroom we had was shared by all four of us, and it seemed someone was always waiting their turn. Clara was the only one who didn't seem to notice, but she was a bit younger, so I figured she would grow out of her ignorance eventually.

Meanwhile, I was so busy thinking of Clara's rude behavior that I didn't consider a consequence of quietly sneaking back to the kitchen to thank Mom for making Weinersnitchel—my favorite meal—as well as for the cake and the gift. In hindsight, I should have listened when she said she would be in shortly to say goodnight.

The moment I rounded the corner toward the kitchen, I stopped short when I heard Mom and Dad having a quiet argument on the other side of the wall. I shouldn't have been listening, but I heard my name mentioned, and curiosity got the best of me. I remained hidden behind the corner and pressed my ear up against the wall to listen.

Mom continued speaking in a harsh voice to Dad, "What are we going to do, Maxwell? They have no records of Annie, and they're going to find out sooner or later that she doesn't belong to us. She'll be taken away."

The words "taken away" were all I heard, or they were all I retained. Suddenly, my world was collapsing in on me. Everything I knew was questionable. I was sure I was misunderstanding what I heard, but I couldn't erase the thoughts plunging through my head. My chest felt tight, and my throat was closing in on itself.

"Let me see the letter, Amelia," Dad said. He sounded nervous, not as nervous as Mom, but not like his usual self.

I heard paper rustling as it was exchanged between them. That noise was deafening compared to the silence that followed. "The state is demanding proof of her birth records. I don't understand why they suddenly need this proof, though?"

A hard, tired sigh spilled from Mom's throat, making her sound strangled. "Maxwell, do not be ridiculous. I just emigrated here a few years ago. You know how this state has been with their records lately. Annie is in public school. Her name is in public records. We knew it was only a matter of time before speculation broke out."

I felt like I couldn't breathe as I continued to listen, frozen in place.

Dad sighed, "Oy, Amelia. I don't know what we're going to do, honey. We must keep her safe, and we will do whatever that means. You know that. I will not let anything happen to that beautiful girl. I promise you, Amelia."

Safe. The word suddenly sounded like a haunting note. I had no clue why I wasn't safe, or why they made it seem as though I wasn't their daughter. My only question was—did they take me? Did they kidnap me? Were *they* the monsters they had warned me about so often? Weekly, I was reminded not to speak to strangers, and especially never to give anyone personal information, including our religion, address, or even my name. At that moment, I think I finally realized why I had to be so careful.

I knew Mom and Dad loved me. They showed it in so many ways. I couldn't recall a day when I didn't feel loved. Mom wasn't fond of saying the words "I love you" out loud, but I hadn't thought much of it. I suddenly began to assume she had an actual reason for avoiding the expression. My thoughts raced. I didn't belong there, and I didn't know what to do.

Deep in thought, through automatic movements, I made my way back to the bedroom, where Clara had managed to settle herself down into bed.

I glanced at her with confusion, studying her blonde hair and light blue eyes that blended seamlessly into her frosty pale complexion. I had never given it any thought before then, but her looks were entirely different from my dark hair and eyes, especially my light olive skin. There had never been much of a reason to consider the difference in our looks because Mom often said, "Every person looks like themselves."

Suddenly, I realized that Clara and I didn't have any similarities. I wondered if that was possible between siblings. It felt as though my thoughts were spiraling out of control, and I wanted to believe that none of what I was assuming could be right. I told myself I must have misheard Mom and Dad because, surely, they would tell me if I wasn't their real daughter. Surely, they would have told me if they had taken me from my birth parents.

Surely.

To continue reading, click here.

ABOUT THE AUTHOR

Shari J. Ryan is a *USA Today* Bestselling Author of Contemporary Romance and Women's Fiction. Shari was once told she tends to exaggerate often and sometimes talks too much, which would make a great foundation for fictional books. Four years later, Shari has written thirteen novels that often leave readers either in tears from laughing, or crying.

With her loud Boston girl attitude, Shari isn't shy about her love for writing or the publishing industry. Along with writing several International bestsellers, Shari has split her time between writing and her longstanding passion for graphic design. In 2014, she started an indie-publishing resource company, MadHat Books, to help fellow authors with their book cover designs, as well as assistance in the self-publishing process.

While Shari may not find many hours to sleep, she still manages to make time for her family. She is a devoted wife to a great guy, and a mother to two little boys who remind her daily why she was put on this earth.

For more information:
Web: www.sharijryan.com
Email: authorshariryan@gmail.com
Facebook: /authorsharijryan
Twitter: @sharijryan
Make sure you join her Twisted Drifters Reader Group at:
https://www.facebook.com/groups/ShariJRyanVIPReaderGroup/

Sign up for my newsletter:
https://www.sharijryan.com/subscribe

Made in the USA
Monee, IL
09 April 2021